EPISTEMOLOGY and METAPHYSICS for QUALITATIVE RESEARCH

SAGE was founded in 1965 by Sara Miller McCune to support the dissemination of usable knowledge by publishing innovative and high-quality research and teaching content. Today, we publish over 900 journals, including those of more than 400 learned societies, more than 800 new books per year, and a growing range of library products including archives, data, case studies, reports, and video. SAGE remains majority-owned by our founder, and after Sara's lifetime will become owned by a charitable trust that secures our continued independence.

Los Angeles | London | New Delhi | Singapore | Washington DC | Melbourne

EPISTEMOLOGY
and METAPHYSICS
for QUALITATIVE
RESEARCH

Tomas Pernecky

Los Angeles | London | New Delhi
Singapore | Washington DC | Melbourne

Los Angeles | London | New Delhi
Singapore | Washington DC | Melbourne

SAGE Publications Ltd
1 Oliver's Yard
55 City Road
London EC1Y 1SP

SAGE Publications Inc.
2455 Teller Road
Thousand Oaks, California 91320

SAGE Publications India Pvt Ltd
B 1/I 1 Mohan Cooperative Industrial Area
Mathura Road
New Delhi 110 044

SAGE Publications Asia-Pacific Pte Ltd
3 Church Street
#10-04 Samsung Hub
Singapore 049483

Editor: Jai Seaman
Editorial assistant: Alysha Owen
Production editor: Tom Bedford
Copyeditor: Audrey Scriven
Indexer: Cathy Heath
Marketing manager: Sally Ransom
Cover design: Shaun Mercier
Typeset by: C&M Digitals (P) Ltd, Chennai, India
Printed in India at Replika Press Pvt Ltd

© Tomas Pernecky 2016

First published 2016

Library of Congress Control Number: 2015960280

British Library Cataloguing in Publication data

A catalogue record for this book is available from
the British Library

ISBN 978-1-4462-8238-0
ISBN 978-1-4462-8239-7 (pbk)

At SAGE we take sustainability seriously. Most of our products are printed in the UK using FSC papers and boards.
When we print overseas we ensure sustainable papers are used as measured by the PREPS grading system.
We undertake an annual audit to monitor our sustainability.

Contents

Preface

Human beings make sense of the external world through experience and cognition. 'Common sense' recognition would suggest that knowledge, then, is fundamentally the result of our physiological make-up and our cognitive processes. To make this concession is to enter an arena of philosophical problems which have occupied many an intellectual mind. While some have argued that by means of the scientific method it is possible to obtain accurate descriptions of reality, others have advocated that the only thing we can truly know is our ideas. Still others have accepted truth claims that solely pertain to the observable aspects of reality, while others still have rejected the possibility of knowledge altogether. In the quest to account for reality and gain knowledge of it, a number of distinct schools of thought have flourished. This book seeks to provide an accessible overview of the developments in the prevailing philosophical doctrines, and supply the reader with a deeper understanding of the key arguments.

There is an increasing demand on students to possess sound knowledge of various theoretical perspectives and to demonstrate the ability to apply these to research. However, attending to matters of metaphysics and epistemology is undoubtedly one of the most vexing tasks a researcher faces. In the pursuit of carefully articulating a philosophical stance, one has to make sense of legacies spanning the course of centuries in a very short period of time, grapple with intricate vocabularies, and digest complex ideas. Many arrive at this juncture without any philosophical background, unequipped to deal with this formidable task. The subtler ambition of this text, therefore, is to bring out the philosopher in the qualitative inquirer by examining a variety of topics that have been pivotal in the philosophy of science.

Several important tenets underpin this project. The first has to do with the notion that there is a 'better' or an 'accurate' way of doing qualitative research. To claim methodological superiority is in itself a manifestation of philosophical assumptions of a certain kind. The vantage point adopted in the pages that follow views qualitative inquiry as characterized by different research aims, philosophical assumptions, varying levels of usefulness, and a range of attitudinal factors – including claims to truth. It does not seek to advance any particular school of thought on qualitative research. This point ought to be raised upfront as some readers may be enmeshed in the traditions of specific communities of qualitative practice. Secondly, this book is not a book about paradigms. Quite the contrary, it is argued that paradigms, as they have been construed in the literature, represent a rigid conceptual organization of ideas, and as such are limited in capturing philosophical diversity. The third tenet arises out of the first two as an appeal to building an environment that nurtures academic freedom, creativity, and the expression of a range of philosophical and methodological choices. Taken together, these three undercurrents crystalize in the final chapter in the form of an invitation to contemplate a post-paradigmatic approach to research.

The central thesis of this text is the claim that philosophy develops across multiple continua, whereby ideas may not only be of a similar (or similar enough) sort, but also diverge and occupy different planes. It is inadequate to speak of one realism, empiricism, rationalism, and idealism univocally; rather, there is a multiplicity of perspectives, and these have evolved and spilled over into other territories to give rise to modified outlooks. Consequently, it would be misleading to suggest that all constructionists, for example, are anti-realists through and through, that all researchers drawn to hermeneutics and phenomenology are anti-objectivists, and that all idealism goes hand in hand with subjectivism. Dichotomies of this breed no longer serve the qualitative researcher of today, who is called to navigate increasingly challenging and heterogeneous philosophical terrains.

The volume is divided into four parts and eight chapters. Parts I and IV are centered on qualitative research, enfolding Parts II and III, which attend to epistemological and ontological problems. Whereas the first chapter establishes the overall premise and erects a conceptual skeleton for thinking about metaphysical and epistemological issues, the final chapter reinforces the extent to which philosophy plays an integral role in the research process in its revisiting of some of the covered topics. Much of the content is built around the core philosophical considerations delineated in Figure 1.3 in Chapter 1. Indeed, this figure may serve as a guide for mapping the main epistemologies. Following that, the chapters in Part II examine the differences between the rationalist and empiricist approaches to knowledge, that is, positivism and postpositivism (Chapter 2); the epistemologies of scepticism, idea-ism, and idealism (Chapter 3); German idealism, phenomenology, and hermeneutics (Chapter 4); and realisms and anti-realisms (Chapter 5).

The third part of the book, titled Intangible Realities, addresses some of the neglected domains of qualitative research. Chapter 6 on social ontology examines how it is possible for social facts such as money and tourists to exist. This chapter should be particularly important for social science and humanities researchers, who study social facts as opposed to natural facts. Building on previous discussions, it also shows that academics can be stronger or weaker realists with regard to different entities. For instance, one can be an ontological realist about rocks and trees, but not about professors and tourists; one can be a realist about atoms and mathematics, but not about moral codes; and one can also be a realist or anti-realist about all of the above. Chapter 7 ventures into the territory of quantum mechanics and outlines nine theories about quantum reality. It is argued that if we are to speak of reality with some degree of relevance in the twenty-first century, then attending to the philosophical problems entwined with the quantum world has an important place in the discourse.

Finally, the reader should be aware that this is not a complete philosophy of science, only a selection of the most pressing concerns for qualitative researchers. While the chapters are compiled to offer a general understanding of the key epistemological stances and metaphysical problems, the volume is not intended as an exhaustive resource. Instead, each chapter includes a list of recommended literature for furthering one's knowledge on the subject. It is also important to emphasize here that this is not a methodological text: its focus rests with metaphysical and epistemological questions, such as what there is and what can be known about it. Although the content is organized as a whole, each chapter can also be used independently as a focused resource. Regardless of their philosophical orientation and choice of methods, *Epistemology and Metaphysics for Qualitative Research* should be a useful companion for social science researchers and students interested in qualitative inquiry.

Acknowledgements

This book has been in the making for nearly two years since its inception, and I would like to acknowledge the people who have contributed, in different ways, to that process. These are the philosophers, scientists, artists, and intellectuals whose work has left a profound impression on me but who are too numerous to be listed here. Some are cited in this book, and I admire them for their clarity of thought. My appreciation goes to Ross Klein, who offered comments on several chapters; Keith Hollinshead, for a critical reading of Chapter 1; and Robert Nola, for valuable insights on Chapter 5. A big 'thank you' goes to my editor Mona-Lynn Courteau, whose work is always outstanding, Jai Seaman, Alysha Owen, Tom Bedford, Sally Ransom and Audrey Scriven at SAGE, and the reviewers – particularly to Kellee Caton for her constructive feedback. Last but not least, my appreciation extends to all the postdisciplinary, disobedient, rebellious, and probing minds not afraid to challenge the norm. These come from all walks of life and continue to inspire me.

PART I
Qualitative Inquiry and Philosophy

A concept is a brick. It can be used to build the courthouse of reason. Or it can be thrown through the window. What is the subject of the brick? The arm that throws it? The body connected to the arm? The brain encased in the body? The situation that brought brain and body to such a juncture? All and none of the above. What is its object? The window? The edifice? The laws the edifice shelters? The class and other power relations encrusted in the laws? All and none of the above.

(Gilles Deleuze & Felix Guattari, *A Thousand Plateaus: Capitalism and Schizophrenia*, 2014)

One

Introduction: Situating Metaphysics and Epistemology in Qualitative Research

Epistemology and metaphysics are the fundamental philosophical pillars of any research. While most human beings make epistemological and metaphysical judgements on a daily basis, unless engaged in a scholarly activity, the average person does not contemplate complex philosophical questions, such as whether invisible subatomic particles can be said to exist or the possibility of social reality. Rather, we[1] trust our senses and take our perceptions for granted. This introductory chapter prepares the ground for our inquiry centred on the problem of knowledge and reality within the wider qualitative landscape. The chapter begins by signposting some of the key views and events that have contributed to the ways in which qualitative research unfolds today. A secondary, but no less important, aim is to provide a critical assessment of the increasingly challenging philosophical terrains students and academics must navigate. It will be argued that most conceptual schemata are limited in their capacity to capture the complexity and richness of the diverse streams of philosophical thought that have emerged and evolved over the past two millennia, and that those schemata responsible for the current paradigmatic dominance are too limiting to accomplish this task. As qualitative research becomes a more heterogeneous blend of various philosophical stances in an intricate web of interests, principles, ideals, and values, it is no longer sufficient to speak of only one way of embracing realism or absolutism, of only one type of objectivism, or to take a univocal approach to constructionism,[2] idealism, hermeneutics, or phenomenology. There are a multitude of philosophical and methodological horizons which require us to think in terms of flows and continua as opposed to rigid frameworks. Although there have been a number of useful conceptual structures devised to assist scholars in blending philosophical decisions with methodologies and methods, and although these models will continue to play an important role in qualitative research, they come with limitations. In order to demonstrate the various ways in which philosophical assumptions can be organized to guide research, this chapter will concentrate on Crotty's (1998) structure of the research process, Lincoln and Guba's (2000) outline of alternative inquiry paradigms, and Lally's (1981) anatomy of metatheoretical and epistemological assumptions in social science. These frameworks have been selected for their popularity and to demonstrate their conceptual range. This chapter concludes with a delineation of the core concerns raised along the way, upon which subsequent chapters are built.

Multiple histories of qualitative research

Qualitative research, as defined for the purposes of this book, is a mode of inquiry capable of accommodating a wide array of philosophical perspectives and methods, stretching on an attitudinal continuum from *means* to *orientation*. This notion is discussed in more detail in Chapter 8, nonetheless it is imperative to establish upfront that it would be too simplistic to conceive of qualitative research purely in terms of choosing a set of methods. Rather, there are a number of considerations which determine the shape and scope of one's project, including the research aims; the researcher's or one's own philosophical assumptions, values and moral sensitivities; the impact on local communities and co-researchers' lives; and, for some, also the critical engagement with issues of emancipation, empowerment and silencing – intertwined with the act of inquiry. Therefore, there is no single correct approach to qualitative research, and this text does not seek to offer a simple definition that would accurately capture the immense variety of qualitative works. Such a reductionist ideal would miss the point and be counterproductive for the task before us.

To articulate the different discourses and to show that qualitative research is a vibrant area benefiting from a multitude of voices, Brinkmann, Jacobsen and Kristiansen (2014), who refer to it as a 'field', have chosen to offer not just one historical account of it but a variety of histories. Their multi-faceted approach yields as many as six types of historical accounts of qualitative research: conceptual, qualitative, internal, marginalizing, repressed, social, and technological. In this section we briefly explore some of their differences.

With respect to the conceptual history of qualitative research, although the term itself is a relatively recent one, the notion of it originates in the ideas of our philosophical predecessors who put in place the early philosophical building blocks. Brinkmann et al. (2014) take note of the Enlightenment thinkers who distinguished between the qualities ('qualia') and the quantities ('quanta') of things. For instance, they call attention to Johann Wolfgang von Goethe (1749–1832), who argued as early as 1810 that there is a difference in the study of colours according to Newtonian optics and how colours are experienced through the human senses.

In Goethe's view, the latter, embodied experience was just as significant as the physics of colour perception, and his *Theory of Colours* is described by Brinkmann et al. as an early qualitative phenomenological study. Other philosophical giants, including Descartes, Locke, and Hume, saw the need to distinguish between primary qualities, those that are independent of observers, and secondary ones, which are observer-dependent. This early separation between 'appearances' and the 'intrinsic properties' of objects is, in contemporary terms, formulated as the problem of objectivism versus subjectivism, and will occupy us later in the book.

We can go beyond Brinkmann et al. and probe even deeper into our historical past. The ancient philosophers pondered many of the fundamental philosophical questions about knowledge with which we still grapple today. For example, the proponents of scepticism, such as the Greeks Sextus Empiricus and Pyrrho, contested the 'givens' of perception and radically undermined the views of the empirically oriented philosophers. Likewise, the philosophical ideas put forth by the proponents of relativism, including Protagoras, and later Wittgenstein, Feyerabend, and many others, played a major role in shaping the discourse between the doctrines of realism and anti-realism. And therefore, as commented by Laudan, 'struggles between realist and relativist perspectives span the entire history of epistemology' (1997: 139). When we adopt a longitudinal approach to qualitative research, we realize that it is in many ways a continuation of the older debates – albeit fuelled by contemporary concerns, novel theoretical perspectives, and innovative methods.

The second, internal history of qualitative research focuses our attention on the dedicated qualitative thinkers from inside the field. Here, Brinkmann et al. (2014: 20) outline what they call the 'three philosophical foundations of qualitative research': the German tradition of *Verstehen*, with figures such as Friedrich Schleiermacher (1768–1834), Wilhelm Dilthey (1833–1911), and Hans-Georg Gadamer (1900–2002); the phenomenological tradition of Edmund Husserl (1859–1938); and the North American traditions of pragmatism, Chicago sociology, Erving Goffman's (1922–1982) dramaturgical approach, symbolic interactionism, and ethnomethodology. These traditions, of course, come with an elaborate list of intellectuals – each making a contribution to what have become rather heterogeneous and at times radically different schools of thought. Later in this book we will see that there is not just one phenomenology but rather a variety of strands of phenomenological thought, that there is not just one symbolic interactionism but rather many approaches within this tradition (Herman and Reynolds (1994) noted that there were up to 15 varieties), and that there is no one univocal hermeneutics, idealism, or constructionism.

The third, marginalizing history of qualitative research is a reminder that qualitative researchers have been subjected to hostile attitudes by scientifically oriented, or what are frequently called positivistically inclined, academics for whom qualitative research does not meet the criteria of scientific inquiry. In this regard, what is refreshing in the work of Brinkmann et al. (2014) is their acknowledgement of positivism as being too quickly dismissed and typecast as the enemy of qualitative inquiry. Pointing out that not all positivists are opposed to qualitative research, the authors comment that 'when qualitative researchers distance themselves from positivism, they most often construct a straw man [sic] and rarely, if ever, go back and read what early positivists such as Comte, Schlick, or Carnap in fact had to say about research and human experience' (2014: 31). This is a key point. We will follow this critical line of thought throughout this book, with Chapter 2 focusing in on the doctrine of positivism and other varieties of empiricism and addressing some of the misconceptions surrounding these.

In the fourth, repressed history of qualitative research, Brinkmann et al. provide an analysis of the discipline of psychology as a way of demonstrating that the qualitative tradition has been 'forgotten by the official journals and handbooks of psychology to an extent that makes it resemble repression' (2014: 32). The authors argue that the qualitative character of such research as Piaget's work with children, Gestalt psychologists' investigations into perception, Merleau-Ponty's phenomenology of the body, and Bartlett's work on remembering is often omitted and 'almost always neglected and repressed' (2014: 32). This leads them to the realization that, in charting various disciplinary developments, qualitative research has not always been noted as having played a significant role, or even any role at all – a wholly unjustified view.

The fifth, social history of qualitative research underscores the necessity to take into account the social, cultural, economic, and historical contexts within which qualitative research takes place. This approach is an invitation to consider not only cultural and social movements, which undoubtedly created new opportunities for scholars to think and express themselves differently (particularly in the 1960s and 1970s), but also soft forms of power. Brinkmann et al. caution against the naïve conception of qualitative inquiry simply as 'progressive' or 'emancipatory', and explain that qualitative market research, for example, has become a powerful tool in the manipulation of consumers' desires and behaviour. This is a critical reminder that qualitative research is now firmly embedded in our social life and is applied for different purposes and agendas, including those that are economic and political.

The last type of history of qualitative research is the technological one. It makes allowance for the kinds of devices researchers utilize to gather, manage, and make sense of qualitative data. From digital voice recorders to the latest software programs, many contemporary researchers rely on a wide array of technological innovations (Brinkmann et al., 2014). It is increasingly common for scholars to work with electronic data, blogs, mind maps, transcription programs, and computer-assisted qualitative data analysis software (CAQDAS) such as NVivo. Moreover, technology has been widely embraced and amalgamated into relatively novel approaches and methods, such as visual methodologies (e.g., Hughes, 2012; Rogers, 2013; Rose, 2012). Of course, as Brinkmann et al. point out, there are a number of issues related to the use of technology. Its critics are concerned that the use of software programs to manage and analyze qualitative data may lead to a certain type of analysis being favoured over others. Nonetheless, the twenty-first century qualitative researcher can be not only a *bricoleur* (Denzin & Lincoln, 2005) but also a techno-savvy problem solver who understands that technology is useful and necessary in a digital era. And if we consider that we 'think through, with, and alongside media' (Hayles, 2012: 1), then much of the future research in humanities and qualitative social science is likely to rely on and incorporate the use of technology. However, there are philosophical implications researchers ought to consider when adopting numerical approaches to qualitative data, some of which are discussed in Chapter 8.

In addition to the types of histories noted above, an account of the developments in qualitative research can be also organized around a focus on specific geographical areas. Flick (2009), for example, explains that in Germany, advances on the front of qualitative research were marked by methodological consolidation and a focus on procedural questions, whereas across the Atlantic, qualitative researchers were more concerned about the issues of representation and the politics and practice of interpretation. He remarks that particularly towards the end of the 1970s, German qualitative researchers reduced their reliance on the translations of American works (what he calls the 'import of American developments') and began to develop original research focusing on the application and analysis of interviews. By the 1980s, Schütze's (1977) *narrative interview* and Oevermann et al.'s (1979) *objective hermeneutics* had become pivotal in the development of an original approach to qualitative research in Germany. The 'historical moments' delineated by Denzin and Lincon (1994) stand as rather unique and specific to the North American context.

The 'historical moments' of qualitative research in North America

Norman Denzin and Yvonna Lincoln (1994) worked diligently to map several 'historical moments' in qualitative research. These have become a popular way of chronologically marking specific ideas and concerns over the past decades. As noted in the previous section, the *moments* correspond to developments within the qualitative communities in North America, and have been outlined as follows: 'the traditional (1900–1950); the modernist or golden age (1950–1970); blurred genres (1970–1986); the crisis of representation (1986–1990); the postmodern, a period of experimental and new ethnographies (1990–1995); postexperimental inquiry (1995–2000); the methodologically contested present (2000–2004); and the future (2005–), which is now' (Denzin, 2010b: 13). In the view of Denzin and Lincoln, qualitative research has reached the *eighth* moment, which 'asks that the social sciences and the humanities become sites for critical conversations about democracy, race, gender, class, nation-states, globalization, freedom, and community' (Denzin & Lincoln, 2011a). We shall not describe each moment here, for this has now become the habit of nearly every text on qualitative research, but we will address some of the concerns and misconceptions surrounding these moments.

The act of conceptually dividing qualitative research into different periods or 'moments', and framing these in terms of 'progress', has been questioned – particularly by scholars within the field of ethnography (Atkinson et al., 1999, 2003; Atkinson et al., 2007; Delamont et al., 2000). Atkinson et al. argue that it is misleading to assume that the early ethnographic figures saw their work as 'positivist', stating that they are not convinced that 'the kind of intellectual history repeatedly sketched by Denzin and Lincoln is wholly adequate' (2003: 21). Furthermore, they posit that Denzin and Lincoln's chronological view 'does a disservice to earlier generations of ethnographers' (2003: 197), and that 'it is far from clear that there ever were such monolithically positivist and modernist phases' (2003: 26). In their opinion, it would be incorrect to assume that all ethnography in past generations 'was conducted under the auspices of a positivistic and totalizing gaze as it is to imply that we are all postmodern now' (2003: 27). Atkinson et al. make an important point about the impossibility of capturing the development of qualitative research by designing a neat chronological system according to which all qualitative scholars progress in a linear fashion. Nonetheless, Denzin and Lincoln acknowledge that the various historical moments overlap and operate simultaneously, and further clarify these as marking 'discernible shifts in style, genre, epistemology, ethics, politics and aesthetics' (2011a: 16, see note 7). It would indeed be problematic if Denzin and Lincoln were to claim a kind of linearity.

As far as ethnographic work in sociology and anthropology is concerned, according to Atkinson et al. (2003), qualitative research is a 'variegated domain of activity', and the authors contrast the *diehard traditionalist*, driven by reliability, validity and clear criteria, with the *Old Guard*, described as the methodological pioneers of the 1950s and 1960s, and the *Avant Garde*, representing the adherents of new ethnography since 1985. We learn that the postmodern Avant Garde scholars have questioned the universal criteria for objectivity, the authority of the researcher, and the difficulties with neutral and independent representations of the social world. They are largely relativists, 'inherently political', and thoroughly sceptical about 'the authority and legitimacy of more conventional notions of methodology, epistemology, and research practice' (Atkinson et al., 2003: 12). However, and this is an important 'however', the issues raised by the earlier scholars – the pioneers of the field – are still valid and pertinent today. The point to be made is that it would be erroneous to think that each instance of qualitative research has to conform to any particular *historical moment*. These moments are more fittingly grasped in terms of preferences, trends, directions, tensions, and discussions within certain communities of qualitative practice.

The four schools of symbolic interactionism

It has been well documented in the literature that anthropology and sociology were the disciplinary forerunners of qualitative research, and that it was largely the early ethnographic researchers who saw the need to study the richness and diversity of people's experiences, unique settings, customs, and traditions. The foundations of the theoretical perspective in sociology called *symbolic interactionism* were laid down mainly by George Herbert Mead (1863–1931), for whom the most crucial aspect about human society was that it was 'made up of persons with selves', whereby the Self (see Mead, 1913) denoted something that emerged as part of social interaction and thus become a social product (Reynolds, 1993: 58). We can distinguish between four key strands of contemporary symbolic interactionism, represented by the Chicago, Iowa, Indiana, and Illinois schools (Pascale, 2011). Taking brief stock of some of the historical antecedents is useful for understanding the current debates, tensions, and approaches to qualitative research.

The Chicago School and the Iowa School

During the 1920s and 1930s the ethnographic studies conducted by the Chicago School were influential in establishing qualitative research as an important tool in other domains of inquiry as well. Herbert Blumer later cemented the term 'symbolic interactionism' during his tenure at the University of Chicago and formulated the methodological position on which this term rests (see Blumer, 1986 [1969]). Most scholars practising symbolic interactionism agree that human beings have the capacity to develop and use symbols as a way of communicating and interacting with others, and that they also have the ability to self-reflect and perceive of themselves as objects (Herman, 1994). In other words, one becomes the object of one's own actions (Reynolds, 1993). Whilst these views are generally shared by many symbolic interactionists, the point of divergence lies in the methods seen as preferable for the study of humans and society. The formation of two distinct approaches began in the 1960s with the Chicago School, led by Herbert Blumer, and the Iowa School, founded by Manford Kuhn (Meltzer & Petras, 1970).

On the level of methodology, Blumer and the Chicago School promoted the observation of social processes, whereas Kuhn and the Iowa School viewed such methods as inadequate, labelling them 'high-class journalism' because they failed to reveal the generic principles of human behaviour (Weckroth, 1989: 213). The scientifically-driven programme at the Iowa School in the area of social and behavioural sciences was largely empirical in character, and guided by 'quantifiable measurements within target samples' (Katovich et al., 2003: 119). Katovich et al. explain that Kuhn believed that 'the hard work of an interactionist and pragmatic science (Mead, 1938) would prove invaluable and would replace the more esoteric expressions of interactionist ideas' (2003: 120). In addition, Prus notes that Kuhn was interested in developing 'standardized measures of human behavior and deriv[ing] causal statements concerning human conduct, with the eventual goal of predicting and controlling human behavior' (1996: 77).

What this means with respect to the study of people and society is that these schools mark two distinct philosophies. Drawing on the analysis of Herman (1994), we can say that the approaches advocated by the Iowa School are more deterministic, that they employ a causal model of social organization, and that the Self is viewed as the result of systems and structures, which are the focus of inquiry. From this standpoint, structures – once created by individuals – become somewhat stable phenomena. The role and utility of the methods employed by the Iowa School, then, is to help us understand the causes of human behaviour. According to Kuhn, 'people's behaviors were seen as caused by the sets of the self-attitudes they had internalized with respect to this or that role' (Prus, 1996: 77). On the other hand, the Chicago School saw social structures as *emergent* phenomena, which come into being through the active agency of individuals – shaping and co-creating social realities. The Self, within the Chicago School of approaches, was understood to be the result of mutual interpretations (Herman, 1994). It is worth noting that Herbert Mead had a profound influence on the research and scholarly perspectives within the Chicago tradition of sociology (Blumer, 1979); we need only consider his views on the relation of individual Selves to the social whole to appreciate the impact of his thought:

> The self is something which has a development; it is not initially there, at birth, but arises in the process of social experience and activity, that is, develops in the given individual as a result of his relations to that process as a whole and to other individuals within that process [p. 135] [...] The process out of which the self arises is a social process which implies interaction of individuals in the group, implies the preexistence of the group. It implies also certain co-operative activities in which the different members of the group are involved. It implies, further, that out of this process there may in turn develop a more elaborate organization than that out of which the self has arisen, and that the selves may be the organs, the essential parts at least, of this more elaborate social organization within which these selves arise and exist. (Mead, 1934: 164)

In terms of its chronological developments, it is useful to emphasize that after the Second World War interactionist sociology at the University of Chicago continued to flourish, developing into a number of research styles that later became known as 'fieldwork' and 'ethnography' (Atkinson & Housley, 2003). Besides Mead and Blumer, there were many other influential researchers, such as Howard Becker, Erving Goffman, Anselm Strauss, W. Lloyd Warner, Everett C. Hughes, and Gary A. Fine. Indeed not all sociologists associated with the Chicago School can be said to have belonged to the same intellectual tradition, as pointed out by Atkinson and Housley (2003). Some followed the work of Mead and Blumer, some the empirical sociological research programme of W.I. Thomas and Robert Park; others were influenced by both.

The Indiana School and the Illinois School

There are two other influential institutions in the field of symbolic interaction-ism: Indiana University and the University of Illinois. The Indiana School, led by Sheldon Stryker, is often perceived as a revised version of the Iowa School programme because it follows rigorous empirical methods and draws largely on quantitative approaches and mathematical models. Herman-Kinney and Verschaeve (2003) note, however, that there has been a shift from positivism to pragmatism, and hence more flexibility in the use of both quantitative and qualitative methods. The Illinois School is the home of Norman Denzin, who, despite having trained at the University of Iowa under Manford Kuhn, followed a more ethnographically oriented approach to symbolic interactionism and pro-duced a version that draws on postmodern and poststructural theories (Pascale, 2011). Denzin's (2001) *interpretive interactionism* continues to focus on interactive processes on the basis that people can be understood through their interactions. His work combines ethnography with hermeneutics, but also includes moral and political concerns. According to Denzin, the researcher has an important and active role to play in the acts of interpretation and knowledge production; this theme has also arisen in his later work, such as *The Qualitative Manifesto* (2010b).

From this quick glance, we can appreciate the extent to which the Chicago School influenced the early stages of qualitative inquiry and the interpretive tradi-tions. The Chicago School became the philosophical–theoretical basis for many of the perspectives that are popular in qualitative research today – from phenomeno-logical inquiries into people's experience and hermeneutics to social constructionist and pragmatist perspectives. Norman Denzin continues to be the leading author-ity on interpretive interactionism and is well regarded for his work in qualitative research internationally. The Iowa and Indiana schools favour positivist and quan-titatively oriented methods. Prus (1996) argues that the 'new' Iowa School (which was led by Carl Couch until 1994) pays little attention to the individual's perspec-tive, and that the Indiana School follows the path of scientific rigour, equations, and quantitative modelling (see, for example, Schneider & Heise, 1995).

The increasingly challenging qualitative terrains

The proliferation of qualitative inquiry is reflected in the growth of original research papers, journals, and books, and also specialist seminars, workshops, and conferences. There is now a large pool of widely accepted works by scholars invested in qualitative ways of thinking and knowing (see, for example, Atkinson et al., 2003; Bogdan & Biklen, 2007; Creswell, 2013; Crotty, 1998; Denzin & Lincoln, 2011b; Hesse-Biber & Leavy, 2010; Leavy, 2014; Lincoln & Guba, 1985; Maxwell, 2012, 2013; Patton, 2002; Silverman, 1997, 2013, 2015; Slife & Williams, 1995; Tashakkori & Teddlie, 2010). In addition, there is body of specialist literature catering to the needs of qualitatively oriented academics within different disciplines, subdisciplines, and fields of study. However, with the increased popularity of qualitative methods comes greater diversity (Patton, 2002) and complexity (Atkinson et al., 2003) among qualitative methodologists and theorists. Denzin, for example, is known for embracing a postmodern and poststructural stance, Lincoln sees herself as an 'avowed constructionist' (Denzin & Lincoln, 2000: xi), Maxwell (2012, 2013) favours qualitative inquiry informed by philosophical realism, and many researchers using mixed methods prefer to describe themselves as pragmatic thinkers. This suggests that qualitative research is an umbrella term capable of accommodating a wide range of philosophical stances.

Yet there has been a growing awareness of qualitative research as being too complex, muddled, and confusing (Atkinson et al., 2003), and that it can be paralyzing for novice researchers (Seale, 2002). Not only is there an immense amount of information to digest, there is also a lack of consistency among scholars in the way they deploy terminology. As Merriam (2009) observes, philosophical and methodological concerns have been variously called 'traditions and theoretical underpinnings', 'theoretical traditions and orientations', 'theoretical paradigms', 'worldviews', 'epistemology and theoretical perspectives'. Furthermore, the list of typologies and approaches claimed as underpinning qualitative research can be equally overwhelming. Creswell's (2013: 8–10) summary shows that qualitative inquiry has become a conglomeration of methods, methodologies, theoretical perspectives, and epistemological assumptions, all of which have been bundled together and given the label 'qualitative approaches'. Moreover, whereas in Denzin and Lincoln's (1994, 2000, 2005, 2011b) handbooks we see a neat separation of ontological, epistemological, and methodological assumptions in terms of guiding paradigms, Patton (2002) seems to take the opposite approach, refusing to separate paradigms from philosophies, theoretical orientations, and design strategies. He argues that the 'distinction between paradigmatic, strategic, and theoretical dimensions within any particular approach are both arguable and somewhat arbitrary' (2002: 80). Under the label of 'theoretical traditions and orientations', he lists positivist, realist, and analytic induction approaches, ethnography, phenomenology, ecological psychology, hermeneutics, symbolic interaction, constructivism, grounded theory, and even chaos and complexity theory. These examples amply demonstrate that navigating the qualitative terrains can indeed be a challenging task. In the next section, we examine three different conceptual schemata that continue to hold relevance today, and in the last section of this chapter, we offer another framework – one that tackles the core metaphysical and epistemological issues.

Crotty's research design process

The concern over mixing up philosophical, methodological, and theoretical views, and the call to distinguish among the different elements that make up the research process, are not new. Nearly two decades have passed since the publication of Michael Crotty's *The Foundations of Social Research*, yet one still finds that methodologies, perspectives, and approaches are 'thrown together in grab-bag style as if they were all comparable terms' (Crotty, 1998: 3). The point Crotty strove to emphasize was that constructionism, for example, is not the same as phenomenology, which is not the same as case study. They each have a place in the hierarchy of the research process (he calls it 'different process elements'; 1998: 4). The conceptual categories offered in Figure 1.1 are therefore a helpful starting point for novice researchers, as they aim to equip academics with the confidence to combine complex philosophical ideas with practical steps. The figure shows the four interconnected elements of research as envisioned by Crotty. These are epistemology, theoretical perspective, methodology, and methods. Epistemology is the theory of knowledge: it signals to the researcher the available theoretical perspectives and suitable methodologies and methods. A theoretical perspective is described as 'the philosophical stance informing the methodology and thus providing a context for the process and grounding its logic and criteria' (1998: 3). Methodology is the overall strategy for reaching the research goal(s), whereas methods are the techniques or tools that help researchers collect and analyze data. In Figure 1.1 we can see that by following this model, one can employ constructionism as the epistemology, symbolic interactionism as the theoretical perspective, ethnography as the methodology, and participant observation as a method. Moreover, it is apparent that the research design process is one that should not be taken lightly. It needs to be a carefully mediated activity that culminates in a design that has been well thought through and is reinforced by a strong degree of correspondence between the four elements. Consequently, when working with Crotty's schema, a researcher who aims to provide an objective account of a social phenomenon may be discouraged from proposing a study that combines, say, the epistemology of constructionism with the theoretical perspective of phenomenology. We are told that the path that starts with the epistemology of objectivism – the view that there are objective and mind-independent facts about how things really are – leads, in a 'typical string' (1998: 5), to the theoretical perspective of positivism and to quantitative methods. This way, survey research and statistical analysis might be employed to obtain a sufficient amount of data and confidence so that findings can be generalized to the population at large. Similarly, Crotty argues that symbolic interactionism is 'thoroughly constructionist in character' (1998: 4), leading him to propose a pathway from constructionism to symbolic interactionism to ethnography to participant observation. We already know, however, that there are different schools of symbolic interactionism (such as the Iowa School), and therefore we must treat claims of symbolic interactionism as 'thoroughly constructionist' with caution. The problem before us is that there are multiple pathways and combinations that are not obvious, and in fact not even permitted, within Crotty's model.

The distinction between objectivism and subjectivism has traditionally divided quantitative and qualitative researchers, with the quantitative aligned with objectivism and the qualitative with subjectivism. This characterization glosses over the fact that qualitative research can also be driven by objectivity, and underpinned by realism where philosophical assumptions are concerned. Objectivism can be found in nearly all philosophical orientations and methodological approaches, including idealism, hermeneutics, phenomenology, and even constructionism. Thus, one can indeed abide by the principles of objectivism and realism while engaging in hermeneutic research, as demonstrated in Chapter 4.

Another problem with Crotty's model is that the subjective–objective divide has been gradually replaced by the notions of *intersubjectivity* and *intentionality*.[3] We will devote an entire chapter to social ontology later in the book, but for now suffice it to say that most social scientists concur, to varying degrees, that meaning is constituted in collaborative ways with other agents, recognizing that we do not think and interact in isolation. This means that it is no longer sufficient to contrast objectivism with subjectivism, especially when subjectivism is taken as the view that 'meaning is created out of nothing'[4] (Crotty, 1998: 9). To claim that social facts, such as money, presidents, and tourists, are socially constructed does not (inherently) warrant subjectivism: in epistemology, social constructionism can be compatible with objectivism. In other words, a number of scholars have argued that it is possible to have objective knowledge about socially constructed social facts (e.g., Lawson, 2015; Nola & Sankey, 2007; Searle, 2010). But since

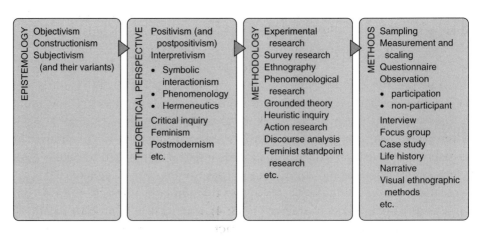

Figure 1.1 Crotty's elements of the research design process

Source: Adapted from Crotty (1998: 5).

objectivism and constructionism are juxtaposed by Crotty as competing episte-mologies in Figure 1.1, we are left with a somewhat muddled perspective.

The vigilant reader will notice that missing in Crotty's schema is ontology. Crotty states that 'ontological issues and epistemological issues tend to emerge together' (1998: 10), informing the theoretical perspective. Although Crotty takes a materialist stance, proclaiming that 'the world is there regardless of whether human beings are conscious of it' (1998: 10), it might be less clear to the novice researcher what precisely ought to 'emerge' philosophically with regard to ontol-ogy and in conjunction with epistemology. We will see in the chapters to come that different ontological entities have 'emerged' to varying degrees among differ-ent thinkers. One can be a realist not only about rocks and trees, but also about numbers, universal laws, social facts, electrons, and so forth. Much confusion and ambiguity can arise if we are not careful about discerning between what kinds of things are claimed to exist.

Overall, Crotty's framework remains a valuable tool for organizing the different elements in a research process; nonetheless, it fails to thoroughly capture the una-voidable complexity of philosophical thought and the spectrum of possibilities in research design.

Qualitative research as 'paradigms'

The word 'paradigm' has become an inevitable part of any researcher's vocabulary. Despite its revival in the twentieth century by various philosophers of science and the popularity it continues to enjoy among scholars today, it had been used rather sporadically and with somewhat varying meanings in the preceding his-torical periods. In his introduction to the fiftieth anniversary edition of Thomas Kuhn's *The Structure of Scientific Revolutions*, originally published in 1962, Ian Hacking (2012) traces its origins to the Greeks, who used the word *paradeigma* to suggest a 'best possible example'. The closest translation of the term is thus 'exemplar'. Hacking notes that 'paradigm' was also employed by members of the Vienna Circle in the 1930s, and was known to appear in the writings of Ludwig Wittgenstein. But it was Kuhn who brought it to the fore of philosophical debates and 'single-handedly changed the currency of the word' (Hacking, 2012 [1962]: xvii). Kuhn himself explained *paradigms* as 'accepted examples of actual scientific practice' (2012 [1962]: 11). He proposed that these exemplars – bound up with sci-entific theories, laws, instruments, and experiments – provide the necessary basis for scientific traditions and the formation of particular scientific communities. Paradigms, according to Kuhn, could be observed historically, and represented communities of scholars who shared similar principles, practices, and traditions (e.g., models, exemplars, generalizations). As he put it, 'Men [sic] whose research is based on shared paradigms are committed to the same rules and standards for scientific practice. That commitment and the apparent consensus it produces are prerequisites for normal science, i.e., for the genesis and continuation of a particular research tradition' (2012 [1962]: 11). Figures such as Copernicus, Newton, and Einstein played a role in transforming the scientific imagination 'in ways that we shall ultimately need to describe as transformation of the world within which scientific work was done' (2012 [1962]: 6).

In the domain of qualitative research, the notion of paradigms has been established and cemented in on a global scale largely through several landmark texts, of which the most influential have been *Naturalistic Inquiry* (Lincoln & Guba, 1985), *The Paradigm Dialog* (Guba, 1990), *Fourth Generation Evaluation* (Guba & Lincoln, 1989), and the numerous editions of the *Handbook of Qualitative Research* (Denzin & Lincoln, 1994, 2000, 2005, 2011b), as well as the paperback editions of *The Landscape of Qualitative Research* (see, for example, Denzin & Lincoln, 2013). Following Kuhn, scholars committed to advancing qualitative inquiry gave the notion of paradigm a predominantly philosophical and methodological meaning. This is most apparent in the description of the paradigm, or 'interpretive framework' (Guba, 1990), as 'a distillation of what we *think* about the world (but cannot prove)' (Lincoln & Guba, 1985: 15), and as a combination of ontological, epistemological, and methodological assumptions (Denzin & Lincoln, 2011a). By using the term 'paradigm' in this fashion, Lincoln and Guba were able to separate various philosophical and methodological concerns into distinct categories. The ongoing process of reorganizing qualitative research according to paradigms has reinforced a conceptual schema that has been in place for nearly three decades.

There is now a widely accepted order that sees qualitative inquiry as organized according to four key paradigms: positivism, postpositivism, critical theory, and constructivism (Guba & Lincoln, 1994). These have been gradually developed in the literature over the past two decades (e.g., Lincoln et al., 2011: 100) to accommodate new directions and concerns, as shown in Table 1.1. Denzin and Lincoln (2011a) see qualitative researchers as situated within four key abstract interpretive paradigms: positivist and postpositivist,[5] constructivist–interpretive, critical (Marxist, emancipatory), and feminist–poststructural. In addition, they have been expanding the paradigm territories in order to accommodate 'specific ethnic, feminist, endarkened, social justice, Marxist, cultural studies, disability, and non-Western-Asian paradigms' (2011a: 13). This shows that contemporary qualitative inquiry is firmly set in the grooves of paradigms. Hacking comments that '[t]oday, it is pretty hard to escape the damn word [paradigm], which is why Kuhn wrote even in 1970 that he had lost control of it' (Hacking, 2012 [1962]: xix). Qualitative researchers have perhaps also lost control over the use of the word, demonstrated by phrases like 'qualitative paradigm' (e.g., Carter, Lubinsky, & Domholdt, 2013; Hatch, 2002; Hesse-Biber & Leavy, 2010; Mouton & Marais, 1988; Tappen, 2010), suggesting that qualitative research as a whole has become a paradigm.

As with Crotty (1998), the achievements of Lincoln, Guba, and Denzin are not to be diminished, for they have provided a system of categorization based on selected philosophical assumptions that can be combined with certain

Table 1.1 Lincoln and Guba's basic beliefs of alternative inquiry paradigms

Item	Positivism	Postpositivism	Critical Theory	Constructivism	Participatory
Ontology	naïve realism – 'real' reality but apprehendible	critical realism – 'real' reality but only imperfectly and probabilistically apprehendible	historical realism – virtual reality shaped by social, political, cultural, economic, ethnic, and gender values; crystallized over time	relativism – local and specific constructed realities	participative reality– subjective-objective reality, co-created by mind and given cosmos
Epistemology	dualist/objectivist; findings true	modified dualist/ objectivist; critical tradition/community; findings probably true	transactional/ subjectivist; value-mediated findings	transactional/ subjectivist; co-created findings	critical subjectivity in participatory transaction with cosmos; extended epistemology of experiential, propositional and practical knowing; co-created findings
Methodology	experimental/ manipulative; verification of hypotheses; chiefly quantitative methods	modified experimental/ manipulative; critical multiplism; falsification of hypotheses; may include qualitative methods	dialogic/dialectical	hermeneutical/ dialectical	political participation in collaborative action inquiry; primacy of the practical; use of language grounded in shared experiential context

Source: Adapted from Lincoln et al. (2011: 100).

methodologies and methods. Problems arise, however, when the paradigms (in Table 1.1) are interpreted in a rigid fashion and compartmentalized into static schemata. Creswell, for example, comments on the inflexibility around the ways in which paradigms have been presented in the literature, noting that they are 'reinforced by the discrete boxes around different paradigm stances' (2010: 54). In other words, each column in Table 1.1 is taken as describing the definitive, discrete options available to researchers in terms of specific ontological, epistemological, and methodological assumptions.

Guba and Lincoln (1994: 116) have claimed that the basic beliefs associated with paradigms are 'essentially contradictory', and have consistently maintained that paradigm commensurability is not possible (Lincoln et al., 2011). While we will not take up the issue of incommensurability here, it must be pointed out that this claim is not only controversial but also immensely problematic. For paradigms to be incommensurable (see, for example, Kuhn's (2012 [1962]) claim that successive scientific paradigms are methodologically, conceptually, and even rationally incomparable), it is a logical necessity that these differ substantially in their tenets. Yet the way the paradigms are formulated in Table 1.1 does not meet this criterion because they are not necessarily mutually exclusive. It is beyond our scope to systematically analyze all of the tables that seek to categorize paradigms in Denzin and Lincoln's handbook(s), but we must address at least the main drawbacks.

For example, on the level of ontological claims, the positivists, we are told, believe in 'real' reality, whereas the constructivists are relativists believing in 'local and specific co-constructed realities' (Lincoln et al., 2011: 100). The question then arises as to what 'real reality' stands for. The answer seems to be 'nature'. If we are speaking about objects existing externally and independent of the mind (materialism), then we can argue that there is no difference between, say, positivism and constructionism. Guba and Lincoln state that 'for constructivists, either there is a "real" reality or there is not (although one might wish to resolve this problem differently in considering the physical versus the human realms)' (1994: 116), leaving us to wonder whether all constructionists are Berkeleyan idealists who question external reality altogether. This, of course, would be unfortunate, as most constructionists are metaphysical realists or materialists content to accept external reality, as we will see in Chapter 6. To claim that social realities are constructed is not to deny the existence of rocks and trees – a point made explicit by Searle in his book *The Construction of Social Reality* (1996: 10). The acknowledgement of metaphysical realism can also be found in the writings of other constructionists, such as Burr (1998, 2003) and Gergen (2009). Therefore, what Lincoln and Guba call 'real' reality, assuming that they are referring to external objects, is available to scholars of diverse philosophical footing, including social constructionists (who they refer to as 'constructivists').

Another problem is that ontology is at times explained in terms of, and conflated with, semantics. For instance, in one of their matrices, the ontology of positivism is described as a 'belief in a single identifiable reality', followed by the statement that 'there is a single truth that can be measured and studied' (Lincoln et al.,

2011: 102). Truth, however, is a property of propositions or sentences – it is not an ontological but a semantic feature, such as when we speak of the truth-value of scientific statements. In other words, 'truth' denotes the semantic correctness of statements about reality (i.e. correspondence theory of truth). For some, truth can also be an epistemic notion (i.e. coherence theory of truth, pragmatist approaches to truth, etc.). For the logical positivists, truth had to do with propositions verified empirically, known as the principle of verification (discussed in Chapter 2).

Similarly, when – in describing the ontology of postpositivism – the authors say that for the postpositivists, '[t]here is a single reality, but we may not be able to fully understand what it is or how to get to it' (2011: 102), in fact, what they are discussing is no longer solely ontology. Understanding what something is, and how to get to it, is different from claiming that something is or exists: to *understand* what things are pertains to knowledge claims; to ponder *how to* obtain knowledge about the world pertains to methodology and methods. Here, we can argue again that there is always *something* that exists for all thinkers, except perhaps the idealists, solipsists, and extreme subjectivists.

By considering the notion of objectivism, we can further demonstrate that paradigms, as presented by Lincoln et al. (2011), are not fully adequate. In Table 1.1 objectivism is mostly associated with positivism and postpositivism. However, neither positivism nor postpositivism is as strongly associated with objectivism as is scientific realism – the strongest form of realism available to any scholar. Scientific realism claims that scientific knowledge about both observable and unobservable (theoretical) entities ought to be treated as a true and accurate description of reality (Sankey, 2008). Historically speaking, the positivists were not prepared to commit to unobservable entities as knowledge (atoms, for example), and these reservations have attracted accusations of subjectivism. As Laudan famously proclaimed, '[O]ne of the best-kept secrets of the philosophical era between the 1930s and the early 1960s was that the positivists themselves were radical subjectivists about methodology and epistemology' (1996: 15). Phillips and Burbules (2000) have similarly pointed out that it would be misleading to view positivists as realists because many took an anti-realist or non-realist stand. In addition, as Phillips explains, the logical positivists 'did not have much time for the notion of absolute truth, and they wanted to remain close to the raw phenomena of experience' (2000: 166). In fact, logical empiricism/logical positivism have traditionally stood opposed to scientific realism (Godfrey-Smith, 2009). Therefore, it would be misleading to assign the label of objectivism equally to the realists, logical positivists, and postpositivists (an issue explored in Chapter 2). It would also be equally limiting to claim that constructionist and hermeneutic inquiry is subjectivist (as per Lincoln et al.'s suggestion in Table 1.1), for we have already established in our analysis of Crotty's model that there is such a thing as objective hermeneutics.

With regard to the methodological matrices in Table 1.1, we have to exercise additional caution in light of the numerous ways in which philosophical traditions can be implemented in the research process. If we take phenomenology (discussed in more depth in Chapter 4) as an example, the fact that the *Encyclopedia of Phenomenology* (Embree, 1997) lists 28 phenomenological figures and 40 major phenomenological topics suggests a rich tradition that may not so easily be compressed into one or two paradigms. There are at least four dominant strains in phenomenological approaches: realistic phenomenology, constitutive phenomenology, existential phenomenology, and hermeneutic phenomenology (Moran & Mooney, 2002). Husserl's (1965 [1910], 1970, 2001 [1900/1901]) eidetic reduction and focus on the study of *essences* are not the same as Heidegger's (1962) and Gadamer's (1976, 2004 [1960]) hermeneutic concerns, such as their emphasis on the structural interpretation of foreknowledge. Moreover, phenomenological and hermeneutic inquiry may be driven by objectivity – we need only consider Paul Ricoeur and Gunter Figal's 'objective turn' in hermeneutic phenomenology (see Figal & Espinet, 2014). Thus, the ways in which the paradigms in Figure 1.1 are composed presents a limited philosophical–methodological vista.

In summary, whether at the level of ontological, epistemological, or methodological considerations, any attempt to capture the complexity and richness of philosophical thought by means of distinct paradigms must ultimately reach its limits. Guba and Lincoln ought to be commended for taking on a task of such mammoth proportions. However, as some of the limitations above suggest, there is scope for loosening the paradigmatic grip on qualitative inquiry to accommodate a broad range of philosophical and methodological amalgamations.

Lally's anatomy of metatheoretical and epistemological assumptions in social science

In addition to Crotty's (1998) structure of the research process and Lincoln and Guba's (2000) paradigmatic matrix, there is another schematic representation worthy of mention, one which seeks to integrate philosophical thought into social science. The application of philosophy to sociology is not an easy task even for the seasoned academic (often under the influence of the community of practice to which she[6] belongs), let alone for students who have a relatively short amount of time at their disposal to grasp the ideas proffered by various philosophers. As a way of providing a pedagogical strategy, Jim Lally (1981) created a model that enables students to engage with the process. He developed an axial schema onto which he mapped epistemological assumptions to demonstrate how questions in the philosophy of science can be applied to, and may feature in, sociological inquiry (see Figure 1.2). The model consists of two axes: a horizontal axis that bisects the *subject–object* distinction and a vertical axis that differentiates between '*Analysis of the "Is"*' and '*Analysis for the "Ought To Be"*'. In erecting this basic structure, Lally placed all those philosophers for whom *man* [sic] was 'the key unit of sociological analysis' on the left (for example Kant, who contended that man is the *subject* of all knowledge), and on the right those thinkers who took the existence of man as 'shaped by his environment', and for whom the focus of inquiry is not the subject but social structures and social 'facts' (Lally, 1981: 6). In other words, on the left side reside those thinkers who took the *subject* or the Self to be the central focus of inquiry, while on the right the primary focus is on the environment, structures, and systems – taken to shape human action and behaviour. With regard to the vertical axis, the upper area represents the study of existing social reality, labelled as the analysis of the 'Is'; the lower region gathers thinkers whose primary interest was to expose society's flaws 'as a prelude to having it changed fundamentally' (1981: 7). As we move towards the bottom of the vertical axis, the focus shifts to the analysis of the 'Ought to Be'. For Lally the vertical axis was as important as the horizontal because:

> [...] it divides between those who see themselves as doing science (whether of the natural science variety as in Positivism or of a peculiarly *social* science variety as in Interactionism) as that term is generally understood and those who see these 'sciences' as part of the problem. Those above the axis tend to write off those below as ideologists. Those below to tend to write off those above as dabbling in superficialities while all around them cruelty and crises obviously abound and the human condition grows rapidly worse. (Lally, 1981: 7)

The key 'paradigms' in Lally's schema are *interactionism* and *emancipationism* on the 'subject' end and *positivism* and *structural determinism* on the 'object' end. It is worthwhile pointing out here that the variables used by Lally are adjusted to address sociological concerns, including the listing of major sociological influences. Another interesting feature is that some philosophers occupy more than one quadrant: Husserl and Dilthey, for instance, are listed under interactionism and emancipationism, Marx under emancipationism and structural determinism, and Weber under interactionism and positivism. Based on the outline of propositions that define each quadrant, we could further enlist other intellectuals and assign Foucault, Habermas, and Gramsci the label of emancipationists. Omitted in Lally's list, but important to note, are also many female scholars, including Hannah Arendt, Ágnes Heller, Simone de Beauvoir, Regina Becker-Schmidt, Nancy Fraser, bell hooks, Martha Nussbaum, Judith Butler and Seyla Benhabib.

Despite some initial usefulness, the predicament of Lally's model is that, like the previous two, it fails to provide a complete picture. For example, it is possible to describe some proponents of social constructionism as interactionists (e.g., Kenneth Gergen) but also as structural determinists (e.g., John Searle). We will examine the difference between Gergen and Searle in more depth in Chapter 6. What becomes clear in all of the models noted thus far is that any attempt to contain, say, constructionism, in a paradigmatic straitjacket leads to a very narrow understanding. Similarly, the brief outline of the four schools of symbolic interactionism in the previous section would suggest that symbolic interactionism is too diverse and complex to be restricted to a single quadrant. For instance, the differences between the Chicago and Iowa schools are too great to place both on the

ANALYSIS OF THE 'IS'	
INTERACTIONISM	**POSITIVISM**
Propositions:	**Propositions:**
1. There are fundamental differences between the natural and the social sciences. Therefore the methods of the former are not directly applicable to the latter. 2. There can be no conclusive disproof of a theory. 3. There is no objective social reality independent of a knowing human subject. 4. Social reality is a continually emerging phenomenon. Change is omnipresent.	1. The phenomena dealt with by the social sciences are qualitatively no different from those of the natural sciences. Hence, the methodology of the latter is appropriate for the former. 2. The principle aim of sociology is to formulate a system of empirically grounded theories that will ultimately be used for accurate prediction of social phenomena. 3. An empiricist epistemology in which knowledge of an object consists in apprehending its essence by a process of abstraction (generalizing) from the concrete object is appropriate for scientific sociology.
Key enterprise: Analysis of behaviour at the level of meaning. **Ontology:** Social reality as produced and emergent. **Philosophers:** Kant, Husserl, Dilthey. **Major sociological influences:** Weber, Mead, Simmel.	**Key enterprise:** Causal explanation and cumulative theory building. **Ontology:** Social reality exists 'out there' independent of human knower. **Philosophers:** Hume, Locke, Mill, logical positivists. **Major sociological influences:** Durkheim, Weber.

SUBJECT	OBJECT
EMANCIPATIONISM	**STRUCTURAL DETERMINISM**
Propositions:	**Propositions:**
1. Sociological theory is not, nor should it attempt to be, value-neutral. Positivist assertions to the contrary contribute to the mystification process. 2. Sociological theory must be united with political practice. 3. The crux of the sociological enterprise should be a mood of meaningful social criticism and a spirit of continuing self-reflection aimed at demystification and significant social change.	1. The key to understanding the observable social world lies in understanding the structure which underlies that world of appearance. 2. Empiricism is not scientific and is not an appropriate methodology. 3. Acceptable sociological explanation can be arrived at only by concentrating on the *objects* which constitute the social structure. The role of the knowing subject is minimised. 4. Significant social change can be brought about only by effecting change at the level of the infrastructure.
Key enterprise: Intervention in consciousness and discourse. **Ontology:** Social reality as mystification and manipulation. **Philosophers:** Hegel, Husserl, Dilthey, Marx, Wittgenstein. **Major sociological influences:** The Frankfurt theorists.	**Key enterprise:** Mapping structural relations and contradictions. **Ontology:** Social reality as underlying structure. **Philosophers:** Rousseau, Marx, Bachelard, Saussure (linguist). **Major sociological influences:** Marx.

ANALYSIS FOR THE 'OUGHT TO BE'

Figure 1.2 Lally's anatomy of metatheoretical and epistemological assumptions in social science (adapted from Lally, 1981: Figure 1 (p. 8) and Figure 2 (p. 10))

'subject' side of the continuum. The Iowa programme is closer to the right-hand spectrum on the subject–object axis because its concerns lie with structures (what Lally calls the 'object') and not the Self. Furthermore, the Illinois School and Denzin's interpretive interactionism would be more appropriately situated in the paradigm of emancipationism within the 'Ought to Be' region because it takes a hermeneutic turn and makes a strong claim about the role of research in facilitating change and action. There is hope for a better and more just world (the 'Ought to Be'), and the researcher is not a distanced observer but instead takes an active part in this project. Denzin's recent 'call to arms' is undoubtedly a powerful form of academic activism. Consequently, symbolic interactionism can be stretched into different corners in Lally's model as not all interactionists sit comfortably in the upper-left region in Figure 1.2. Understood more broadly, interactionism is a 'broad approach to sociology' and a 'sociological perspective that has had multiple origins and inspirations' (Atkinson & Housley, 2003: 1).

The contrast between the schemas created by Crotty (1998), Lally (1981), and Lincoln et al. (2011) shows that there are various ways in which theoretical and philosophical issues can be framed. It also demonstrates the difficulty of encapsulating the concerns and ideas for which various philosophers have been known, and which are not so easily organized under only one label, or one set of parameters, or one conceptual framework. The danger of compartmentalizing qualitative research into distinct paradigms is that we lose sight of the subtler varieties and close the doors to other ways of thinking and knowing. Schemata and models are designed to organize academic practice – they structure the ways in which research proceeds as well as what knowledge we produce and how we produce it. The comparison of the models is an exercise not only in vigilance but also in celebrating the conceptual minds that have played a pivotal role in the shaping of qualitative research and social science. The final section of this chapter will offer an additional conceptual framework which may prompt the student to ponder metaphysical and epistemological concerns.

An alternative approach to metaphysical and epistemological concerns

The most fundamental philosophical questions for any inquirer to deal with are what exists, whether we can know that it exists, and if so, how. These problems have intrigued many philosophers and have led to the formation of various doctrines, including solipsism, scepticism, idealism, rationalism, empiricism, and realism. We will explore these in more detail in the chapters that follow, but for our present purposes, consider this question: *Is there an external world with objects such as rocks and trees and other planets that exists independent of our cognitive faculties?* This question is an invitation to metaphysical or ontological concerns. Metaphysics[7] is the 'the theory of reality and the ultimate nature of all things';

it extends to all kinds of entities, including God or gods and the spiritual realm (Solomon & Higgins, 2010: 7). In this book, our focus will remain on the types of entities, categories, and structures that have been the object of scientific interest, such as physical matter, numbers, universals, and the laws that govern nature. The term 'ontology' was invented in the seventeenth century to capture the science of being (van Inwagen, 2013). Ontology is a field of metaphysics that is concerned with the study of being or that which is. According to Solomon and Higgins (2010), ontology includes a hierarchy of levels of reality to determine what is believed to exist, undeniably, in the external world. As an exercise in ontology, they suggest pondering the extent to which the following may be considered as real: trees, numbers, atoms, geometric shapes, love, beauty, galaxies, consciousness, music, the theory of relativity, human rights, and colours. We realize that not all of these items are real in the same sense: some have physical properties, some are appearances, some are abstract and theoretical concepts, and some are produced by our senses. The aim of ontology, therefore, is to answer 'what is *most* real, what is *most* basic, and what is to be accounted for in terms of what' (Solomon & Higgins, 2010: 111). Having this basic understanding will serve us well when we explore the metaphysical and ontological battles between the rationalists and the empiricists in Chapter 2.

To put these ideas into practice, at the level of metaphysical concerns, qualitative researchers can distinguish between two contrasting positions: materialism/metaphysical realism and immaterialism/metaphysical idealism. Materialism is the view that material objects exist in the external world 'independently of the minds of perceivers'[8] (Musgrave, 1993: 122). In some literature, materialism is used synonymously with another term, physicalism, introduced in the 1930s by Otto Neurath and Rudolf Carnap (both members of the Vienna Circle). This term denotes the thesis that everything in the world conforms to the condition of being physical (Stoljar, 2009). To accept physicalism is to assert that everything can be reduced to a set of physical properties – that ultimately, everything is matter. In order to simplify our inquiry, we will employ the term 'metaphysical realism' to designate the broader view that matter exists. Metaphysical realism, in its basic form, makes the claim that 'there is a world that exists independent of the mental' (Lynch, 2002: 59). This view is compatible with the chief tenets of realism, including the claims that 'the world contains ingredients whose existence does not depend either logically or causally upon any form of cognition or perception' (Stroll, 2000: 96) and that 'reality is indeed "out there" and existing independently of us and our understanding of it' (Gorman, 1992: 24). While throughout this book we shall not maintain a strict distinction between the words 'ontological' and 'metaphysical', we shall use the latter to capture the broader inquiry into that which is.

Metaphysical realism is the opposing view to *metaphysical idealism* or *immaterialism*. If metaphysical realism claims that matter exists independent of the human mind, metaphysical idealism must be the notion that 'everything is mental or an aspect of, or dependent on, the mental' (Alston, 2002: 97). Metaphysical idealism and immaterialism is most strongly captured in the philosophy of George Berkeley (1685–1753), who is commonly associated with the view that matter does not exist and that we can only have certainty about our *ideas*. Debate abounds among philosophers about the degree to which Berkeley is believed to have rejected the existence of matter. Musgrave clarifies that Berkeley was denying 'that stones or doors exist as material objects external to minds', while on the other hand conceding that 'stones and doors exist, or are real things, but they consist of particular collections of ideas in people's minds' (1993: 127). In the words of Rickless, Berkeley's argument can be formulated as follows: ' [...] if sensible objects are nothing but collections of ideas and the only kinds of things there are in the world are minds, ideas, and sensible objects, then the only kinds of things there are in the world are minds and ideas' (2013: 1). The upshot of this, is that for the materialists there is something external to the mind (i.e. matter) causing us to have sense data, whereas for Berkeley, whatever the cause of sensations is, this could well be the mind (or spirit). On the level of metaphysics, Berkeley shifts our focus from the immediate perception of external objects to sense data and ideas. Following his philosophy, therefore, what there *is* and what we can *know*, are appearances, ideas, or collections of ideas. In this respect, an idealist thinker would hold that 'what we call "reality" is something which depends for its existence upon our own minds' (Gorman, 1992: 24). Broadly speaking then, idealism purports that sensible objects (such as rocks and trees) and their properties are mind-dependent entities; immaterialism tells us 'that there is no such thing as material substance, there is no senseless, unperceiving thing in which sensible properties inhere' (Rickless, 2013: 1). We will return to Berkeley in Chapter 3, but for the time being, this is what the philosopher himself had to say on the issue:

> We see only the appearances, and not the real qualities of things. What may be the extension, figure, or motion of anything really and absolutely, or in itself, it is impossible for us to know, but only the proportion or relation they bear to our senses. Things remaining the same, our ideas vary, and which of them, or even whether any of them at all, represent the true quality really existing in the thing, it is out of our reach to determine. (Berkeley, 2008 [1710]: 70)

With respect to metaphysical concerns, thus far we have established that metaphysical realism or materialism ought to be contrasted with metaphysical idealism or immaterialism (this has been suggested previously also by Crotty, 1998; Gorman, 1992; Stroll, 2000). This is depicted visually in Figure 1.3. To return to the question posed earlier ('Is there an external world with objects such as rocks and trees and other planets that exists independent of our cognitive faculties?'), we should be able to formulate two clear responses. One may either state that there are indeed objects that exist independent of any person's consciousness (i.e., metaphysical realism), or one may assert that what exists are ideas and sense data (i.e., metaphysical idealism). However, there is also a third response, and perhaps the most extreme, which not only utterly denies the existence of matter, it also rejects the existence of other minds – namely, other thinking subjects. This philosophical stance is called *solipsism*. It is the view that material objects have no existence other than in our consciousness, and that 'the only real existent is the *self*' (Ellis, 1999: 439).[9] Solipsism's claims are so extreme that it would be difficult to find a contemporary philosopher willing to defend its thesis. Ellis (1999) tells us that Kant, for example, saw solipsism as a scandal to philosophy, and that Schopenhauer deemed all solipsists to be madmen. More recently, Musgrave (1993: 104) called it the 'lunatic version of idealism'. He also pointed out the necessity of distinguishing solipsism from idealism because some commentators have mistakenly accused some idealist philosophical figures, such as Hume and Berkeley, of solipsism.

Mainly for logical reasons, solipsism is less likely to be popular in the social sciences than in a natural science such as theoretical physics. If one were to deny the existence of other human beings, then there would be little point in any research activity at all. Put differently, solipsism undermines the academic endeavour and refutes itself as a legitimate metaphysical stance. Vernes sums it up nicely by stating that according to the solipsistic thesis, 'We are the only person in existence. Correction: I am the only person in existence and I wonder why I am trying so hard to communicate my remarkable thoughts to you' (2000: 92). In Figure 1.3 solipsism is therefore separated out from the two main positions of metaphysical realism and metaphysical idealism. The question of whether or not it is possible to know anything other than our sense impressions will occupy us in Chapters 3 and 4. For the time being, we shall reiterate that on the level of metaphysical concerns, the key choice is between materialism/metaphysical realism and immaterialism/metaphysical idealism, as shown by the continuum in Figure 1.3.

Figure 1.3 is organized into four tiers, each representing a layer of specific philosophical concerns. The first tier deals with western metaphysical concerns, the second with western epistemological concerns, the third with non-western and indigenous philosophical views, and the fourth with additional theoretical concerns. In keeping with our present focus on metaphysical issues, the first tier simply considers what exists. In order to make epistemic claims, we have to be

----

CORE WESTERN METAPHYSICAL (ONTOLOGICAL) CONCERNS [TIER 1]

Views about what there is and is not (e.g., the existence of matter).

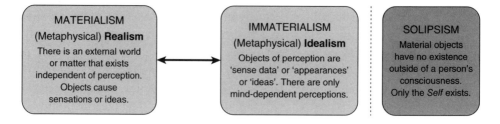

CORE WESTERN EPISTEMOLOGICAL CONCERNS [TIER 2]

Views about what can be known, the scope and sources of knowledge and its limitations.

1. **EMPIRICISM** → Knowledge derives a *posteriori* from experience of observable entities.

2. **RATIONALISM** → Knowledge derives a *priori* from logic and reason.

3. **REALISM**

   – DIRECT REALISM → Knowledge of the external world is direct as perceived through the senses (also called *naïve* realism).

   – INDIRECT REALISM → Knowledge of the external world is indirect (also called *causal* or *representative* realism).

   – SCIENTIFIC REALISM → Scientific theories describe the world as it really is, including both observable and *unobservable* entities.

4. **IDEA-ISM** → Knowledge is limited to *sense data* and *ideas* (i.e., the content of the mind).

5. **SCEPTICISM** → No knowledge is possible; we shall suspend judgement about the possibility of knowing anything.

CAVEAT: Most epistemological stances can be traced to the doctrines outlined above. For example, constructivism can be understood as a form of Kantian idealism whereby reality is cognitively constructed. Social constructionism can be understood as a form of idea-ism, postpositivism as a form of rationalism, and logical positivism as a form of empiricism.

NON-WESTERN EPISTEMOLOGIES [TIER 3]

African, East Asian, Native American, First Nations, Māori, Mesoamerican, Polynesian, Indian, and other epistemologies.

ADDITIONAL CONCERNS AND (THEORETICAL) FRAMEWORKS [TIER 4]

What is claimed to exist (in metaphysical and ontological terms) and to be known (in epistemological terms) is subject to other factors which may form an important, and for some inevitable, part of the inquiry. These include social, cultural, historical, political, and ideological influences as well as various critical lenses.

> - The sociology of knowledge
> - Deconstructionism
> - Critical theory
> - Queer theory
> - Race theory
> - Indigenous critical theory
> - Postmodernism
> - Poststructuralism
> - Symbolic interactionist approaches
> - Critical hermeneutics
> - Philosophical hermeneutics
> - Etc.

For some thinkers the concerns listed in Tier 4 can, but do not always have to, form a fundamental part of inquiry. Knowledge is contingent upon political, ethical, and economic ideals, and inseparable from discourses of power (e.g., Foucault, 1977). It can be deconstructed vis-à-vis race theory, queer theory, indigenous critical theory, and critical hermeneutics. Furthermore, various symbolic interactionist approaches may offer different strategies for the study of human behaviour and social interaction.

Figure 1.3 Core philosophical considerations for qualitative research

clear about the *what* – the object – of knowledge, which, as we have already seen, can range from numbers and colours to atoms and rocks. Therefore Tiers 1 and 2 mark the difference between the metaphysical/ontological status of the objects of knowledge and the ways in which we can know about the world (epistemology).

Epistemology, taken as a theory about knowledge, asks such questions as, 'What kind of knowledge do we believe will be attained by our research? What characteristics do we believe that knowledge to have? [...] How should observers of our research [...] regard the outcomes we lay out before them? And why should our readers take these outcomes seriously?' (Crotty, 1998: 2). We can see that Tier 2 is organized according to five core epistemological concerns: empiricism, rationalism, realism, idea-ism, and scepticism. It is necessary to bear in mind here that not all of these are preoccupied solely with epistemic issues: some are much broader philosophical doctrines that are also concerned with ontology, ethics, methodology, and methods (this will become clear later on in this book, such as when we discuss realism in Chapter 5). In Figure 1.3, we concentrate only on the epistemic dimension of these philosophical stances.

Historically, there have been two ways by which knowledge claims can be rationally justified: empiricism and rationalism (Gorman, 1992: 21). On the one hand is the view that knowledge can only derive from experience (empiricism), and on the other that the source of knowledge is reason (rationalism). Opposed to both of these claims is scepticism, whose adherents at minimum refrain from making any judgement about beliefs and knowledge (alethic scepticism), but may go so far as to claim that no knowledge is possible at all (this dogmatic variety is called Academic scepticism). In order to defend empiricism, Locke, Berkeley, and Hume, the well-known trio of British empiricists, played a major role in developing the theory of 'sense data', which has come to be known as idealism in metaphysics or ontology and idea-ism in epistemology (Musgrave, 1993). We have already established that idealists hold 'that we can simply make no *sense* of the existence of something *independently* of its existence as known by us, as mediated through our minds' (Gorman, 1992: 25; emphasis in original). For example, if a devout realist were to demonstrate that material objects exist by lifting up her foot and proclaiming 'this is my foot', as Stroll (2000) points out, the idealist would respond that the foot is merely a collection of sensations. Furthermore, because sensations are *ideas* and thus mental entities, the foot can never have a mind-independent status (Stroll, 2000). When we use the term *idea-ism* in making knowledge claims, as noted in Figure 1.3, we espouse the view that 'what we are immediately aware of in perception are appearances, or ideas or sense-data' (Musgrave,1993: 96). Idea-ism as an epistemological doctrine thus states that we can only have knowledge or immediate information about ideas and sense data – it is a thesis about the nature of perception, 'not a metaphysical thesis about what exists' (Ladyman, 2002: 144). This distinction is important because idealism inevitably presupposes idea-ism in epistemology, but we shall see that not all idea-ists are necessarily idealists.

The doctrine we have yet to address in Tier 2 is realism. We have already seen that with respect to ontology and metaphysics *metaphysical realism* makes claims about the existence of objects. The metaphysical or ontological realist 'affirms the existence (or reality) of a largely mind-, experience-, language-, concept-, theory-, and practice-independent world' (Pihlström, 2014: 252). Thus, rocks and trees exist regardless of our ability to perceive them, touch them, describe them, and theorize about them. In addition to this metaphysical claim, on the level of epistemic concerns, realism also has something to say about knowledge and methods of arriving at truth. Scientific realists are the ones that make the strongest claims about knowledge. Scientific realism is a doctrine fuelled by the aim of science to produce *true theories* about observable and theoretical entities (Sankey, 2008). It is the strongest realist position because its proponents hold that the aim of science is to discover the truth about the world (Nola & Sankey, 2007), and therefore a notable characteristic of scientific theories is that they not only correspond to reality, they also accurately or truthfully describe it. In other words, scientific realists are committed to there being 'a literally true story of what the world is like' (Giere, 2005: 150). Psillos's statement that 'there are no better explanations of the success of science than the realist one' (1999: 97) underscores the high esteem in which some scientists hold scientific realism. In addition to scientific realism, Figure 1.3 also includes direct and indirect realism, and additional varieties will be explored in Chapter 5. Put simply, direct realism is the naïve view that the world is how we perceive it directly via our senses; indirect realism is the view that we can only have indirect knowledge of the external world as things are not always how they appear to us.

Tier 3 acknowledges non-western epistemological outlooks. It would take several volumes to cover all the world's theories of knowledge, but it is important to at least recognize that these exist by inserting an additional layer to Figure 1.3. The numbering of the tiers does not imply that Tier 3 is less important in the hierarchy of philosophical views. Indigenous scholars, for example, may situate their work in the western tradition (i.e., Tiers 1 and 2) but they can also ground their inquiry in non-western philosophy (i.e., Tier 3). In addition, those academics operating from an ethno-epistemological standpoint (for further clarification see Maffie, 2013) may approach western epistemology as one among many epistemological undertakings, together with African, East Asian, Native American, First Nations, Mesoamerican, Polynesian, Indian, and other epistemologies. This book can be viewed as an overview of the developments in western philosophical thought, and the reader invested in non-western schools of thought may wish to complement it with other works that specifically address other theories of knowledge (e.g., Denzin et al., 2008; Devy et al., 2014; George, 1999; Kincheloe & Steinberg, 2008; Meyer, 2003; Phillips, 2012; Sandoval, 2000; Semali & Kincheloe, 1999; Smith, 1999).

Tier 4 attends to additional theoretical concerns. These are called 'additional' in order to emphasize that they do not replace, but rather can be added to, Tiers 1, 2 and 3. In other words, all forms of inquiry are underpinned by some type of metaphysical and epistemological claim, and these can be enriched by a range of theoretical concerns. Depending on the nature of the research project, these theoretical concerns can (but do not necessarily have to)[10] play a pivotal role in the formulation of the philosophical assumptions. For instance, following the writings of Habermas, Foucault, and Gadamer, a researcher can assert that the search for knowledge ought to include a critical analysis of the 'obvious' because the ways in which knowledge is produced, and what is often represented, are driven by various interests (e.g., political, ethical, economic). Moreover, because these interests are not so easily divorced from social realities, the role of the inquiry is to critically examine and deconstruct such influences. Hence researchers can draw, for example, on critical hermeneutics as a way of examining the issue of power and domination. The types of concerns listed in Tier 4 extend to critical indigenous theory, race theory, gender theory, and numerous other issue-based theories that can be located within distinct intellectual movements such as poststructuralism and postmodernism.

Finally, before we continue our inquiry into that which is, whether we can know something, and if so, how, it is necessary to reaffirm the scope of this text. Due to its specific focus on philosophical issues and the limited space available, this volume only attends to the metaphysical and epistemological problems noted in Tiers 1 and 2. Their content will be discussed in depth in the second part of the book: Chapter 2 will examine empiricism and rationalism; Chapter 3 will look at scepticism, idealism, and idea-ism; Chapter 4 will survey German idealism, phenomenology, and hermeneutics; and Chapter 5 will unpack the different forms of realism and anti-realism. In the third part of the book, we will address some of the neglected domains of qualitative research. In Chapter 6, we will explore social ontology through the work of John Searle and articulate how it is possible for social facts, such as money, presidents, professors, and tourists, to exist. We will also contrast between different attitudes towards social constructionism in order to debunk some of the myths and misconceptions associated with it. In Chapter 7, we will venture into the territory of quantum mechanics and outline nine theories about quantum reality. This exercise will allow us to ponder some of the problems with claims of absolutism and universalism. Finally, Chapter 8 will offer a summary of this book's key points and propose that qualitative inquiry can be imagined on an attitudinal continuum from 'means' to 'orientation'.

Notes

1. Rather than using 'I' and drawing the attention to the author, the term 'we' was chosen deliberately to include the reader in the philosophical explorations.
2. The terms 'constructionism', 'social constructionism', and 'constructivism' are often used interchangeably and inconsistently in the literature – a problem that has been addressed elsewhere (see, for example, Pernecky, 2012). Throughout this book we will use the terms 'constructionism' and 'social constructionism' when discussing the collective generation of meaning, and when speaking about socially constructed reality and/or knowledge (particularly in Chapters 1 and 6). We reserve the term 'constructivism' for the meaning-making activity

of the individual mind – in other words, for the cognitive processes of the mind (for example, Kant's constructivist outlook, examined in Chapter 4). However, a number of commentators in qualitative research use the word 'constructivism' to express the notion of socially constructed knowledge/reality, i.e., constructionism, such as Guba and Lincoln (1994), Denzin and Lincoln (2011a), and Lincoln et al. (2011), when they speak of the constructivist paradigm.

3. Regarding intentionality, there are two opposing views: one that understands mental states as 'directness' or 'aboutness' (notable in the work of Franz Bretano, Edmund Husserl, and lately, John Searle), and another which rejects the mind–world and subject–object dualisms and the traditional representationalist account of practice (Heidegger's Dasein as being absorbed in the world) (Dreyfus, 1993).

4. Crotty adds that meaning is not derived entirely out of 'nothing'; he explains that in subjectivism, meaning can come from one's dreams, one's religious beliefs, 'primordial archetypes', 'the conjunction and aspects of the planets', etc. (1998: 9). One can argue, however, that the latter are examples of intersubjectivity. Religious beliefs, for instance, are socially constituted and accepted by individuals.

5. This can be a confusing term as 'postpositivism' is sometimes used to denote a modified pro-positivist attitude to knowledge but also an anti-positivist stance, which is how we will use the term in this book (e.g., in Chapter 2).

6. To include all sexes, we will alternate between 'he' and 'she' throughout the book.

7. It is pertinent to note that because of the strong hold religion had over science until the Age of Enlightment (1650s to 1780s), the terms 'metaphysics' and 'metaphysical' were strongly interconnected with the realm of the 'divine'. This association can still be observed today, particularly in religiously oriented literature. In this book we will employ the term mainly in reference to reality and being with respect to scientific knowledge.

8. Musgrave explains that there is a strong and a weak view of materialism (see 1993: 122). We shall follow the weaker view, which states that material objects exist (as opposed to the stronger view, which states that only material objects exist).

9. According to Ellis, one can further differentiate between metaphysical and epistemological solipsism: the first suggests that only the *Self* exists, while the latter 'advances the modest claim that the Self is the source of all knowledge of existence' (Ellis, 1999: 439). In addition, Musgrave (1993) notes that many philosophers have adopted the 'methodological solipsism' of Rudolf Carnap, which begins with metaphysical solipsism but eventually establishes the existence of external objects and other minds.

10. Not all qualitative work is motivated by critical theory and some scholars may simply wish to use qualitative research as a method. We will return to this issue in the concluding chapter and distinguish between qualitative research as a *method* and as an *orientation*.

PART II
Key Epistemological and Metaphysical Problems

Discussion is impossible with someone who claims not to seek truth, but already to possess it.

(Romain Rolland, *Above the Battle*; cited in Pratt, 2008)

Two

In Search of Truths: Empiricism Versus Rationalism

The defining question of epistemology – *How is knowledge possible?* – is an invitation to thinking about how anybody is to know anything about anything (Cassam, 2009: 3). This problem of vast epistemological scope cannot be addressed by a single book, let alone in one chapter. It is possible, however, to explore some of the developments in thought about knowledge, and with this aim in mind, focus on the two rival doctrines that became the building blocks for scientific knowledge: rationalism and empiricism. This chapter commences by noting the importance of mathematical truths in establishing rationalism as the accepted worldview for nearly 2,000 years. It explains the difference between the rationalist and empiricist approaches to knowledge by situating these within broader historical debates, and outlines the main arguments advanced by their adherents on each side. The second part of the chapter examines the more contemporary manifestations of empiricism and rationalism through the epistemologies of positivism and postpositivism. It will be shown that the core values of empiricism evolved into logical empiricism, and that the principles of rationalism have been revived in Karl Popper's postpositivist critique of positivism. In addition to delineating the key tenets, the chapter will also survey the ramifications for social science research. A summary and implications for qualitative research will be offered at the end.

On the importance of mathematics

The quest for knowledge is one of the most admirable attributes of human beings. Although modern humans have survived in nature for nearly 200,000 years, as a species, we only started to form a coherent understanding of the external world in the last 3,000 years. For much of our existence, observable occurrences in nature and unexplained events were ascribed to the work of spirits and given mystical explanations. Our existence was ruled by belief. With the formation of societies and organized religion, such phenomena continued to be comprehended and explained by invoking the supernatural. Solar eclipses, for example, were seen by most ancient civilizations as a bad omen, and were linked with death, wars, famine, and disease (Steel, 2001). The use of myths was part of most cultures, including African, Mesopotamian, Indonesian, Greek, Roman, Zuni, Aztec, and Celtic societies. These were religious narratives about various aspects of reality that transcended the possibilities of common experience (Leeming, 2005). This understanding of the world influenced human behaviour, culture, and traditions in all parts of the world. Nature, then only poorly understood, was seen as chaotic and dangerous.

It was the Greek conception of the universe that set in motion the intellectual growth of humanity, and importantly, the search for scientific explanations. The Greek influence, particularly on the western civilizations, is undeniable, as it introduced many of these societies to theatre, drama, and architecture, as well as democracy, philosophy, and mathematics. Today, it is perhaps not with great enthusiasm that qualitative researchers view mathematics, mostly due to its affiliation with quantitative approaches. Yet, mathematics and geometry did play a fundamental role in the development of western philosophical thought, and, as we will see later in the book, continue to enjoy this privileged position in the field of quantum mechanics. The search for things-in-themselves at the quantum level, which is both a scientific and a philosophical endeavour, is mainly possible because of mathematics. Hence, not only did mathematics change our view of nature, its application seems inevitable for unlocking the remaining mysteries of the universe:

> From the days of Pythagoras and Plato down to those of Kant and Herbart the mathematical sciences, and especially geometry, have played so important a part in the discussions of philosophers as models of method and patterns of certitude, that philosophy cannot but be extremely sensitive to any change or progress occurring in the views of mathematicians. (Schiller, 1896: 173)

There are many books on the history of mathematics, but its rollercoaster journey is perhaps best depicted in *Mathematics: The Loss of Certainty* by Morris Kline (1982), whose insights are valuable for the task ahead. Concerning broader philosophical debates, mathematics can be understood as initiating the quest for finding objective truths, and in its early days, it was held as reality itself. Kline tells a story of a science that, for a long time, provided the security of certainty, but eventually had to face the realization that mathematical formulas were not *truths*, and that there was not only *one* mathematics according to which the universe works, but *many* mathematics. Even more damaging were assertions that the application of mathematics was determined by experience – a claim intensified by the fact that it was mathematicians themselves proposing that mathematics is the outcome of sensory experience, and that it originates in the mind of the beholder. Therefore, the 'story' of mathematics is not only important with respect to appreciating its developments as a science, it is also fundamental in thought about mathematics on the philosophical front.

As noted, the ancient Greeks were the first to challenge belief in the supernatural forces and the divine order of things in the universe, and thus marked the distinction between supernatural and natural explanations of phenomena (Kline, 1982). Although the Babylonians and Egyptians knew mathematics and astronomy and even had some medical knowledge, it was the Greeks who advanced the rational theory of nature. Reason was firmly applied by the Greeks not only to mathematics but also to justice, education, and other aspects of social life. In fact, much of what we know today – and the ways in which many societies operate – has been erected upon the pillars of reason. The departure from religious conceptions of the universe[1] was a new attitude that embraced secular, rational, and critical thinking. The Greeks were motivated to understand the *Logos* of the world, 'the underlying law that made all things in the universe run as they do' (Lightbody, 2013: 7). This drive to discover how things *really* are by applying specific methods suggests that it is in ancient Greece that we start to see the beginnings of what in contemporary terms is called *realism* and *objectivism*. The magnitude of this shift in human thought, whereby for the first time in our existence nature was believed to be rationally ordered, is emphasized by Kline:

> All phenomena apparent to the senses, from the motions of the planets to the stirrings of the leaves on a tree, can be fitted into a precise, coherent, intelligible pattern. In short, nature is rationally designed and that design, though unaffected by human actions, can be apprehended by man's mind. (Kline, 1982: 10)

In light of this newly emerged worldview, the physical world operates independent of human beings, who, nonetheless, can understand how it works. For the Greeks, there was an order according to which the universe functioned independent of man's mind, but which was within reach through rational processes. Importantly, they believed that there was a specific means of accessing the workings of nature – and this means was none other than mathematics (Kline, 1982). The early mathematical organization of nature developed by the Pythagoreans, led by Pythagoras (c. 585–500 BCE), can be seen as the first attempt at a rational explanation of the world we see. And to appreciate just how much the Pythagoreans were serious about numbers and mathematics, we only need to consider the oath that they swore by the Tetractys, which goes as follows:

> I swear in the name of the Tetractys [the numbers 1, 2, 3, and 4, particularly valued by Pythagoreans] which has been bestowed on our soul. The source and roots of the overflowing nature are contained in it. (Kline, 1982: 14)

Figure 2.1 Triangular, square, and pentagonal numbers (adapted from Kline, 1982: 13)

It is worth pointing out that the early Pythagoreans believed that the external world was made up of mathematical shapes. Numbers were not mere theoretical entities or abstract ideas (as we tend to think if them today): they were points or particles which, when arranged, would form various geometric figures (triangles, squares, pentagons). Numbers were seen as inherent in things and thus nature as corresponding to geometric figures, as shown in Figure 2.1. Following the Pythagorean doctrine, therefore, all natural phenomena exhibited mathematical properties, and numbers were conceived as 'the matter and form of the universe' (Kline, 1982: 12). The extent to which this was applied to other aspects of their life, such as music, is discussed in the textbox below.

As the science of mathematics developed, the later Pythagoreans and Platonists affirmed more and more strongly the notion of 'absolute truths'. Plato (c. 428–348 BCE), for example, distinguished between the world of objects and the world of ideas. While the material world was flawed, the *Ideal* world was perfect, and it was here that absolute and unchanging truths could be found (Kline, 1982). His ideal world of *forms* was vastly different from everyday life, susceptible as it was to change, turmoil, and inconsistency: 'For Plato, the world of everyday sensory experience was not the "real" world. The real world for Plato – reality – was a change-less ideal world that could be perceived only by the intellect' (Huerta, 2005: 20). Notably, for the Platonists, numbers and the science of mathematics were not merely the means for understanding nature: mathematics was nature itself, 'the reality about the physical world' (Kline, 1982: 29). Relating these views to our discussion on metaphysics and ontology in Chapter 1 (see Figure 1.3), we can understand Plato's idealism as a strong metaphysical claim which saw mathematics at the core of the structure of the universe. In other words, mathematics was not only a lens though which worldly phenomena could be explained, it was also one of the foundational pillars upon which the universe was erected. Thus, true reality was a 'nexus of math-ematical laws' that could be verified by employing sensuous experience (Lodge, 2001: 117). Importantly, it was only through rational analysis that this *Ideal* world could be accessed.

A rationalist view of music in Ancient Greece

The Ancient Greeks believed that music, like all else in the physical world, was subject to mathematical laws. Musical theory, Gozza explains, was a mathematical discipline, whose characters were 'not sounds but numbers, and the ratios between numbers defined the relationships between sounds' (2000: 1). To produce pleasant or harmonious tunes was a matter of choosing the 'right' numbers. Pythagoras experimented with strings, water-filled glasses, vases, pipes, and finally a single string stretched over a sounding board, thereby discovering the following consonances: 'by dividing the string in two parts, one of which double ($^2/_1$), then one and a half ($^3/_2$) and finally one and a third ($^4/_3$) times longer than the other, and plucking them, two notes of different pitch can be heard at a distance, respectively, of an octave (C-C), fifth (C-G) and fourth (C-F)' (Gozza, 2000: 4). In other words, harmonious sounds are generated by dividing the string into equal parts.

Aristotle (384–322 BCE), another key figure of ancient Greek philosophy, did not share the Platonian outlook. Unlike Plato, he saw material objects, not numbers, as the source of reality, and was interested in actual observation and classification of the natural world. As Kline (1982) explains, to Aristotle, mathematical concepts were only abstractions of the real world. He emphasized universals and general qualities that can be abstracted from real things. To obtain these, he proposed that inquiry must '"start with things which are knowable and observable to us and proceed toward those things which are clearer and more knowable by nature". He took the obvious sensuous qualities of objects, hypostatized them, and elevated them to independent, mental concepts' (1982: 17). This contrast between Plato and Aristotle is not insignificant, as each paved the way to distinct philosophical stances. If Aristotle is to be seen as the forerunner of scientific inquiry, and perhaps as one of the first naturalists and empiricists, Plato can be depicted as the opposite, mainly for his abstract metaphysics. Plato's world of Ideas later became attractive to Christian thought, giving rise to Christian Platonism (Huerta, 2005). Although Plato has been the target of criticism – for example, Mayr (1982: 304) calls him the 'great antihero of evolutionism' with a 'deleterious impact on biology through the ensuing two thousand years' – we shall not descend into trivial accusations, but rather keep our minds open in order to appreciate the varied strands of philosophical thought. What we can take away from this brief analysis is that for Plato, *truth* resided in the abstract and was accessible by rational thought, and could not be obtained by observation and the methods of empiricism – thus opposing the view of Aristotle.

Deductive reasoning and the rollercoaster ride of mathematics

The popularity of geometry and mathematics, and the reason why they were so prominent, can be attributed to a specific method of reasoning devised by the Greeks: that of deductive proof. This method came to be accepted as the only way to obtain truths about the universe. Geometry became a *deductive* science due to the work of Euclid of Alexandria (fl. 300 BCE), who organized rules for computing lengths, areas, and volumes into a body of knowledge so effectively that geometry became the most bullet-proof branch of science for the centuries to come (Ryan, 2009). He established an axiomatic system which consisted of definitions, postulates, axioms, and theorems. Put simply, Euclid defined the terms he used (e.g., points, angles, lines, planes – 'a line is a breadthless length'); wrote 12 axioms or statements of self-evident truth (e.g., if equals be added to equals, the wholes are equal); he delineated five postulates – the basic suppositions of geometry (e.g., all right angles equal one another); and formulated nearly 500 theorems or geometrical statements (e.g., straight lines parallel to the same straight line are also parallel to one another) (Norton, 2013). The significance of his method is that the theorems were deduced *logically* from the definitions, axioms, and postulates. Euclid's deductive, axiomatic method therefore did not rely on empirical evidence; it was purely logical. And although the truth of the theorems was not necessarily self-evident, 'it was guaranteed by the fact that all the theorems had been derived strictly according to the accepted laws of logic from the original (self-evident) assertions' (Ryan, 2009: 1). Euclid's intellectual achievement was so crowning that Euclidean geometry was to become the foundation for a predominant view of the world for the next 2,000 years.

Mathematical investigation of nature continued well into the eighteenth century with many other scientists, including Isaac Newton (1642–1727), who insisted on mathematical descriptions of the world. It is worth emphasizing that until then, Euclidean geometry was the *only* possible geometry. Kline explains that Euclidean geometry was held in such high esteem because it was the first to be deductively established, and also because its theorems had been found to be 'in perfect accord with the physical facts' (Kline, 1982: 78). Euclidean geometry encapsulated the conviction that there was only one truth about space. With the discoveries of new, non-Euclidean geometries and algebras in the eighteenth and nineteenth centuries, such as double elliptic and hyperbolic geometries, which offered equally valid explanations of space, a crisis in mathematics was sparked. The consequences of these discoveries were of immense importance: there now seemed to be multiple truths about space and thus the external world at large. In addition, arithmetic and algebra suffered a similar blow with the appearance of quaternions, matrices, and other new, unusual algebras: 'The very fact that new algebras appeared on the scene made men doubt the truth of the familiar arithmetic and algebra' (Kline, 1982: 92).

It would be a major omission not to bring into the picture of this crucial period two other influential philosophers who challenged the privileged position of mathematics. These are Immanuel Kant (1724–1804) and David Hume (1711–1776), and we will examine both in more detail in Chapter 3. Kant questioned both the inherence of mathematical/geometrical laws in the universe and the notion of universal design by God. Even more scandalous were Hume's ideas, as he rejected both, proposing that all knowing is facilitated by the human senses. Kant and Hume's contesting views contributed to the slow demise of mathematics as the central organizing principle of the external world, and the eventual dismissal of the previously held universal truths. In other words, they undermined the primacy of rationalism and the notion that truths about the world are only obtainable by rational thought. On these events, Kline remarks that 'by destroying the doctrine of an external world following fixed mathematical laws, Hume had destroyed the value of a logical deductive structure which represents reality' (1982: 75).

Among those who challenged the ultimate status of mathematics was Hermann von Helmholtz (1821–1894), who delivered one of the strongest critiques yet. He proclaimed that arithmetic cannot be determined *a priori* – that is, before experience – because only experience can tell us in which situations it does apply and in which it does not (Kline, 1982). Consider that, when we speak of physical phenomena, it is not at all clear *a priori* that 1+1=2 is always applicable. For instance, we may add one yellow tomato to one red tomato and agree to have two tomatoes, however, if we merge one bowl of tomato soup with another bowl of tomato soup, we would not end up with two bowls of tomato soup. Likewise, adding yellow colour to red colour does not produce two yellows or two reds, rather, it may produce a different shade (orange), suggesting again that 1+1=2 does not hold in all scenarios. Hence, the laws of arithmetic do not always apply nor accurately describe phenomena in nature.

Qualitative researchers may be interested to know that there were mathematicians who have argued that mathematics was an invention in the same way literature or banking was (Hersh, 1997). For this group of thinkers, mathematics had nothing to do with universal truths: it was a cultural enterprise. Indeed, for many cognitive scientists today, numbers express nothing more than ideas. According to Lakoff and Núñez, for example, the cognitive science of mathematics rules out that mathematical objects are real and 'objectively existent entities', rather they are dependent on embodied human cognition: '[s]ince human mathematics is all that we have access to, mathematical entities can only be conceptual in nature, arising from our embodied conceptual systems' (2000: 366).

The story told through the example of mathematics is a significant one. The long-held belief that mathematics was the key to understanding the secrets of the universe, and that mathematics existed in an *ideal* world outside space and time, not only inspired rationalism, it was also one of the main arguments against empiricism. Accordingly, truths about the workings of the universe were to be grasped deductively by the rational mind, without the need for experience. This conception eventually collapsed under the weight of a competing view, which insisted that mathematics, including its axioms and theorems, was determined by human experience. Mathematical truths and mathematics as a whole thus became secondary to knowledge grounded in observation. This epistemic conflict can be formulated as the battle between pure reason and empiricism.

Reason versus experience

To be able to assert that a proposition is true, it has to be justified. This important realization is credited to Plato, who defined knowledge as *true belief*. Plato held that knowledge was a form of belief – 'true belief accompanied by an account'

(Hoitenga, 1991: 1). Consider, for example, that for a long time, people were content with the belief that the Earth was flat and shaped like a disk. It wasn't until approximately 500 BCE that Pythagoras challenged this conception when he made detailed observations of the constellation Ursa Major, and inferred from these that the Earth had to be spherical (Clark & Clark, 2004). The idea of a flat Earth, however, was revived again during the Early Middle Ages, and in the fifth century CE, Father Lucius Lactantius condemned the notion of a spherical Earth as heresy (Carey, 1988). The notion of a flat Earth was 'true' because it was stated to be so in the scriptures. This episode demonstrates that the fundamental distinction between knowledge and mere belief (or dogma) rests on the recognition that beliefs can be false. In order to justify that a belief is true, it must meet certain criteria and be supported by evidence.

The question of what constitutes sufficient proof for propositions to be true was the subject of fervent discussion between two medical schools in Ancient Greece as early as 300 BCE. Frede (1990) explains that the dispute was over the supremacy of experience, advocated by the empiricist doctors (the *empeirikos*), and logic, advanced by the rationalist doctors (the *logikos*). The rationalists held that knowledge had to be an achievement of reason because experience alone could not amount to medical knowledge. On the other hand, the empiricists argued that to *know* was a matter of observation, correct remembering,[2] and application. This involved a 'specialised kind of experience' – comparable to technical knowledge – that drew mainly on use of the senses and memory (1990: 226). Furthermore, Frede tells us that the empiricist regarded *reason* as unreliable and untrustworthy, and as far as knowledge was concerned, doctors prescribed medicine not because of some kind of theoretical reasoning but because it was proven to be effective in experience. If a remedy proved successful in experiments (i.e., when tested in practice) that was all that was required as a criterion for knowledge. Hence the debates about the nature of knowledge and how it is justified (i.e., debates over inductive versus deductive thinking) date all the way back to antiquity.

With the achievements of Euclid of Alexandria, reason and mathematics eventually came to dominate the intellectual scene and laid the foundations for a worldview that prevailed for nearly two millennia. The spread of the Catholic doctrine meant that scientific advancements, including mathematics, as we have seen earlier, came to be seen as revelations of God's creative process, including that He 'designed the world in accordance with mathematical principles' (Kline, 1982: 58). Empiricism, both as a philosophy of science and as a method, was dormant for most of the Middle Ages. In this historical period, all philosophical, scholastic, and cultural activities were controlled by the Church. To contradict the teachings of the Church was to commit heresy. Galileo (1564–1642), for example, had to appear before the Inquisition in Rome for embracing the work of Copernicus (1473–1543) and for suggesting that the Earth and planets revolved around the Sun. During the Renaissance, universities were ecclesiastical organizations either supervized by or strongly connected to the Church (Rüegg, 2004), and all profound thinkers from that period were likely to be theologians by profession (Moody, 1975).[3] From Descartes, Pascal and Kepler, to Copernicus, Galileo and Newton, mathematical knowledge as absolute truth was a reflection of God's magnificence. Scientific discoveries, therefore, were not taken as the triumph of human beings and their ability to unravel the ways in which nature operates so much as testimonies to the greatness of God.

Not surprisingly, the Middle Ages and much of the Renaissance period were marked by speculation, and the interpretation of many natural phenomena involved a belief in the supernatural. This can be seen most strikingly in the area of medicine, where a paucity of medical knowledge and a poor understanding of the causes of diseases meant that conclusions were drawn based not on empirical evidence but rather on superstitious beliefs. Like universities, hospitals were religious establishments and the doctors and nurses assisting patients were members of religious orders (Rogers, 2011). Medical 'knowledge' and education in medieval universities were based on the translated writings of Roman physician Aelius Galenus (130–200 CE), whose work dominated western medicine for nearly 1,300 years (Rogers, 2011). In other words, not much progress was made in medicine during the first millennium. In the following centuries there were only pockets of experimental methods, such as at the Medical School of the Bologna University (founded around 1063), known to have lectures on Latin, Greek, Arabic, and Hebrew medical literature (Moroni, 2000). Notable among its faculty was Mondino Dei Liuzzi (1270–1326), who conducted first-hand examinations of the human body (Carlino, 1999). A more widespread return to empiricism only began in the sixteenth century, with new advances being made by means of experimentation and observation – such as the groundbreaking discoveries based on dissections, exemplified in the work of Andreas Vesalius (1514–1564), a Flemish professor of anatomy. Rogers highlights the magnitude of these developments using the example of William Harvey (1578–1657):

> Harvey's discovery of the circulation of the blood was a landmark of medical progress. The new experimental method by which the results were secured was as noteworthy as the work itself. Following the method described by the philosopher Francis Bacon, he drew the truth from experience and not from authority. (Rogers, 2011: 37)

Given that opposing the Church could lead to punishment by death, only determined intellectuals like Harvey dared proffer that religious knowledge was less important than knowledge of nature (Cook, 2010). Nonetheless, a growing number of thinkers, scientists, and practitioners began to see how limiting it was to stick with views of nature that were heavily underpinned by the doctrines of the Church. With growing acceptance of the Copernican theory and the writings of Galileo Galilei, Pierre Gassendi (1592–1655), and Marin Mersenne (1588–1648) came a gradual shift towards scientific thinking, and eventually a fundamentally different view of the natural world (Wilson & Reill, 2004). This exhilarating period was to be known by two names: the Scientific Revolution (1500–1700) and the Age of Enlightenment (1650–1800).

The Cartesian method and a priori knowledge

As part of our general overview of the rationalist–empiricist debate, we cannot pass over one of the pivotal figures in the philosophy of science – seventeenth-century philosopher and mathematician René Descartes (1596–1650). In contrast to those who supported the idea of scientific knowledge as mainly stemming from observation and experience, Descartes held that *true* knowledge was the product of reason and logic. He was interested in *a priori* truths and believed that 'by its own power the intellect may arrive at a perfect knowledge of all things' (Kline, 1982: 45). The Cartesian method describes the rules for 'employing rightly the natural capacities and operations of the mind' (Copleston, 1958: 73). Following Descartes' ideas, the only way to acquire *a priori* knowledge is through *intuition* and *deduction*. Intuition (sometimes called 'mental vision') refers to the operation of the mind 'in which a proposition is perceived all at once or in a moment, and so clearly and distinctly as to be certain or indubitable' (Loeb, 1986: 246). The illustration Descartes gives in Rule III, for example, is the ability of a human being to mentally intuit that a triangle is bounded by three lines (Sasaki, 2003). One only has to be attentive to grasp this truth – an example of Descartes' contention that entering this attentive state is all that is needed to access what he called 'first principles'.

Furthermore, there was a difference between the cognitive operations of *intuitive* and *deductive* reasoning. For Descartes, the concept of *intuition* was 'knowledge at rest', while *deduction* referred to a 'mental movement toward knowledge' (Groarke, 2009: 310). Groarke clarifies that *intuition* was to be understood as 'an instantaneous, all-at-once illumination', and *deduction* as a kind of 'movement or succession' (2009: 310) – in other words, a mental activity performed by the inquirer. Deduction or logical inference, then, implies movement or a step-by-step process; intuition does not require movement at all. Intuitions or first principles are a 'product of looking' (2009: 311).

According to Schouls, Descartes considered himself to be doing the work of 'proper' philosophy, which involved 'seek[ing] out the first causes and the true principles from which reasons may be deduced for all that we are capable of knowing' (1989: 28). By comparison, the empiricists, who became the pioneers of the Enlightenment, were reluctant to share Descartes' conviction. The astronomer, mathematician, and physicist Galileo Galilei, for example, argued that in physics, 'first principles must come from experience and experimentation' (Kline, 1982: 48). It was through observation of nature that the mind could create concepts and make sense of external phenomena. Galileo also criticized Descartes' method for its lack of ability to predict. Galileo was not so much interested in the cause of why something happens as he was in establishing descriptive formulas – describing phenomena mathematically (Kline, 1982). Descartes, in turn, perceived Galileo's reliance on observation and the senses as a methodological weakness. It should be noted that Descartes was not against experimentation per se: he simply did not agree that it was the essence of science, 'did not think of science as a cumulative activity' (Ree, 1974: 43).

The distinction between the truths of the mind (e.g., Descartes) and truths based on experimentation (e.g., Aristotle, Galileo, Francis Bacon) is captured by the terms '*a priori* knowledge' and '*a posteriori* knowledge'. *A priori* justifications rely on rational intuitions or insights; they are based on reason alone and include mostly abstract concepts and mathematical calculations (Russell, 2007). Take for example the statement 'a bachelor is an unmarried man'. We do not need to carry out an empirical study to confirm that all bachelors are unmarried men; it is a self-evident statement because the notion of 'unmarried man' comes with the term 'bachelor'. Likewise, in the view of rationalists, mathematical truths, such as $1 + 1 = 2$, are self-evident and do not require observation. *A posteriori* knowledge, on the other hand, is knowledge derived from sense data. In their support of this notion, empiricist philosophers denied the claim of *a priori* mathematical knowledge, arguing instead that mathematical truths are analytic (expressing relations between ideas) or based on experience (Ladyman, 2002).

In summary, the proponents of rationalism, including Plato, Descartes, Malebranche, Spinoza, Leibniz, Hegel, and others, are often associated with *a priori* knowledge. Many rationalists perceived a mind–body dualism, holding that the mind is different from the body, and therefore, sense perception and mental experiences are of secondary importance. They insisted on the distinction between reality (only accessible through reason) and appearances (Nelson, 2013b: xiv). On the other hand, empiricists such Aristotle, Berkeley, Locke, Hume, and the positivistically inclined thinkers argued that knowledge derives from sensory experience and observation. As a rule, knowledge that is not *a priori* and founded on reason alone must be *a posteriori*. The following section will further explore the shift towards an *a posteriori* view of science and trace the rise and fall of logical positivism.

Positivism and logical empiricism/positivism

The revitalization of empiricism can be situated within two overlapping epochs in the history of the west noted earlier: the Scientific Revolution and the Age of Enlightenment (or simply 'the Enlightenment'). The Scientific Revolution has been described by historians in many ways, but it generally represents radical changes in humans' conception of nature, the shift from the Medieval period, and the emergence of modern science (Applebaum, 2000). Here the word 'revolution' is not being used in the traditional sense as there was no specific event in time and space. Rather, as Shapin clarifies (1996: 1), it was coined by the French historian Andre Koyré in 1943 to mark a historical period in time when 'the world was made modern'. The Enlightenment is intertwined with, and was influenced by, the Scientific Revolution, but as a term refers more specifically to the social, political, and economic changes in European societies in the eighteenth century. The Enlightenment is perhaps most fittingly described as a 'set of attitudes' underpinned by criticism and 'a growing questioning of traditional institutions, customs, and morals' (Love, 2008: xiii).

The key events associated with the setting in of the Scientific Revolution are Copernicus's heliocentric model of the solar system (approximately 1543 CE), Newton's idea of a mechanical universe (1687 CE), and the appearance of new methods and approaches to the study of natural phenomena (Rogers, 2011). With the prevailing views of the world changing, it was inevitable that scientific and philosophical conceptions would also be subjected to modification. Unlike the rationalists, the empiricists were unified in the conviction that the only way to discover facts about the universe was to search for them in nature. They 'held firmly to the principle that knowledge *about the outer world* must come from the outer world, and so can be acquired only by observation and experiment' (Jeans, 2012: 37). In Britain, empiricism gained full momentum in 1660s with the Royal Society's embracing of a novel outlook, described by Wolfe and Gal as 'an open, collaborative experimental practice, mediated by specially-designed instruments, supported by civil, critical discourse, stressing accuracy and replicability' (2010: 1). This was a move towards scientific knowledge predicated on observation of the material world and experiments. The most well-known empiricist was Francis Bacon (1561–1626), dubbed the father of empiricism, and the British trio of John Locke (1632–1704), George Berkeley (1685–1753), and David Hume (1711–1776), who became influential in the eighteenth century, and whose influential ideas we shall focus on in Chapter 3. For the time being, we continue to examine the chronological developments of empiricism, which take us to *positivism* and, later, the *logical positivism* of the twentieth century.

Positivism has its roots in empiricism, drawing ideas from Ludwig Wittgenstein (in particular his work *Tractatus Logico-Philosophicus*), Gottlob Frege, Betrand Russell, and the early British empiricists. Locke and Hume in particular were labelled 'fundamental craftsmen of modern empiricism' (Levine, 2006: 171). The term 'positivism' was coined by French philosopher Auguste Comte (1798–1857). Among his many achievements, such as building the foundations of the discipline of sociology, Comte is known for his Law of Three Stages (Comte, 1858), which puts forward the idea that every branch of science passes through three stages: the theological stage, the metaphysical stage, and the positive stage. Hung (2014), distilling Comte's ideas, explains that during the theological stage, science grapples with natural phenomena by employing supernatural agents such as spirits, devils, gods, and ghosts; the second, metaphysical stage marks an advancement inasmuch as the 'supernatural' becomes more abstract, and the language changes to refer to inanimate agents (e.g., mass in Newton's mechanics); at the third, mature or positive stage, science becomes the practice of positivism. Comte's notion of positivism, within the context of the Law of Three Stages, suggests an ascription to humans of a level of maturity in their search for knowledge. Bourdeau (2013) further comments that, in Comte's view, the first stage is necessary, the second transitory, and the last a positive state whereby the mind no longer looks for causes of phenomena, but instead seeks to understand the laws governing them.

Bourdeau (2013) emphasizes that, contrary to popular belief, Comte's positivism was not a philosophy of science, but a political philosophy whose goal was to reorganize society. This vision is most evident in Comte's *First System of Positive Polity* (Comte, 1875). With respect to the development of scientific knowledge, Comte did not believe that there was an overarching purpose to nature and saw no room for any metaphysical or theological explanations in science. Instead, he argued that 'the only legitimate practice in science is the observation and generalization of constant conjunctions of natural phenomena or events' (Hung, 2014: 314). The value of science, Comte believed, lay in the use of the positive method, be it observation in astronomy, experimentation in physics, or comparison in biology (Bourdeau, 2013).

Despite the distinction drawn between the rationalists and the empiricists, and although the positivists and empiricists shared common ground, it would be erroneous to presume that *all* empiricists and positivists agreed about *a priori* and *a posteriori* knowledge. For some, empiricism did not necessarily mean a complete departure from reason. As pointed out by Jeans (2012), Locke and Hume, and later on Whitehead and Russell, did not object to the idea that mathematical truths could be obtained by intuition, that is, *a priori*. In this regard, one can distinguish between a *mild* version of empiricism – the willingness to accommodate logic under certain circumstances – and a *strong* version that dismissed the idea of *a priori* knowledge altogether. John Stuart Mill (1806–1873) was a prime example of nineteenth-century *strong* empiricism. As Jeans elucidates, Mill rejected the notion of any knowledge as *a priori* and refused to accept intuitive knowledge as a whole, including mathematical truths. He maintained that 'the laws of arithmetic embodied generalizations derived from observations of actual objects, while geometry dealt merely with idealizations of objects of experience' (Jeans, 2012: 36). In other words, the notion of mathematical objects could not be imagined without their representation in the natural world (e.g., a line), and so mathematics and logic, Mill argued, had to be founded on experience. Reluctant to entertain the idea of axiomatic principles (embraced by Euclidean followers such as Descartes), this is what he had to say about axiomatic truths:

> It is not necessary to show that the truths which we call axioms are originally *suggested* by observation, and that we should never have known that two straight lines cannot inclose a space if we had never seen a straight line [...] Without denying, therefore, the possibility of satisfying ourselves that two straight lines cannot

inclose a space, by merely thinking of straight lines without actually looking at them; I contend, that we do not believe this truth on the ground of the imaginary intuition simply, but because we know that the imaginary lines exactly resemble real ones, and that we may conclude from them to real ones with quite as much certainty as we could conclude from one real line to another. The conclusion, therefore, is still an induction from observation. (Mill, 1858: 153-5)

Mill's views paint a clear picture of the different epistemic outlooks represented by the rationalists on the one hand and the empiricists on the other. His empiricism is often labelled 'extreme' because he regarded mathematical truths as empirical generalizations and all knowledge as being derived inductively (Rollinger, 1999). Logical positivism, which we define next, differed from empiricism and the work of Mill only in degree and in that, only an inquiry which could be verified by experimentation or logic was scientifically meaningful. All else was held by the logical positivist as scientifically meaningless.

Key tenets of logical positivism

In the early twentieth century, groups of intellectuals started to meet on a regular basis in Vienna and Berlin. These gatherings, which stretched through the 1920s and 1930s, came to be known as the Vienna Circle and the Berlin Circle. The Vienna Circle was led by Moritz Schlick and the Berlin Circle by Hans Reichenbach. Among the original members of the Vienna Circle were Otto Neurath, Friedrich Waismann, Hans Hahn, Olga Hahn, Victor Kraft, Philipp Frank, Kurt Reidemeister, and Herbert Feigl; later, it was joined by other prominent thinkers such as Gustav Bergmann, Béla Juhos, Karl Menger, Richard von Mises, Edgar Zilsel, Kurt Gödel, Rudolf Carnap, and Alfred J. Ayer (Stroll, 2000). In Berlin, Hans Reichenbach led the Society of Scientific Philosophy. Reichenbach preferred the term 'logical empiricism' as opposed to 'logical positivism' to distinguish his programme from the one in Vienna (McGrew et al., 2009). The members of the Berlin Circle included Carl Hempel, David Hilbert, Kurt Grelling, and Richard von Mises.[4] Apart from the German and Austrian gatherings, there were intellectuals in other parts of Europe known to support the positivist views, such as in Prague and Warsaw. During the wars, some of the scholars migrated to Britain and the United States (e.g., Carnap became a professor at the University of Chicago and Reinbach at the University of California). The extent to which the logical positivists exerted influence over scholarly communities and dominated much of philosophical thought is captured by Sarkar (1996: ix) in his assertion that they established a 'temporary hegemony over academic philosophy'.

It is useful to be aware that the terms 'logical positivism' and 'logical empiricism' tend to be employed interchangeably in the literature.[5] Another label that is used for the logical developments in the philosophy of science is 'neopositivism'.

We will use the term 'logical empiricism' to capture the continuation of empiricism in the twentieth century, reflecting that all the representative thinkers were united in their vision to eliminate 'metaphysical nonsense from empirical science' (Rosenberg, 1999: 12) and align philosophy with other 'genuinely scientific disciplines' (Uebel & Richardson, 2007: 4). Uebel explains that, in general, the philosophy of science espoused by logical empiricists treats *a priori* knowledge and any form of metaphysical intuition as unintelligible (Uebel, 2013). Furthermore, logical empiricists made a distinction between the empirical sciences (such as physics, biology, and the social sciences) and the formal sciences (such as logic and mathematics). This was a key part of their strategy to renew empiricism 'by freeing it from the impossible task of grounding logical and mathematical knowledge' (2013: 90). This way the first principles (i.e., axioms and postulates) could be recognized by the positivists in mathematics, for example, but were to be rejected in science. In this respect, logical empiricism made no allowances for anything but logic and empirical science: 'Any claim that was neither logic nor able to be adjudicated by empirical means was rejected by the logical empiricists as "meaningless" or "cognitively insignificant," whatever its noncognitive (for instance, emotional) appeal' (Sarkar, 1996: ix). There are three core principles that underpin the tenets of logical positivism. These can be formulated as (1) the distinction between analytic and synthetic statements, (2) the principle of verification, and (3) a reductive thesis. Drawing on the analysis of Stroll (2000: 65–70), we can expand upon these as follows.

The distinction between analytic and synthetic statements

There is a sharp distinction between *analytic* and *synthetic* statements. For example, 'All bachelors are single' is a tautologous and self-evident statement. The meaning of the world 'bachelor' directly implies that we are speaking about a single male. However, it is a different statement altogether to utter that 'All bachelors are mortal'. This statement cannot be viewed as self-evident because its truth can only be established through observation and experimentation – what logical positivists call *sense experience*. To determine whether or not it is true that bachelors are mortal we have to investigate the world (i.e., experience has shown us that human beings can die). In the philosophy of science, such a proposition – one that entails empirical investigation in order to confirm its truth – is called a *synthetic statement*. These are often synonymous with the terms 'factual', 'empirical', 'contingent', and '*a posteriori*'. On the other hand, the truth of a statement that is self-evident (like 'All bachelors are single') emerges from the direct meaning of its constituent words. These are called *analytic statements* and are synonymous with the words 'necessary', 'tautological', and '*a priori*' (Stroll, 2000: 65). Importantly, for the logical positivists no proposition can be both synthetic and analytic.[6] The conclusion they drew, as Stroll explains, was that 'analytic propositions do not give us any information about the world, that is, that they lack existential import' (2000: 66). Hence, only synthetic propositions are informative about reality and 'true when what they assert corresponds to the facts' (2000: 66). This meant that the rationalist tradition advanced by the philosophy of Plato, Descartes, Spinoza, Hegel, Bradley, and others, could be rejected because it drew heavily on reason.[7] Positivists held that any knowledge about the external world had to be based on sense experience and observational data because reason alone could not yield facts about natural phenomena. Stroll summarizes this:

> [I]f the positivists were right, namely, that all truths of reason were empty of factual content, the rationalist tradition was wholly misguided. In effect, this was a powerful defence of empiricism. (2000: 66)

The principle of verification

According to Stroll, the principle of verification enabled the logical positivists to dismiss not only metaphysical propositions but also humanistic disciplines in general. Why? Because they could not produce cognitive propositions. For instance, statements in poetry are not verifiable in the same way the laws of physics are. They may have a poetic meaning, but they are not scientifically significant, as Stroll (2000) explains. The positivists held that propositions had to be empirically verifiable (i.e., verifiable in principle). The principle of verification asserts that 'no sentence that refers to a "reality" transcending the limits of all possible sense-experience can have any cognitive significance' (2000: 68). Put differently, anything that is not verifiable empirically was seen as of no scientific value. Amid some disagreement, the positivists came up with several formulations of the verification principle. The basic idea was that it denoted the view that observation and empirical verification had to show that something was either *true* or *false*. The verification principle was later challenged by a new theory introduced by Karl Popper, that of *falsification*, which we will address in the next section. Another, but no less vital, feature of logical empiricism was that knowledge could never be certain – only *probable* and based on given evidence (Stroll, 2000).

The reductive thesis

For the positivists, observation was at the core of the scientific method and thus had a special meaning, albeit not unanimously agreed upon. Stroll outlines their divergent views: (a) observation as direct apprehension of visual sense data (a phenomenalistic interpretation arising from the work of earlier empiricists such as Locke, Hume, and Russell, and emphasized by Carnap and Ayer); (b) observation of physical objects (a physicalistic interpretation of positivism advanced by

Neurath); and (c) observation based on either A or B (known as the 'principle of tolerance', advanced mainly by Carnap in 1937 in *The Logical Syntax of Language*). In broad terms, the main premise of the reductive thesis is that 'all factual knowledge can be reduced to observable data' (Stroll, 2000: 70).

A key aspect of logical positivism was the theory of *phenomenalism* advocated by A.J. Ayer (not to be confused with *phenomenology*, discussed in Chapter 4). Phenomenalism is the empirical thesis which states that unless statements are confirmed or verified by experience they are nonsensical. According to phenomenalism, therefore, the statements 'Plato was a great philosopher' and 'The Higgs boson is the smallest particle' are not verifiable in experience and should be excluded from scientific statements. Musgrave (1993) describes Ayer as a representative of twentieth-century idea-ism because he advocated the theory of sense data and argued that we can only know what is presented to us in consciousness.

The inductive and hypothetico-deductive methods

A typical distinction between the rationalists and the empiricists is that the first promoted the method of *deduction* and the latter the method of *induction*. The method of induction is a logical process for arriving at knowledge about observed phenomena. Despite its popularity among the members of the Vienna Circle, induction was not an innovation of the logical empiricists or logical positivists, instead dating back to their empirical predecessors. We also ought to be careful not to claim, as many texts do, that all positivists adhered to inductivism. For example, this is not true of Neurath or Carnap (Woleński, 1997). Inductive reasoning was promoted and embraced by the founder of the scientific method, Francis Bacon, for whom it played an important role in separating investigations of the scientific sort from unscientific varieties. It was later refined by Mill (1843), who took induction to be a process of 'real' inference:

> In every induction we proceed from truths which we knew, to truths which we did not know: from facts certified by observation, to facts which we have not observed, and even to facts not capable of being now observed; future facts, for example: but which we do not hesitate to believe upon the sole evidence of the induction itself. Induction, then, is a real process of Reasoning or Inference. (Mill, 1843: 225)

The aim of inductive methods is to produce universal generalizations that can be applied to yet unobserved phenomena (Smith, 1998). Inductive reasoning is 'founded on reasoning about cause and effect' (Ladyman, 2002: 38), such as observing natural phenomena and inferring that in light of past experiences, the Sun will rise tomorrow, apples fall toward the ground when ripe, birds can fly, and swans are white.[8] The scientist, immersed in the method of induction, seeks to infer general laws by moving from the particular to the general.

The gathering of observational data becomes the foundation for the building of scientific theories. It is a way of extrapolating general principles from individual observations. This process is depicted in Figure 2.2 (see 'A: Positivist/Verificationism'), as is the method of deduction, which generally follows the reverse process. Whereas induction is believed to broaden and deepen empirical knowledge, deduction tends to be explicative (Vickers, 2013).

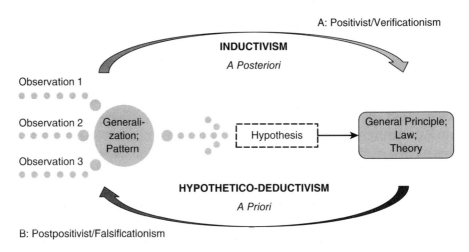

Figure 2.2 The method of induction (and deduction)

The proclamation that induction can lead to scientific knowledge was challenged by one of the greatest[9] philosophers of science of the twentieth century, Karl Popper (1902–1994). Popper, who maintained contact with the members of the Vienna Circle, was critical of the main tenets of logical positivism. He was not necessarily interested in the epistemological concerns of when a theory is *true* and under which conditions it is acceptable, rather his motivation was to distinguish science from what he called 'pseudo-science' (Popper, 1999b: 66). Later, he termed this issue a 'problem of demarcation' and argued that there were fundamental differences between the claims of various types of science. Popper's main point was that some scientific work is radically different from the rest – for example, Albert Einstein's gravitational theory – in that it could lead to knowledge that is neither based solely on observation nor merely generalized from particular instances, as is the case with induction. The role of observation was indeed important in Einstein's work: it could, and indeed did, serve to prove his hypothesis. However, in Popper's view, the very purpose of the scientific method is to use observation to either refute or confirm predictions, and predictions always involve risk (Popper, 1999b).

Popper thus saw a striking difference between the work of Einstein and the theories of other sciences. He held that Marx's theory of history, Freud's psychoanalysis, and Adler's 'individual psychology' were not scientific to the same degree because they were based exclusively on observation – which, in his opinion, was a significant limitation. Positivists used the method of *verificationism*, whereby the role of observation was to verify or confirm theories (e.g., the verification of Freud's theory by clinical observations). The difficulty with this approach, Popper explained, was that certain behaviour displayed by a person counted as yet another case to which a particular theory could be assigned. In other words, the way confirmation was obtained was by 'looking for it' in people's behaviour (Popper, 1999b). This method could only mean that each case that verified or confirmed a theory was nothing more than the case being interpreted through that theory. The biggest flaw pointed to by Popper was the impossibility of testing or refuting psychoanalytic theories. There was no human behaviour that could contradict them. Popper commented on Freud's theory:

> And as for Freud's epic of the Ego, the Super-ego, and the Id, no substantially stronger claim to scientific status can be made for it than for Homer's collected stories from Olympus. These theories describe some facts, but in the manner of myths. They contain most interesting psychological suggestions, but not in a testable form. (Popper, 1999b: 69)

Hence, for the positivists, the function performed by observation was solely confirmatory; theories that arose from observations alone by employing the method of induction were not, in Popper's view, scientific:

> 'Clinical observations', like all other observations, are interpretations in the light of theories [...] and for this reason alone they are apt to seem to support those theories in the light of which they were interpreted. But real support can be obtained only from observations undertaken as tests (by 'attempted refutations'); and for this purpose criteria of refutation have to be laid down beforehand: it must be agreed which observable situations, if actually observed, mean that the theory is refuted. (Popper, 1999b: 70)

Science, for Popper, was a hypothetico-deductive process: scientists were to formulate theories or hypotheses to be tested by experimentation and observation (as noted in Figure 2.2.). It is necessary to reiterate here that the role of observation had a fundamental role to play in Popper's methodology. The aim was not to verify or confirm theories, as in the case of the logical positivists, but instead to falsify, reject, or tentatively accept them (Vickers, 2013). In the words of Popper, 'the criterion of the scientific status of a theory is its falsifiability, or refutability, or testability' (1999b: 69). In other words, a theory could only be scientific if it were possible to test that it could be false. This possibility of proving theories wrong was imperative to his project. Another key aspect of Popper's philosophy was the separation of *truth* from the scientific process. Popper (2005) contends that the confirmation of hypotheses does not necessarily warrant that they are *true*: any theory may be refuted by future experiments, and therefore even the best and most seemingly confirmed theories available to us are, in fact, tentative.[10] As he proclaimed, 'Science is the quest for truth. But truth is not *certain* truth' (Popper, 1999a: 38).

Popper's critique of logical positivism, verificationism, and inductivism has led to him being labelled one of the main figures of *postpositivism*. His view of the scientific method as a hypothetico-deductive process underpinned by falsificationism is illustrated in Figure 2.2 (see 'B: Postpositivist/Falsificationism'). In contrast to the method of induction, Popper's scientific process commences with a theory, proceeds to forming a hypothesis that is tested through observation and experimentation, and finally is either confirmed or refuted. Through a continual process of falsification, successful hypotheses are eventually accepted as *best current theories*. As noted in Figure 2.2, the method for induction and verificationism is commonly associated with logical positivism, whereas the methods for hypothetico-deduction and falsificationism are methodological features ascribed to postpositivism. Knowledge grounded in observation and derived by means of induction is *a posteriori*; knowledge claims formulated prior to sense-observation and obtained via the hypothetico-deductive methods are *a priori*. Popper was a strong proponent of the *a priori* nature of propositions. He held that all knowledge was hypothetical and asserted that '99 per cent of the knowledge of all organisms is inborn and incorporated in our biochemical constitution' (Popper, 1999a: 70). With regard to the doctrine of rationalism, Popper used the term 'critical rationalism'[11] to emphasize that any proposition ought to be subjected to his principle of falsificationism and thought through rationally before being subjected to empirical testing. He contrasted it with 'uncritical rationalism' or 'comprehensive rationalism' – more dogmatic approaches to truth (Popper, 2013 [1945]).

Empiricism and rationalism in the social sciences

A longstanding problem of the social sciences can be expressed in the question of whether or not a conceptual line should be drawn between the social and the natural sciences at all. The answer determines how one conceives of not only social phenomena but also their ontological status, epistemological strategies, methodologies, and methods. The positivists and postpositivists responded with a resounding 'no' and strove to replicate in the social sciences the success of the scientific methods in the natural sciences. According to Bernstein, social science was to become 'a genuine natural science of individuals in society' that would 'diff[er] in degree and not in kind from the rest of the natural sciences' (1983: 27). For example, Otto Neurath, a member of the Vienna Circle, sought to establish the rules for an empirical sociology, and argued there was no difference between the natural and the social sciences as far as cognitive methods were concerned. As further remarked by Kolakowski, 'according to Neurath, the social sciences do not deal with human intentions, experiences, aspirations, or "personalities," but solely with the behaviour of human organisms' (1968: 190). There were also academics such as Max Weber – a pivotal figure of *interpretive* sociology, yet somewhat open to the idea of a scientific model of the social sciences – who claimed that it is possible to 'check the validity of sociological interpretations by appealing to statistical laws based on observations of what happens' (Bernstein, 1983: 27). This claim was rejected by anti-positivist thinkers, the likes of Peter Winch, who maintained that statistics were not the court of appeal for sociological interpretations because a misleading interpretation is still a misleading interpretation. Winch instead argued that:

> What is then needed is a better interpretation, not something different in kind [...] Someone who interprets a tribe's magical rites as a form of misplaced scientific activity will not be corrected by statistics about what members of that tribe are likely to do on various kinds of occasion. (Winch, 2008 [1958]: 113)

To appreciate the epistemic tensions and the numerous dichotomies that prevail to this day, it is necessary to underscore that the nineteenth century marked the debates over whether or not the social sciences should be called sciences at all. Jones (2000: 199) explains that the main dispute was over *humanistic* (*Geisteswissenschaften*) versus *positivistic* (*Naturwissenschaften*) approaches to social science, which led to 'understanding versus explaining', 'interpreting versus explaining', 'reasons versus causes', 'subjective versus objective', 'qualitative versus quantitative', 'sympathetic versus detached', and 'insider versus outsider accounts'. In this regard, many others had much to say on the issue of knowledge production in the social sciences, from critical theorists and interpretivists to social constructionists and hermeneuticians, some of whom we will explore in Chapters 5 and 6. To conclude our exploration of the empirical approaches to the social sciences, there is one more influential scholar whose impact should not go unnoticed: Émile Durkheim.

Émile Durkheim's positivism and the social sciences

Émile Durkheim (1858–1917) was key in establishing a scientific approach to sociology. He belonged to a generation of scholars who were fervent about the creation of new scientific fields and disciplines in what we now call the *social sciences*. During his time, there were multiple and competing views about the ways in which the human world was to be studied. Collins explains that 'it was not at all clear whether these should be part of the biological sciences, or the lineup of political ideologies, or connected to law and public administration [...], or part of the general education taught in the secondary schools' (2005: 106). Moreover, it was not certain whether sociology was to be combined with, or made distinct from, anthropology, social work, and other rival social disciplines such as psychology. His quest to cement the foundation for sociology as a unique discipline led him to 'formulate the character of sociology as dealing with "social facts," the *sui generis* character of patterns of social interaction, constraining the individual from without' (2005: 106). Sociology was to be established as a general science, and its task was to build general theory by empirical comparison and synthesis (Collins, 2005).

In his epistemic quest, Durkheim's (1982) notion of social facts was as 'things' that existed independent of individuals and which were to be studied and explained in terms of the norms, values, and structures within a society. His ambition was no less than for sociology to become a scientific, objective study of social facts as external 'givens' existing independent of individuals. The success of social science lay in adopting the scientific methods of the natural sciences. This conviction is elucidated in Steven Lukes's introduction to Durkheim's *Rules of Sociological Method* (Durkheim, 1982: 3): 'The sociologist must adopt what Durkheim thought was the state of mind of physicists, chemists and physiologists when they venture into an as yet unexplored area of their scientific field'. The extent to which social facts can be claimed to be 'things' that exist independent of individuals will concern us in Chapter 6 when we examine social ontology. In this respect, Durkheim epitomizes a realist and an objectivist view of social phenomena, as expressed by him in the following statement:

> Indeed, we do not say that social facts are material things, but that they are things just as are material things, although in a different way. What indeed is a thing? The thing stands in opposition to the idea, just as what is known from the outside stands in opposition to what is known from the inside. A thing is any object of knowledge which is not naturally penetrable by the understanding. It is all that which we cannot conceptualize adequately as an idea by the simple process of intellectual analysis. It is all that which the mind cannot understand without going outside itself, proceeding progressively by way of observation and experimentation from those features which are the most external and the most immediately accessible to those which are the least visible and the most profound. (Durkheim, 1982: 35-6)

Through a philosophical lens, Durkheim's main legacy is the application of the positivist principles to sociology. The study of social phenomena in general as 'things' or external structures that exist independent of social agents is what is perhaps most characteristic of the positivist, postpositivist, and (scientific) realist approaches to social science. The influence of positivism and postpositivism has been well covered in many qualitative research texts and need not be rehearsed here (see, for example, Denzin & Lincoln, 1994, 1998, 2000, 2003, 2005, 2011b; Guba, 1990; Guba & Lincoln, 1989, 1994; Lincoln & Guba, 1998, 2000). Broadly, positivism denotes the view that the scientific methods of the natural sciences ought to be adopted as a model in the study of human experience, behaviour, and social worlds. The positivistic view, as we have seen, is underpinned by the original ideas of empiricism, which 'establishes the basis for assuming that we can know what is "out there" objectively in the world via our sensory experiences' (Slife & Williams, 1995: 214). Positivistically motivated social science is often characterized by the discovery of fundamental causal laws, careful empirical observation, and value-free research, whereby preference is given to surveys, statistics, and quantitative data – all to be thought through with prudence to secure rigorous and objective knowledge (Neuman, 2011). These postpositivist approaches differ from Popper's rationalism, where the role of observation and experiment is solely to confirm or refute hypotheses.

Summary and implications for qualitative research

The difference between mere beliefs and knowledge is that the former are mere claims which are not supported by sufficient evidence and justified, whereas the latter is furnished by reason, observation, and experiments designed to determine whether propositions are true or false. This chapter has illustrated that the debate over what counts as knowledge and whether or not it is possible to arrive at truth merely by reason, or via observation and experience, goes back to the time of Ancient Greece. The Greeks were the first to abandon a supernatural view of the universe, substituting it with laws, order, and truths that were accessible to humans. The Platonists believed that nature followed a rational order and that it was mathematically structured. Thus any *truth* about the external world was to be deduced logically. This was the beginning of a *rationalist* outlook. It was challenged by the competing standpoint of *empiricism*, espoused by the early empiricists, such as Aristotle, who emphasized the need for knowledge to be based on the observation of real things. They argued that only those aspects of the world that were accessible to the senses and observable could be knowable. The ways in which rationalism manifests in science today reflect the thesis that reality, not merely appearances available to the senses, is revealed through rational thought and can be tested through experimentation. Empiricists, on the other hand, draw their conclusions mainly from observation.

In the social sciences, empiricism is largely exhibited through positivistic approaches to research, whereas rationalism (reformulated as a hypothetico-deductive method by Karl Popper) is most obvious in postpositivistic tactics. Qualitative inquiry underpinned by positivism and postpositivism may, but does not have to, employ computational tools, such as the UAM CorpusTool, which allows researchers to perform comparative statistics. Postpositivist studies tend to formulate theories and hypotheses that can be tested by collecting qualitative data (for example, through interviews) in order for these to be confirmed or falsified. If confirmed, they become the 'best available theories' but remain subject to revision and future refutation. As far as suitable methodologies are concerned, Spencer, Pryce, and Walsh (2014), for example, argue that grounded theory, as formulated by Glaser and Straus, is aligned with positivistic and postpositivistic research.[12] Although it requires data to begin with, these academics hold that 'the foundational assumptions on which traditional grounded theory rests are largely rooted in post-positivism' (2014: 85).

It is necessary to emphasize here that all qualitative research relies on the use of empirical data (observation, interviews, focus groups, etc.). In this regard, the qualitative researcher does not have to be a positivist or a postpositivist, and in fact the vast majority of qualitatively minded academics are philosophically and methodologically opposed to these views. At the level of techniques, the mere deployment of participant observation or interviews (or any other tools) is not sufficient in itself to distinguish between positivist, postpositivist, interpretivist, and constructionist approaches. What sets these apart are the philosophical assumptions that ultimately inform methodological and methodical decisions. As such, a positivist study can draw on interviews with the aim of formulating a theory that could be generalized to a larger population, a postpositivist study can draw on interviews to test a hypothesis, a phenomenological study can use interviews to describe the essence of a phenomenon, a hermeneutic study may seek to understand the emergence of meanings in specific contexts, and a constructionist study can use interviews as a way of expounding the plurality of meanings. It is a common mistake – and indeed false – to assume that the methods popular among qualitative researchers, such as interviews or participant observation, are *inherently* 'qualitative'.[13] It is also important to emphasize that there is a difference between the methods of data collection and the methods of data analysis, a point to which we will return in Chapter 8.

Finally, although it was necessary to highlight the differences between the doctrines of rationalism and empiricism, it is essential to resist the temptation to place all the rationalists in one box and all the empiricists in another. Markie (2015), for example, cautions against the adoption of a simple-minded general classification. To this end, the picture painted in this chapter mainly serves the purpose of revealing the landscape of the core epistemic problems. The final task lies with the researcher who must follow up and immerse herself in the works of individual philosophers whose ideas she may find resonated the most. It is indeed possible to formulate a more complex stance and be a rationalist about mathematics and physics and an empiricist about medicine and social science. It is also possible to be a realist about some things, but not others – a problem we shall pursue in later chapters.

─────────────── **Recommended reading** ───────────────

Casullo, A. (2003) *A Priori Justification*. Oxford: Oxford University Press.
Hung, E. (2014) *Philosophy of Science Complete: A Text on Traditional Problems and Schools of Thought* (2nd edn). Boston, MA: Wadsworth.
Kline, M. (1982) *Mathematics: The Loss of Certainty*. Oxford: Oxford University Press.
Monton, B. & Mohler, C. (2012) Constructive Empiricism. In E.N. Zalta (ed.), *The Stanford Encyclopedia of Philosophy* (Winter, 2012 edn). Retrieved 9 February 2014 from http://plato.stanford.edu/archives/win2012/entries/constructive-empiricism/

Nelson, A. (ed.) (2013) *A Companion to Rationalism*. Chichester: Wiley-Blackwell.

Popper, K. (1999) Falsificationisms. In R. Klee (ed.), *Scientific Inquiry: Readings in the Philosophy of Science* (pp. 65–71). New York: Oxford University Press.

Stroll, A. (2000) *Twentieth-Century Analytic Philosophy*. New York: Columbia University Press.

Uebel, T. (2013) Logical empiricism. In M. Curd & S. Psillos (eds), *The Routledge Companion to Philosophy of Science* (2nd edn; pp. 90–102). Abingdon: Taylor & Francis.

Notes

1. Religion and spirituality did continue to play a fundamental role in ancient Greece, so there was not a complete departure from religion per se. However, the laws of nature could now begin to be developed using rational processes and methods as opposed to natural phenomena being explained through mere 'beliefs'.
2. Of course it goes without saying that reason and logic are necessary for drawing inferences. What we see with the *empeirikos*, as Frede (1990) explains, is a particular conception of reason that is different from how we would employ the term today. Frede likens it to an 'associationist account of thought' whereby knowledge is accounted for solely in terms of memory and senses (1990: 226).
3. In the present day, we think of universities as secular places that strive to foster critical thinking and promote scientific methods of inquiry. However, the process of secularization of universities only began later, in the Enlightenment era.
4. For a complete list of the intellectuals associated with the Vienna and Berlin Circles, see Uebel's entry in the *Stanford Encyclopedia of Philosophy*: http://plato.stanford.edu/entries/vienna-circle/
5. Uebel, for example, notes that it is difficult to make a sharp distinction between the Viennese logical positivism and Berlin logical empiricism, and although some have suggested that Carnap's phenomenalist verificationism and Reichenbach's physicalist verificationism is precisely the difference needed, any such attempt would only mark a temporary difference and misrepresent the changing theories of the Vienna Circle (Uebel, 2013).
6. For the positivists the theorems of mathematics were *analytic* or *a priori*. This view was rejected not only by Mill, but also by White, Quine, and Tarski (for more see Stroll, 2000).
7. Stroll (2000) notes that while the positivists indeed acknowledged the importance of reason in the processes of deduction to allow for the derivation of truths from truths, they viewed reason as playing a facilitative role, not to be confused with an existential application to reality.
8. Of course not all birds fly and not all swans are white, which is why inductive knowledge can never be absolute, only probable (see also Chapter 3).

9. According to the *Stanford Encyclopedia of Philosophy* (see http://plato.stanford.edu/entries/popper/).

10. This view of theories as being potentially false is also called *fallibilism*.

11. For more information on critical rationalism, see www.iep.utm.edu/cr-ratio/

12. Spencer et al. (2014) are quick to point out that grounded theory can be adopted into, and is compatible with, a number of philosophical approaches. This is an important point, but not one that we will examine further here.

13. Some academics contrast quantitative and qualitative methods whereby the meaning of the term 'qualitative' is painted as 'anti-realist', 'anti-positivist', or 'anti-objectivist'. This generalization ought to be avoided as it is misleading. We will examine qualitative research in Chapter 8 in terms of attitudes: as *means* and as *orientation*.

Three

Scepticism, Idea-ism, and Idealism

In the preceding chapter, we looked at the tensions between the empiricists and the rationalists and placed logical positivism and postpositivism on the continuum of these philosophical traditions. In this chapter, our focus shifts toward exploring the doctrines of scepticism, idea-ism and idealism. In the first part, we will take note of two schools of scepticism – Academic and Pyrrhonian – and briefly outline their features, differences and proponents. While on the topic of scepticism, we will also re-visit the philosophy of René Descartes, this time concentrating on the sceptical method, which he employed to determine whether the sceptics were correct in their doubt about knowledge. Idea-ism, discussed next, arises as a response to scepticism about sense data by the British empiricists. It will be shown that idea-ism was an important epistemological stance that informed much of the debate about reality and perception, presented in this chapter as the Two-World Assumption problem. After a close examination of the philosophies of John Locke, David Hume, George Berkeley, and Immanuel Kant, it will be proposed that whereas all of these thinkers can be understood as idea-ists in epistemology, differences must be recognized between their ontological assumptions. The chapter closes with a summary and an exercise in pondering *a priori* and *a posteriori* statements. It is worth emphasizing that qualitative inquiry is not isolated from, but rather informed by, the problems covered in the following pages. By gaining a deeper understanding of the doctrines of scepticism, idea-ism, and idealism, as well as the philosophical issues surrounding perception, we become attuned to the conundrums that preoccupied many great minds.

Scepticism

In Chapter 1, we introduced scepticism as one of the core epistemological outlooks. We must not dwell too much on this doctrine, for there would be very little incentive to carry out research and study the world if we were to deny its existence and the possibility of knowing it. Worse yet, if we were thoroughly sceptical about the worth of our work, scholarly activity would seem pointless. Nevertheless, it is crucial to provide at least a short overview of scepticism to better understand the developments in the philosophy of science that unfolded as a result of the opposition to sceptical thought. There were two ancient schools of scepticism: Academic (also dogmatic) scepticism and Pyrrhonian scepticism. Academic scepticism dates back to Socratic and Platonic times, but was only developed theoretically by Arcesilaus (315–241 BCE) and Carneades (213–129 BCE). It asserts that nothing can be known, that our human senses cannot be trusted to furnish us with reliable knowledge, and that there is no ultimate criterion of true knowledge (Popkin, 2003). This type of scepticism, often called *global scepticism* because of its wide reach, denies all knowledge – i.e., that there is nothing justifiable, rational, or reasonable (Graham, 2008). The Academic sceptics of ancient Greece can be contrasted with their philosophical counterparts, the Stoics, who, following Aristotle, claimed that 'truths' about the world are not only possible but also attainable through observation. There were other schools of philosophy in that period, of which the most prominent were the Epicureans (following Epicurus), the Cynics (following Diogenes), and the logicians of the Megarian School (following Socrates) (Long, 2006). We shall only acknowledge these, staying on course in our exploration of scepticism.

Pyrrhonian scepticism originated in the doctrines of Pyrrho of Elis (360–275 BCE), who has been described as 'a living example of a complete doubter' (Popkin, 2003: xviii). The theoretical developments of Pyrrhonian scepticism are attributed to a later philosopher, Aenesidemus (100–40 BCE). Pyrrhonian scepticism steered a middle path between the Academic sceptics, who held that no knowledge is possible, and the dogmatist philosophers, who claimed that humans can acquire empirical truths. According to Popkin, the Pyrrhonians 'proposed to suspend judgment on all questions on which there seemed to be conflicting evidence, including the question whether or not something could be known' (2003: xix). Whereas the outcome of Academic scepticism tended to be negative and led to dogmatic conclusions – that nothing can be known – in the area of judgement, Pyrrhonian scepticism was 'mute'. Judgements on matters beyond appearances were simply suspended. Aside from the philosophical implications, it was their mental attitude that allowed the followers of Pyrrhonian scepticism to reach a state of *ataraxia* or unperturbedness. Popkin conveys this attitude in the following way: 'The Pyrrhonist, then, lives undogmatically, following his natural inclinations, the appearances he is aware of, and the laws and customs of his society, without ever committing himself to any judgment about them' (2003: xix). Understood, therefore, as an ethically driven doctrine, Pyrrhonian scepticism was believed to lead the ancient Greeks to a state of tranquillity, freedom, and true happiness (Bermúdez, 2008).

Pyrrhonian scepticism remained popular until the time of Sextus Empiricus (a Greek physician and philosopher dated to c. 160–210 CE), who continued the tradition of skilful questioning culminating in the suspension of judgement. Sextus's views were aligned with the Pyrrhonian one. Lammenranta states that the sceptics sought truth but realized along the way that there were disagreements they could not resolve, leading them to them suspend all judgement (Lammenranta, 2008). Sextus's response to the dogmatist philosophers and their attack on scepticism was that it was the dogmatists who would not inquire. Namely, he argued that 'one inquires only when one has the idea (*nomizein*) that one hasn't found the answer' (Fine, 2014: 343). The dogmatists believed they had discovered the answers and were in possession of truths.

During the Middle Ages, scepticism as a philosophy was overshadowed by Platonism and Neo-Platonism, and later, by the revival of Aristotle's work in the twelfth and thirteenth centuries, when it was translated into Latin. Yet it would be inaccurate to claim that scepticism disappeared completely. It can be traced, for instance, to the works of Augustine (354–430 CE), Al-Haytham (965–1040 CE), and Al-Ghazali (1058–1111), plus a handful of other scholastics in the thirteenth century (Bolyard, 2013). Scepticism made a comeback towards the end of the fifteenth century. It played a vital role during the Protestant Reformation in figures such as Girolamo Savonarola (1452–1498) and Martin Luther (1483–1546), both known for criticizing the Church for corruption and opulent lifestyles within the clergy, the selling of *indulgences*, and papal authority – all of which, the reformers argued, had little to do with *true* religion (Popkin, 2003). They were sceptical about the *truths* authorized by the Church.

Scepticism later spread from doubting 'true' religious knowledge to doubting natural knowledge and philosophy, and exerted a profound influence on the intellectual scene in a number of societies. Popkin notes that France in the 1600s, for example, was dominated by scepticism and *probable* knowledge, as opposed to certainty and absolute truths. And it is within this context that we ought to say a little more about René Descartes, who played an important part in shaping the intellectual scene of that period, and was denounced by orthodox and traditional thinkers of French society as a 'dangerous Pyrrhonist' (Popkin, 2003: 158).

Descartes, introduced in the previous chapter as a leading figure of *rationalism,* is perhaps best known for his use of the sceptical doubt. From the outset, we note that Descartes' scepticism was different from the Academic or Pyrrhonian varieties outlined above. In fact, he was disturbed by the suggestion that humans have no access to any truths. With the intent to determine what kind of truths, if any, could be attained, Descartes employed scepticism in a systematic fashion. As emphasized by Popkin, it was *through* the process of doubting (not *after* doubting) that he strove to find indubitable truths, and hence, the foundations of knowledge. Put otherwise, the sceptical *method of doubting* consists of a methodical series of doubts (published in Descartes' *Meditations on First Philosophy*).[1] Descartes used the analogy of a basket full of apples containing some rotten specimens. The apples represented all truth claims, the rotten ones false beliefs. In order to eliminate the bad apples from the basket, he suggested that the best strategy would be to empty the basket and closely examine each apple one at a time, putting the good ones back in and discarding the rest. Only in this way can one be certain that the contents of the basket are good. Similarly, knowledge and truth claims must be systematically scrutinized and subjected to the method of doubt. Through this process of eliminating all unreliable knowledge – including that acquired through our senses (e.g., touch, taste, smell, hearing, and sight), which Descartes viewed as fallible – he arrived at one *truth* that he could not doubt. This was his famous *Cogito, ergo sum*, translated as *I think, therefore I am*. And because anything external to the mind could be doubted, through logic and reason he eventually confirmed other *truths*, such as axioms and mathematical truths (e.g., $1 + 1 = 2$). Descartes' ultimate attempt to avoid scepticism was to 'objectify subjective certitude by attaching it to God', i.e. what is subjectively certain is also certain absolutely and objectively (Popkin, 2003: 156). This way, our knowledge is dependent on an objective God who would not deceive us or entangle us in some demonic trickery.

Descartes had both his followers and his critics. Spinoza was among the early sceptical philosophers to apply the Cartesian method to religion and religious texts. He was a rational thinker sceptical about religious knowledge, but anti-sceptical about scientific knowledge. Although he did not reject the notion of a God, he dismissed the religious knowledge and truth-claims of the Scriptures as 'some odd writing of the Hebrews' (Popkin, 2003: 243). Among Descartes' critics were a number of prominent sceptics of the seventeenth century, such as Simon Foucher, Bishop Pierre-Daniel Huet, and Pierre Bayle – but who were also critical of the views held by other metaphysicians of that era, including Locke, Malebranche, Arnauld,[2] Spinoza, and Cudworth (Popkin, 2003). Pierre Bayle (1647–1706), for example, held against Descartes that all sensory data or ideas are not to be found in the objects themselves but in the mind, and that we cannot trust our belief in the external world by grounding it in another belief in God. Furthermore, if God can deceive us about our sensory perceptions, then he may indeed deceive us about other things too (Lennon & Hickson, 2014).

In addition to the general notion of scepticism as 'doubt' about belief, the sceptics radically undermined the empirical method, and with it, any notion of certitude about reality (ontology) and the possibility of knowing it (epistemology). They maintained that claims to truth about the external world grounded in perception were not to be trusted, and deemed knowledge of physical objects through the sense apparatus to be unreliable. Consequently, the human senses could not be the means to trustworthy knowledge. For example, according to the sceptics, we cannot trust our vision to know the *true* shape of an object. Instead, we get multiple appearances of a thing in viewing it from different angles or from closer or further away. Moreover, appearances vary under different conditions. If we were to look at the same object under infrared light, we would experience yet another sense-datum. Thus, the sceptics would argue that there is no single accurate appearance, but rather as many appearances as there are perspectives, making it impossible to know which one is *true*. Included among the arsenal of sceptical weaponry against

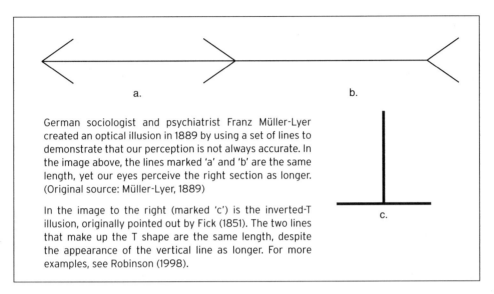

German sociologist and psychiatrist Franz Müller-Lyer created an optical illusion in 1889 by using a set of lines to demonstrate that our perception is not always accurate. In the image above, the lines marked 'a' and 'b' are the same length, yet our eyes perceive the right section as longer. (Original source: Müller-Lyer, 1889)

In the image to the right (marked 'c') is the inverted-T illusion, originally pointed out by Fick (1851). The two lines that make up the T shape are the same length, despite the appearance of the vertical line as longer. For more examples, see Robinson (1998).

Figure 3.1 Examples of optical illusions

perception were also various demonstrations of illusion (see Figure 3.1). Musgrave (1993) gives the example of a stick immersed in a glass of water which appears bent through the glass. Of course we know that the stick remains straight even when immersed – it only appears bent because the water distorts our perception – but this was precisely the point raised by the sceptics: that our perceptions can deceive us. We must therefore question the extent to which knowledge based on sense data can be deemed accurate. Sceptical arguments about the senses kept surfacing in the philosophy of science throughout the twentieth century, and here we shall mention at least Nelson Goodman, who made the following assertion:

> If I take a photograph of a man with his feet towards me, the feet may come out as large as his torso. Is this the way I normally or properly see the man? If so, then why do we call such a photograph distorted? If not, then I can no longer claim to be taking the photographic view of the world as my standard of faithfulness. (1996: 7)

To return to Descartes, his successful attempt to overcome *global* scepticism by using methodical doubting meant that the mind and rational thought were once again rendered secure as legitimate means of arriving at *truths* about the world. The same, however, could not be said of knowledge that relied on sense data. Empirical truths fell short of providing certainty. Smell, sound, colour, and touch-related stimuli were perceived by influential scientists and philosophers, including Galileo, Descartes, and Hobbes, as the *effects* 'produced by the real object on the sentient mind' (Dewey, 1979: 226). Sense data were not held to be accurate in capturing the way the external world *really* was because they were deceptive – hardly reliable as evidence for justifying propositions. The truths of reason reigned over the truths of observation and experience. The rationalist philosophers believed that all human beings must have *innate ideas* that exist *a priori* and as part of our rational make-up. As we saw in Chapter 2, from Plato to Descartes, our knowledge of geometry and mathematics, for example, was proclaimed *innate*. The empiricists found this notion of inborn knowledge obscure and upheld that our knowledge of nature must come from observation. To defend the empirical knowledge of the senses, the British empiricists erected a new line of epistemic defence: what Alan Musgrave (1993) has termed *idea-ism*.

Idea-ism

The empiricists demanded that knowledge be founded on experience, hence *a posteriori*. The notion that human beings are born with certain *a priori* truths was thus unsurprisingly rejected by the empiricists, in particular the trio of British empirical thinkers Locke, Berkeley, and Hume. Although the philosophy of these legendary thinkers is rather diverse, they were united in their commitment to defending the empirical knowledge of the senses. The conviction they shared about the possibility of knowing one's ideas or sense data is what Musgrave (1993) has termed *idea-ism*. Simply put, idea-ism stands for the knowledge of ideas. Their individual scholarly efforts yielded greatly diverging results, and in this section we explore what these are.

John Locke (1632–1704): Indirect realism and primary and secondary qualities

John Locke famously proclaimed that the human mind is like a blank slate or *tabula rasa* on which ideas are recorded. All ideas – what he called 'objects of understanding' – must stem from experience, including axioms, mathematics, and moral principles (Uzgalis, 2014). In Locke's view, no *a priori* knowledge or truths exist prior to experience. He was a metaphysical realist[3] and an atomist (holding that atoms were the smallest particles of matter) who, after Bayle, popularized the notion of objects as having different types of qualities. These were categorized as the *primary qualities* (e.g., shape, size, weight, being in motion or at rest, being one or several in number) and the *secondary qualities* (e.g., colour, taste, odour, sound, texture, temperature) (Musgrave, 1993: 107). This distinction was of immense importance in combating the sceptics. It enabled the separation of the potentially deceiving secondary qualities (including the aforementioned optical illusions) from the primary ones, which Locke believed to exist in objects inherently. Accepting of the natural philosophy of Robert Boyle (1627–1691), Locke painted a picture of the world where all objects are comprised of solid atoms and primary qualities, which could be distinguished from secondary qualities (Stroud, 1980).

However, Locke was not prepared to commit fully to the notion of *certain* knowledge of the world. Although his philosophy marks a departure from Descartes' *a priori* and innate ideas, and a move towards empirical knowledge gained through the senses, Locke believed that knowledge of material objects could only be *probabilistic* and closer to an opinion rather than the *truth* of how things *really* are in the world (Uzgalis, 2014). The reason for this cautious outlook had to do with perception. Locke held that we have only direct knowledge of sense data. In other words, what we observe directly are the *ideas* of primary and secondary qualities. As Musgrave notes, the 'ideas of primary qualities resemble primary qualities (apparent shape and real shape are both shapes), while ideas of secondary qualities do not resemble secondary qualities (apparent colours or colour-sensations are nothing like the properties of surfaces which produce them)' (1993: 114). It is necessary to note here that the ontological claim that objects possess intrinsic properties remains in place; what is at stake is whether our knowledge of these properties comes from *direct perception*. For instance, the yellowness and warmth of fire are secondary properties – perceiver-dependent – and do not really exist in the fire; what really exists are the primary, intrinsic properties of fire that produce these sensations in us, in this case the motion of particles. This means that 'the representation of things is always at best indirect, and since we can never think of things but indirectly, obviously we cannot but also use signs to recollect them or refer others to them indirectly' (Chappell, 1994: 123). Fisher summarizes Locke's outlook:

> The problem, Locke proposes, is that, from sensory experience, we are limited to only ideas of secondary qualities, and these fail to represent truly constitutive primary qualities. So, though we might believe we can judge what those primary qualities are, we have no grounds for certainty about those beliefs. Since, for Locke, knowledge requires certainty, he holds that we cannot know the basic constituents and relations of physical objects. (Fisher, 2003: 580)

Locke maintained a moderate empiricist view in his belief that through observation we can have *probable knowledge*. He was a metaphysical realist for holding that objects have inherent properties and that they exist independent of the mind. As Stroud explained it, 'everything that happens in the world, including our perceiving the colours, sounds, odours, and so on that we do, is caused by the action of physical particles possessing only primary qualities of the sort listed' (1980: 150). What we can take away from Locke's philosophy are two types of perceptual realisms: *direct* or *naïve* realism and *indirect* (also *representative* or *causal*) realism. Direct realism claims that we perceive physical objects directly as they are; indirect realism is the thesis that we only perceive physical objects indirectly, i.e., mediated through our senses. Locke's indirect realism is compatible with metaphysical realism in that he accepts that there are external objects in the world. It asserts that while some sense data are *representative* of the primary qualities of objects (e.g., shape and size), we can only know for certain the relationship between *ideas*. In Musgrave's (1993) view, Locke was therefore one of the first philosophers to be classified as an *indirect* or *causal* realist.

──────────── **Indirect (Causal Or Representative) Realism** ────────────

Physical objects cause sense data or sense impressions. We have direct access to, or evidence of, only sense data, but no immediate access to mind-independent entities or objects as they 'really are'. Consider, for example, the time-lag problem. What we perceive when looking at distant objects, such as planets in our solar system, are light waves processed by our brains. We do not perceive the objects themselves. Because it takes time for light to reach our sense preceptors, it is possible that in the meantime the object will cease to exist. Therefore, our immediate knowledge is only of our sense data. Concerning epistemology, we can only know our ideas (idea-ism). With respect to ontology, indirect realism acknowledges the existence of 'something' to exist and cause sense perception (metaphysical realism). For Locke, these were the primary qualities.

In summary, Locke's philosophy can be outlined as follows: (1) external objects have intrinsic, primary properties; (2) these properties are objective; and (3) we can have *representative* or *probable* knowledge of these. Furthermore, all knowledge is empirical as there are no truths prior to experience; our propositions are formulated through, and grounded in, observations of nature and experiments. This makes our mind a *tabula rasa* or a 'blank canvas' on which ideas are recorded. By stripping objects of their secondary (subjective) mental qualities, we are left with the sense data of the *primary qualities* that *represent* objects as they really are (Uzgalis, 2014). If we were to situate Locke epistemologically (e.g., in Figure 1.3, Chapter 1), we would classify him under empiricism and idea-ism – empiricism because he believed that all knowledge came from experience, and idea-ism because we can know ideas.

Finally, it is necessary to clarify that for indirect realists the human sense is not to be understood as a bias that distorts reality, as we saw with the sceptics; rather, sense data are the only way to know the external world. On this, Locke said, 'Where this perception is, there is knowledge; and where it is not, there, though we may fancy, guess, or believe, yet we always come short of knowledge' (1836: 385). In this respect, Locke was an empiricist, a metaphysical and indirect realist, and an idea-ist, but he certainly was not an idealist. The doctrine of idealism was reinstated by another empirical philosopher, George Berkeley. But before we move on to him, it is valuable to re-affirm the problem of reality on the one hand, and ideas on the other. The issue of reconciling the two can be described as the Two-World Assumption.

The Two-World Assumption

Indirect realism eventually leads us to the epistemological problem of the correspondence theory of truth. Namely, we face the question of whether we can know the world *truly* as it is and whether our knowledge corresponds with reality. By accepting causal realism, we are confronted by 'a gap between the world as we perceive it and the world as it is' (Ladyman, 2002: 141). In other words, indirect realism implies our inability to get hold of a literally true picture of the world because we have no direct access to it. Brown expands on this point further: what we perceive is a causal interaction between a physical object and a perceiver, and although the 'properties that the physical object appears to have are determined by the actual properties of that object [...] none of the properties that a physical object is perceived as having need be intrinsic properties of that object' (1992: 357). Thus, we are not justified in believing that what we perceive 'mirrors' with absolute certainty the world as it really is. To restate the problem before us – if knowledge is to be defined as 'justified true belief', then we are in a capricious position. Following Locke, all that is available to us are representations, ideas, and sensations, and our knowledge is limited only to these. This issue has been presented as the Two-World Assumption problem, which is depicted in Figure 3.2. This problem has been summarized succinctly by Solomon and Higgins:

> We can see the nature of the problem if we restate our assumption in the form of two apparently reasonable claims: (1) there is an external world - that is, a world beyond our beliefs and experiences, which is not affected by what we happen to believe about it, and (2) we cannot ever make direct contact with the world itself but only with the contents of our own minds - with our ideas, our beliefs, our various experiences, and the principles that we find to be necessary truths (such as the principles of logic and arithmetic). (2010: 157)

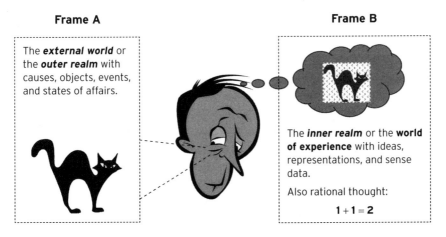

Frame A

The **external world** or the **outer realm** with causes, objects, events, and states of affairs.

Frame B

The **inner realm** or the **world of experience** with ideas, representations, and sense data.

Also rational thought:

$$1 + 1 = 2$$

Figure 3.2 The Two-World Assumption. Concept adapted from Solomon and Higgins (2010: 157)

The problem, as presented in Figure 3.2, is that there is the external world with objects, events, and causes (Frame A) and the internal world of experiences, ideas, and sense data (Frame B). The question of what exists in the external world, and how to reconcile it with our ideas, has been approached and answered in different ways. If we were to begin with the more moderate Pyrrhonian sceptics, the senses cannot be trusted and therefore any judgement about what can be known must be suspended. The more radical Academic sceptics would maintain that knowledge is unattainable and remove any certainty about the existence of an external world. This would imply scepticism about both Frame A and Frame B. Descartes' solution would be to get rid of the 'rotten apples' and only keep the *a priori* truths, those that are certain. He would be doubtful about the content of Frame A, since for all we know it could be an illusion; he would also reject any knowledge in Frame B that is based on sense data. He would, however, accept the *a priori* mathematical truths (e.g., $1 + 1 = 2$), in addition to, of course, the existence of an undeceiving God and his own mind. Locke would be sceptical about the secondary, subjective qualities of external objects, but not about their primary qualities. For him, the content in Frame A exists as far as primary qualities are concerned, plus we can have knowledge of the ideas about it (e.g., size and shape), but we cannot have direct and certain knowledge of the objects of perception. Locke himself proclaimed that:

> [...] since the mind, in all its thoughts and reasonings, hath no other immediate object but its own ideas, which it alone does or can contemplate, it is evident that our knowledge is only conversant about them. Knowledge is the perception of the agreement or disagreement of two ideas. Knowledge then seems to me to be nothing but the perception of the connexion and agreement, or disagreement and repugnancy, of any of our ideas. In this alone it consists. (Locke, 1836: 385)

We have seen that the sceptics attacked direct perception, and hence direct realism, about the external world, telling us that the senses cannot be trusted as a reliable source of truths about reality. The British empiricists Locke, Berkeley, and Hume abandoned the naïve view of direct apprehension of objects, but maintained that we *can* be certain about our *ideas*. They argued that 'the senses give us direct and infallible information about the "appearances" or "ideas"' (Musgrave, 1993: 88). For this reason, Musgrave sees them as representatives of a new form of empiricism that emerged as a response to the sceptical assault on sense data – idea-ism. To appreciate the differences between direct realism and idea-ism, we can put to use the following examples originally presented by Musgrave (1993: 89), altered here to accommodate the content of Figure 3.2:

> **Direct realism**: '*I see a black cat*' [the claim here is that a person is perceiving visually an external object as it is - a black cat].

> **Idea-ism**: '*I am now having or experiencing a visual idea or visual sense datum of a black cat*' [we claim to be immediately perceiving ideas or sense data].

With direct realism, what we perceive matches what there is. The sense data in our mind mirror the objects in the world. With idea-ism, the claim shifts from 'Now I am seeing something' to 'I am experiencing sense datum', which is a critical epistemological move from knowledge of external objects to knowledge of ideas and sense data furnished by our mind (Musgrave, 1993). To sum up the main point, for the idea-ists there is no direct knowledge of the world, only knowledge of ideas. We can be certain about the content of Frame B in Figure 3.2, but not so certain about it matching what there is in Frame A. With respect to Locke, it is fundamental to recognize that ideas are caused by ontologically real, external objects. The other idea-ists, Berkeley and Hume, approached the issue differently. Berkeley removed the primary qualities from the epistemic pedestal, so carefully placed there by Locke, and grouped them with the secondary qualities. In doing so, he removed any glimmer of hope of knowing the world, even going so far as to deny its existence. Hume took Locke's ideas to the extreme, suggesting that our knowledge of reality can be justified neither empirically nor rationally. We shall examine both of these idea-ists in more depth.

George Berkeley (1685–1753): Idea-ism turns into idealism

Thus far we have established that Locke, Berkeley, and Hume opposed the notion of innate ideas and *a priori* knowledge, and that all three were empiricists who in epistemology represent the doctrine of idea-ism. It has also been explained that Locke, adhering to a materialist view of nature, was an idea-ist but not an idealist. The same, however, cannot be said of Berkeley. While Locke was aware of the problem of appearances and distinguished between *primary* and *secondary* qualities – separating the inherent and knowable from the subjective and subordinate – Berkeley objected to this distinction, grouping primary and secondary sense data together and proclaiming that the objects we perceive in the external world are all 'collections of ideas which do not exist unperceived' (Musgrave, 1993: 125). Consequently, he denied that objects undoubtedly exist. With Locke, there was a gap separating the internal realm of *ideas* and the world as it really was; with Berkeley, we lost access to reality completely, with only *ideas* remaining. Berkeley, therefore, is our chief idealist. He took idea-ism to its extreme and denied the existence of a mind-independent world (Musgrave, 1993). This denial, on the level of ontological discourse, is what positions *metaphysical idealism* or *immaterialism* as the competing view to materialism (the notion that there is an external world that exists independently, as shown in Figure 1.3 in Chapter 1). Ladyman (2002) further emphasizes that – in Berkeley's view – the primary properties of objects are as relative and variable as secondary ones because they too are subject to perception and some reference frame. Ladyman sums up Berkeley's argument as follows:

1. We experience only 'ideas' and not material objects (idea-ism).
2. All our ideas come from experience (concept empiricism).
3. The words 'material object' cannot stand for any idea and are therefore meaningless (immaterialism).

Furthermore, Berkeley argued that the supposedly mind-independent objects are, in fact, mind-dependent and only exist when perceived:

a) We perceive such things as trees and stones.

b) We perceive only ideas and aggregates (or collections) of them (idea-ism).

c) These ideas and aggregates cannot exist unperceived.

d) Therefore, trees and stones are ideas and impressions or aggregates of them, and cannot exist unperceived (idealism). (see Ladyman, 2002: 142-5).

It is vital not to confuse idea-ism, which is an epistemological claim, with idealism, which is a metaphysical claim. Locke and Berkeley disagreed on the issue of external objects as having an objective, sovereign, mind-independent status. Berkeley argued that all objects in the world are mind-dependent; Locke held that objects have primary qualities, and that there must be *something* in the object to cause its appearance. Moreover, perception is consistent: it does not vary dramatically from one person to another. Indeed, when 100 people look at a tree, they see the same thing. And when we talk about the Moon, we are talking about one and the same thing, with the same properties (there is only one, it is round, it is bright, etc.). For Locke, the answer lay in the primary properties of objects and an object's 'powers' to produce sensations in us. Berkeley, we note, was also a priest (later named the Bishop of Cloyne) and he provided a spiritual response: that 'God perceives everything all the time and hence ensures the continued existence of the world around us when we are not observing it' (Ladyman, 2002: 146).

This religious account of reality has been criticized by many philosophers and rejected by scientists as a whole. But before we charge against Berkeley's rather extreme views, it is important to emphasize that his philosophical goal was to defeat scepticism. Musgrave (1993) labours this point because he feels that Berkeley is easily dismissed, misunderstood, and underappreciated. Musgrave explains that idealism was the only strategy that could be applied towards preserving the evidence of the senses. Berkeley's solution to the problem of scepticism was 'to give up the distinction between "real things" and ideas, to turn the ideas into the real things – the solution, in a word, is idealism' (1993: 123). In this way, he was able to argue that the least we can have is certain knowledge about our ideas. And while it was easy for the sceptics to attack direct or naïve realism (the view that we can perceive reality directly as it is), it was difficult for them to deny knowledge of ideas.

David Hume (1711–1776): Idea-ism turns into scepticism

The empiricist outlook tells us that we are not equipped with *innate* or *a priori* knowledge. Rather, we learn from experience that the Sun 'rises', that it generates heat, and that if exposed to it for a long period of time unprotected, our skin is likely to get sunburned. This knowledge is not obtainable by reason alone, it requires observation and experience. Hume, like the other empiricists, argued that our knowledge of the external world must be empirical and that all natural phenomena, such as rain, lightning, tornados, and biological processes, have causes. In this respect a great deal of empirical facts are facts about cause and effect. But causation, in Hume's view, was not something humans can observe. Instead, the principle of universal causality is something we *carry to* experience rather than *learn from* experience (Solomon & Higgins, 2010: 164). To illustrate Hume's point, imagine a pencil sitting on a desk. A cat jumps on the desk and plays with it until the pencil reaches the edge of the desk. If the cat were to push the pencil further, we would expect it to fall on the ground. In other words, we would anticipate cause and effect. And here, causation, as Hume pointed out, is something we apply from our past experience. We have no reason to believe that the patterns of behaviour we have observed until now will continue to manifest in the same fashion in the future. It is only due to our past observations that we expect effects to have specific causes. Thus, Hume concluded that 'we never actually see the cause of an event at all; we only see that two events are regularly found together, in "constant conjunction"' (Solomon & Higgins, 2010: 164). And although we think that in causation there are 'necessary connections', we only perceive 'conjoint events', not the connection between them (Ladyman, 2002: 37).

We are not *justified* in believing that when the cat pushes the pencil past the edge of the desk it will fall, other than that is what it has done in the past. Our justification is historical and habitual. And therefore, according to Hume, it is possible that events will not unfold as we expect them to because there are no other guarantees than past experience: 'Since it is logically possible that any regularity will fail to hold in the future, the only basis we have for inductive inference is the belief that the future will resemble the past' (Ladyman, 2002: 40). Hence, with the method of induction we cannot speak of *certain* knowledge – only *probable* knowledge, grounded in previous observations. We also know from the classical examples of the problems of induction that generalizations are only justified so long so they are not contradicted. For instance, our belief that all swans are white is only valid so long as we do not discover that there are also black swans. Hence, the fundamental issue that accompanies inductively derived truths, Hume pointed out, is the lack of justification for inductive practices, leaving it on par with 'animal instinct and habit rather than reason' (Ladyman, 2002: 40). As to the bigger question of whether or not we can be justified in believing in the existence of the external world, Hume's response was equally unfavourable: neither can we appeal to reason to support our belief in it, nor can we prove it with certainty by experience (Solomon & Higgins, 2010). Hume's position, then, is scepticism.

To understand Hume's strategy, known as Hume's fork, Table 3.1 shows that he divided all truths into two categories. These were (a) *a priori* Truths of Reason, and (b) *a posteriori* Matters of Fact (empirical truths). Any other proposed form of knowledge was deemed by Hume as 'sophistry and illusion' (Ladyman, 2002: 33): whatever question we ask, it must fall into one of the two categories provided in the table. If the proposition is abstract and *a priori*, such as a mathematical truth (1 + 1 = 2), it belongs in the category 'Truths of Reason'. If the proposition deals with questions about the external world and requires experience or observation for its verification, it belongs in the category 'Matters of Fact' – for instance, we cannot know that snow is white prior to our experience of snow. Table 3.1 also separates analytic statements from synthetic statements (recall, here, the discussion of positivism in Chapter 2). The statement that 'all bachelors are single' requires no justification by experience because it is a tautological, self-evident statement that is true by definition. In order to know how many legs cats have or at what temperature water freezes, we need to engage in observation and carry out experiments.

Table 3.1 Hume's fork

THERE CAN BE ONLY TWO KINDS OF PROPOSITIONS:	
(A) Truths of Reason	*(B) Matters of Fact*
Concepts or ideas.	Informative about the actual world (empirical).
Analytical knowledge.	Synthetic.
A priori.	*A posteriori* (*a priori* knowledge of matters of fact impossible).
Necessary.	Contingent (subject to chance).
Provable by deduction; negation will contradict the proposition (2 + 2 = 7 is wrong).	Not provable by deduction; only verifiable by the senses, logically unrelated.
Examples: All bachelors are single. Mathematical truths (e.g., triangles have angles totalling 180°; 1 + 1 = 2).	**Examples:** Snow is white. Paris is the capital of France. Cats have four legs. Water freezes at 0 degrees Celsius.
The principle of universal causality?	

Source: Distilled from Ladyman (2002), Musgrave (1993), and Solomon and Higgins (2010).

The crucial part, to which we shall return, is the issue of cause and effects. When it comes to the fundamental question of the principle of universal causality – i.e., the claim that all events in the universe must have a cause – the question arises as to whether it belongs to Truths of Reason or Matters of Fact. Hume's answer is unsettling for both the rationalists and the empiricists. As explained by Solomon and Higgins, we can think of concepts or scenarios of a world without necessary cause. It is rationally possible to conceive of possibilities where events happen at random. We only need to consider the theory of quantum mechanics (discussed in Chapter 7). And so, if causation is not necessarily a Truth of Reason, this leaves us with only one viable option – to place the universal principle of causality in the category of Matters of Fact. The fundamental argument provided by Hume was that the first human being had to learn through experience all of the causes we take for granted, such as that fire burns, water drowns, and apples fall (Solomon & Higgins, 2010). The problem with causality being an empirical truth, however, is that it relies solely on our past observations, and as such is not a reliable guide: it offers no certainty, only probability.[4] The final verdict, therefore, is uncertainty about causation, and hence, uncertainty about nature. When we grasp the implications of Hume's thought, it is no wonder that Howson states 'David Hume published a philosophical argument that was, metaphorically, dynamite' (2000: 1).

In order to ease the mind of the bewildered reader, Ladyman gives a number of responses that have surfaced in the study of the philosophy of science to counter Hume's scepticism of induction. Here we review a selection of the strategies that sought to address the problem of induction distilled from Ladyman's analysis (2002: 40–52):

(1) *Induction is rational by definition*: People use induction to make rational choices on a daily basis, assuming that nature is uniform and that the future will be like the past. For instance, based on our experience that the Sun has risen every morning, we infer that the Sun will rise tomorrow. Although we cannot be fully justified about this form of reasoning (i.e., we are not justified in believing that nature is uniform either by reason or by experience), we can approach Hume's argument as a paradox, and accept that we just don't know how it should be justified.

(2) *Induction is justified by the (mathematical) theory of probability*: Rudolf Carnap and Hans Reichenbach attempted to solve the problem of induction by calculating the probabilities of hypotheses – the degree to which a hypothesis can be confirmed. Although we can never have complete certainty about inferred generalizations, for many scholars getting close to certainty (i.e. high probability) is sufficient for a justification of scientific knowledge.

(3) *Induction is really (a species of) inference to the best explanation, which is justified*: A popular way of solving Hume's problem is inference to the best explanation (IBE), also called the method of *abduction*. It states that based on the known facts available to us, we should adopt the hypothesis that offers the most likely explanation.

(4) *Agree that induction is unjustified and offer an account of knowledge, in particular scientific knowledge, which dispenses with the need for inductive reference*: The most radical approach to the problem of induction is to accept that induction is unjustified and follow Popper's method of falsification, discussed in Chapter 2. Accordingly, instead of verifying theories by finding confirming instances, scientists ought to formulate theories that are in principle falsifiable. Of course, falsificationism comes with a different set of problems, which we will not attempt to address here (see, for example, Ladyman, 2002). Overall, what we can say about the philosophical problem Hume put before us is that no conclusive answer has been offered to date. Nevertheless, many scientists are content with the responses formulated to date, including the ones listed above.

Idealism and metaphysical realism

Before progressing any further in our exploration of Immanuel Kant's attempts to reconcile empiricism with rationalism, a brief overview of the developments in the eighteenth to twentieth centuries is well advised. Until the early 1900s and the publication of Moore's 'The Refutation of Idealism' (Moore, 1903), idealism in its many forms (e.g., post-Berkeleyan, post-Kantian, post-Hegelian) was the prevailing mode of philosophy (Stroll, 2000). Much of the discourse on reality and metaphysics revolved around the problem of reconciling the mind (ideas, sense data, appearances, phenomena) with the external objects (the things-in-themselves). Stroll explains that Moore made a key distinction between the act of perceiving and the objects themselves, arguing that while the first was mind-dependent the latter was not. Material or physical objects were therefore proclaimed to exist, and the doctrine of idealism, together with continental philosophy (e.g., Nietzsche, Hegel, Heidegger, Husserl, Gadamer, Foucault, Derrida), was on the decline (Braver, 2007). Twentieth-century philosophy was dominated by analytic thought, which appealed to logic and mathematics (advanced mainly by Frege, Russell, and Moore). In this philosophical environment, the scientific view and new forms of realism and logical positivism took centre stage (Stroll, 2000). We noted the continuum in the developments on the front of rationalism and empiricism in Chapter 2. The focus of this section is the philosophical thought of eighteenth-century idealism.

Idealism

In the widest sense of the term, idealism begins with the claim that there is an inseparable tie between whatever there may be in the external world and the human mind. It is a tie that is so strong that external objects are denied a mind-independent existence: the world and its phenomena depend on the mind – leaving no room for objectivity and the sovereign existence of things. Metaphysically speaking, idealism stands in opposition to the doctrine of metaphysical realism and materialism, which states that the world 'goes on' regardless of the activities of the human mind. In other words, the world exists autonomously and objectively. We have seen that Berkeley reduced reality (external objects) to *ideas*, turning him into a prime example of a dogmatic idealist who advocated metaphysical *immaterialism*. With reference to the Two-World Assumption in Figure 3.2, Berkeley would only acknowledge Frame B (ideas and sense data), denying the objective existence of things, causes, and events in Frame A.

Idealism is different from idea-ism in that the latter pertains to epistemology, whereas the former deals with entities, objects, and the philosophical investigation of what there *is* in the world. Idealism thus addresses only ontological and metaphysical concerns and must not be confused with idea-ism. It is important to hold onto this distinction because not all idea-ists are idealists, but all idealists are idea-ists. John Locke is an example of an idea-ist who was not an idealist; he held an atomist and materialist view of the external world, where objects had primary, intrinsic qualities. To put this more succinctly, idea-ists can accommodate, if not demand, *metaphysical realism*, but they are cautious about making any knowledge claims over and beyond what is given to us in experience. In this respect, Immanuel Kant, one of the greatest philosophers of the eighteenth century, was another idea-ist who strove to advance not a subjectivist but a realist view of the world.

Immanuel Kant (1724-1804): Bridging the rationalist-empiricist divide

Before Kant, the competing doctrines were rationalism and empiricism. The rationalists based knowledge on reason and logic, the empiricists on observation and experience. With the British empiricist Hume, we saw that there were either necessary Truths of Reason, such as mathematics, or Matters of Fact, grounded in observation and experiment. Kant thought that on their own rationalism and empiricism were insufficient epistemologies, and he brought the two together by introducing a previously non-existent category of *synthetic a priori* knowledge. Whereas in Hume's view, statements had to be either analytic and *a priori* or synthetic and *a posteriori*, Kant was convinced that some truths were both *synthetic* and *a priori*. Yet Kant did not just merge rationalism with empiricism. As Dicker (2004) explains, he combined elements of both, whilst profoundly transforming the previously held views – so much so that their implication and meaning were altered to accommodate his transcendental idealism. And therefore it is accurate to say that Kant's philosophy 'both *rejects* rationalism and empiricism yet *incorporates* elements of rationalist and empiricist thought' (Dicker, 2004: 4). Understood this way, Kant's philosophy is 'not entirely or exclusively either subjective or objective idealism; rather, it is a relatively coherent synthesis of both forms, which preserves and negates elements from each' (Beiser, 2002: 20). As these are complex ideas to grasp, Table 3.2 summarizes the different types of knowledge proposed by Kant.

Prior to Kant, the rationalists had argued for knowledge to be *analytic* and *a priori*. This notion is demonstrated in Table 3.2 in the quadrant marked no. 1. Analytic *a priori* statements are those statements that are true or necessary without the need for experience to verify them. For example, principles of mathematics and geometry were held by Descartes and Hume to be analytic *a priori* truths. We may also recall Chapter 2, where we learned that Plato and the rationalists believed that the universe was structured mathematically – endowing mathematics with a privileged *a priori* status. Kant disagreed. He argued instead that most mathematical and geometric knowledge is synthetic *a priori*, moving it from quadrant no. 1 to quadrant no. 2. The only mathematical/geometric truths that remained analytic *a priori* were the axioms of Euclidean geometry; postulates and propositions

Table 3.2 Kant's types of knowledge

Judgements	A priori (independent of experience)	A posteriori (dependent on experience, empirical)
ANALYTIC (true by definition; rational, intuitive, certain)	**1. Analytic a priori judgements** are certain and true by definition and independent of experience. ✓ NECESSARY TRUTHS ✓ UNIVERSAL TRUTHS ✓ DO NOT GENERATE NEW KNOWLEDGE **Examples:** All bodies are extended. Every effect has a cause. A is A.	**4. Analytic a posteriori judgements** **DO NOT EXIST**
SYNTHETIC (not true by definition; additional information or action required)	**2. Synthetic a priori judgements** are certain and necessary when combined with experience (e.g., we have to add the numbers seven and five to arrive at knowing that it is twelve). ✓ NECESSARY/UNIVERSAL + SYNTHETIC ✓ GENERATE NEW KNOWLEDGE **Examples:** 7 + 5 = 12. A straight line is the shortest distance between two points.	**3. Synthetic a posteriori judgements** are solely based on experience or observation and provide new knowledge. ✓ NOT NECESSARY ✓ NOT UNIVERSAL ✓ GENERATE NEW KNOWLEDGE **Examples:** All bodies are heavy. Aristotle was a student of Plato. Not all swans are white.

Source: Distilled and adapted from DeLong (1998: 39).

were, in Kant's view, *synthetic a priori* (DeLong, 1998). In other words, he proposed that it is an analytic *a priori* truth that a triangle must have three sides; however, the subsequent proposition that the angles of a triangle have to add up to 180° is not true by virtue, and therefore not *a priori*. Similarly, the statement 7 + 5 = 12 belongs to a class of *synthetic a priori* statements. We know that the numbers 7 and 5 must add up to another number, but this number is not something we have knowledge of *a priori*. We have to do the work of adding 7 plus 5 to find out the number in question. Therefore, the concept of '12' is not contained *a priori* within the equation. We can adopt a similar approach to other geometrical truths, such as 'A straight line is the shortest distance between two points'. In this case, the concepts of 'short' and 'straight' are not given *a priori* – they, too, have to be ascertained *a posteriori* (DeLong, 1998).

Moving on to the other regions in Table 3.2, quadrant no. 3 represents synthetic and *a posteriori* knowledge that stems from observation and experience. Given our previous discussion on the method of induction, we know that synthetic *a posteriori* statements are not necessarily true, only probable. They do, nevertheless, provide us with new knowledge (i.e., new natural species). The category of analytical *a posteriori* statements was rejected by Kant, and indeed by most philosophers. It does not exist because if we were to claim that a statement is analytic – i.e., true by definition – no experience is required to verify it. If a proposition is true by definition, it belongs to the category of analytic *a priori* statements. If it has to be justified in experimentation or observation, it belongs to synthetic *a posteriori*.

Kant regarded synthetic *a priori* judgements to be the 'best kind' because they combined the best of both – the certainty of *a priori* truths and empirical knowledge (Trudeau, 1987). As mentioned earlier, Kant perceived empirical and rational truths on their own as too limiting: knowledge that was solely empirical (quadrant no. 3) was neither reliable nor certain, and knowledge that was solely analytical and *a priori* (quadrant no. 1) generated no new insights. This means that Kant did not believe that rationalism and empiricism as separate epistemologies offered a satisfying solution to knowing the world (Trudeau, 1987). It was in the union of the synthetic and the *a priori* that human beings were to attain the best knowledge possible. Trudeau uses an analogy of diamonds to underscore the significance of Kant's achievement, and to illustrate Kant's view on synthetic *a priori* statements, in what he calls the 'diamond theory' of truth (see Figure 3.3). To obtain the visual notion of a diamond shape, we simply remove the redundant analytic *a posteriori* judgements from the picture and rotate the previous exhibit (Table 3.2).

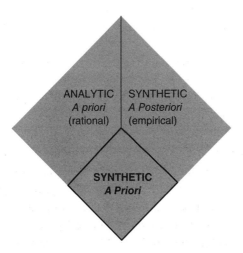

Figure 3.3 The Diamond Theory of Truth

This figure depicts Trudeau's notion of Kant as a 'diamond hunter':

'People have always longed for truths about the world – not logical truths, for all their utility; or even probable truths, without which daily life would be impossible; but informative, certain truths, the only "truths" strictly worthy of the name. Such truths I will call diamonds; they are highly desirable but hard to find' (Trudeau, 1987: 114).

Source: adapted from Trudeau (1987: 110).

Synthetic *a priori* truths were Kant's gems in the crown of knowledge. The truths that fall into this realm were necessary and universal, but even more than that, they contributed to new knowledge. From a broader epistemic stance, these truths were not only subjective (derived from people's experience of the world) nor only objective (analytical statements), instead subjectivity and objectivity were fused into a new category – Kant's synthetic *a priori*. It has been argued that Kant joins the idea-ists in epistemology, as knowledge comes from ideas and not directly from the objects themselves. Ontologically, however, situating Kant is more complex. On the one hand, he tends to be characterized as an idealist for holding that we cannot know the world mind-independently: in Kant's view, the only possible knowledge was knowledge of appearances that manifest as phenomena. On the other hand, he speaks of the *things-in-themselves* and a mind-independent *noumenal* realm. In order to examine his position on reality, we must open another chapter in this book and explore what precisely was at stake for the German idealists. This will form a large part of Chapter 4.

Summary and implications for qualitative research

This chapter attempted to cover a long historical period, from the time of ancient Greek scepticism to eighteenth-century empiricism and idea-ism. From the sceptics, we have learned that we ought not to trust our senses. What we see in our everyday life may not necessarily be how things are. Direct perception can be misleading and does not lead to certain knowledge about the world. The sceptics would thus refrain from making any judgements about truths, and some would go as far as to deny reality.

With the philosophy of John Locke we learned that it is possible to distinguish between primary and secondary properties of objects, and that the first are the objective features of things that do indeed exist in the world. George Berkeley challenged Locke on this distinction and deemed both primary and secondary qualities as subjective and arbitrary. With his philosophical quill he removed any notion of mind-independent reality, and with it also the existence of rocks, trees, and galaxies. All became ideas. Yet despite Berkeley's radical views, the man of modern science has come to realize that he was correct in his claim that primary properties (as defined by Locke) were not true representations of external objects. In this way, 'even mass is now regarded as a secondary property produced by the "rest mass" of things in a certain frame of reference' (Ladyman, 2002: 144). The primary properties we know to exist today thanks to theoretical physics cannot be experienced by the human senses.

This chapter has described the empiricist threesome of Locke, Berkeley, and Hume as idea-ists, for all shared the view that all that can be known with certainty is the content of our mind. Whereas Locke distinguished between primary and secondary qualities of objects and espoused metaphysical realism, Berkeley turned to idealism by reducing external objects to sense-ideas. Hume then reinstated scepticism and radically undermined the method of induction and the certainty of empirical and rational truths. Any knowledge, in Hume's view, could only be probable. We saw in Chapter 2 that empiricism did not vanish, with new waves emerging in the nineteenth and twentieth centuries. These were the positivists and logical positivists. Idea-ism as a theory of knowledge was extended to also accommodate the philosophy of Immanuel Kant. He introduced the notion of synthetic *a priori* statements – described here as the 'diamonds' in the truths about the world, whose uniqueness stems from being a specimen of both reason and empiricism.

Aside from outlining the key philosophers, this chapter introduced many concepts and further built on the notions of *a priori* and *a posteriori* knowledge and *analytical* and *synthetic* statements. Table 3.3 offers a list of statements as a way of recapitulating some of the philosophical terrain covered thus far. These are intended not to test accuracy, but to provoke us to think about the problems of philosophy and ponder the ways in which these have been, and can be, tackled. Some questions, the eager reader will notice, may be answered in more than one way, depending on whose philosophical viewpoint we follow. For instance, before Kant the mathematical equation 1+1=2 was held to be an *a priori* truth and the most likely choice would be 'A'. After Kant and the arrival of the synthetic *a priori*, the equation became a combination of both 'A' and 'B', leading us to a different answer. We can also think of examples of twentieth century mathematicians convinced that mathematical concepts and properties exist independent of the human mind, such as Hilbert Church and the theoreticians working under the pseudonym 'Nicolas Bourmaki'. And of course there have been scientists known to argue that mathematics is no different from any other creative activity – proposing that mathematics is a human creation (e.g., Percy W. Bridgman, Richard Dedekind, Karl Weierstrass, William R. Hamilton, and Arthur Cayley).[5] Among the philosophers who deemed mathematics to be a product of culture were Ludwig Wittgenstein, Imre Lakatos and Paul Ernest. Overall the correctness of the answers thus largely depends on the philosophical assumptions adopted, and as we have seen in this chapter, there have been several responses.

Table 3.3 also includes statements that may be of particular interest to qualitative researchers. Several of the statements deal with social reality (as opposed to nature), and are therefore not natural facts but social facts. These include statements such as 'This is a US dollar banknote', 'They are tourists', 'This is sustainable', and 'Paris is the capital of France'. We will discuss social facts in detail in Chapter 6, but it is also valuable to ponder these questions in the context of this chapter. With regard to the discourse on *a priori* and *a posteriori* knowledge, we can ask, for example, how do we know that someone is a French citizen, that Paris is the capital of France, that what I am holding in my hand is a US dollar banknote, and that something is sustainable? Does this knowledge come before or after experience?

Through this chapter, we know that *a priori* truths do not require experimentation or observation for justification. Conversely, we also know that the source of *a posteriori* knowledge is experience, including social and cultural experience.

Table 3.3 Statement assessment

STATEMENT	Is either: (A) A Priori / Analytical (B) A Posteriori / Synthetic	Can be justified: (A) Deductively (B) Inductively
She is a professor	A or B?	A or B?
All bachelors are single	A or B?	A or B?
All swans are white	A or B?	A or B?
1 + 1 = 2	A or B?	A or B?
God exists	A or B?	A or B?
The principle of causality	A or B?	A or B?
This is sustainable	A or B?	A or B?
They are tourists	A or B?	A or B?
Paris is the capital of France	A or B?	A or B?
This is a US dollar banknote	A or B?	A or B?
He is a French citizen	A or B?	A or B?

It would seem, then, that the questions above cannot be solved by applying logic or reason alone. There is nothing logical about someone being a professor or a tourist; neither is it logical for an action to be deemed sustainable. Therefore, social facts cannot be *a priori* – they must always be *a posteriori* statements. Furthermore, we know from Chapter 2 that analytical statements are self-evident. An example of a tautology is the sentence 'All bachelors are single'. This is an analytical statement because it is true in every possible situation and in any interpretation. There are no circumstances in which a bachelor is not single. Social facts are different. Social facts are not self-evident tautologies. Rather, we come to realize that not every person is a tourist, a professor, or a French citizen, and that not all green pieces of paper are US dollar banknotes. Whether or not someone is a tourist is contingent on that person's actions, behaviour, and something called *collective intentionality*.[6] Likewise, whether the object in my hand is money is contingent on it meeting certain criteria. We are not born with innate ideas of US dollars; we acquire this knowledge socially. Therefore, all social facts must be synthetic *a posteriori* statements. The implication for qualitative research is that because qualitative scholars study social facts, as opposed to minerals or molecules, they deal with synthetic *a posteriori* knowledge.

Recommended reading

Bermúdez, J.L. (2008) Cartesian skepticism: Arguments and antecedents. In J. Greco (ed.), *The Oxford Handbook of Skepticism* (pp. 53-79). New York: Oxford University Press.
Bolyard, C. (2013) Medieval Skepticism. In E.N. Zalta (ed.) *The Stanford Encyclopedia of Philosophy* (Spring, 2013 edn). Retrieved 28 February 2015 from http://plato.stanford.edu/archives/spr2013/entries/skepticism-medieval/

Greco, J. (2008) Skepticism about the external world. In J. Greco (ed.), *The Oxford Handbook of Skepticism* (pp.108-28). New York: Oxford University Press.
Ladyman, J. (2002) *Understanding Philosophy of Science*. London: Taylor & Francis.
Musgrave, A. (1993) *Common Sense, Science and Scepticism: A Historical Introduction to the Theory of Knowledge*. Cambridge: Cambridge University Press.
Solomon, R.C. & Higgins, K.M. (2010) *The Big Questions: A Short Introduction to Philosophy* (8th edn). Belmont, CA: Wadsworth, Cengage Learning.
Trudeau, R.J. (1987) *The Non-Euclidean Revolution*. Boston, MA: Birkhäuser.

Notes

1. For a recent edition of this work, see, for example, Michael Moriarty's (2008) translation.
2. Arnauld, Malebranche, and Berkeley 'regarded it as their mission to destroy the sceptical menace, "the spectre haunting European philosophy"' (Popkin, 2003: 261).
3. In the sense outlined in Chapter 1 – as a materialist believing in the objective existence of objects that have primary qualities.
4. Popper (see Chapter 2) would further point out that because truths based on induction cannot be falsified, they are not scientific.
5. For a detailed discussion see Kline (1982).
6. See Chapter 6 for an explanation of collective intentionality.

Four

German Idealism, Phenomenology, and Hermeneutics

This chapter builds on the last, pursuing our exploration of the developments on the front of idealism within the German tradition. Because the terms 'idealism' and 'idealist' have been attached to thinkers of various schools of thought and liberally applied in the literature, we commence with a short re-examination of the differences between idealism and idea-ism. In the preceding chapter, we already introduced Berkeley as the leading representative of the idealist doctrine. In order to complete the list of the key idealists, a few more names must be added. Idealism as a metaphysical thesis about what there *is* (in the world) starts with the teachings of Plato and his distinction of material vs immaterial objects. Over the centuries, his philosophy caught the attention of a handful of other scholars, of whom the most debated and well-known are the aforementioned George Berkeley, Gottfried Leibniz, Immanuel Kant, and the German post-Kantian idealists who came to dominate much of the nineteenth century. We will organize them according to the idealist–idea-ist distinction and show that German idealism was propelled by a critique of subjectivism. Post-Kantian idealism in particular was concerned with the proof of the reality of the external world. The latter part of the chapter will examine the continued interest in 'experience' within the traditions of phenomenology and hermeneutics. Here we will take advantage of what we have learned about realism and idea-ism and apply it to phenomenology and hermeneutics. It will be shown that hermeneutics and phenomenology do not (inherently) belong to a single alternative inquiry paradigm (as suggested in Figure 1.1, in Chapter 1), and that the choice of methods is tied to either a realist or idea-ist conception of knowledge and interpretation.

Idealism

Idealism is an intricate set of metaphysical views. There is no common idealist position or particular doctrinal commitment adhered to by all idealists. In the words of Tom Rockmore (2007: 23), 'at most, there are only idealists, who defend different theories that typically are, or at least reasonably might be, described as forms of idealism'. Noting, for example, the variations within German idealism, Beiser (2002) distinguishes between sceptical idealism, empirical or dogmatic idealism, transcendental idealism, subjective idealism, critical or formal idealism, absolute idealism, and higher idealism. Resonating with Rockmore's view, he states that 'such is the diversity and complexity of the period that there is not a single doctrine to which all thinkers adhere, and which could be described for the same reasons as "idealism"' (Beiser, 2002: 11). Moreover, the term 'idealism' has many connotations and has been a source of confusion in particular for analytically trained philosophers who fail to distinguish German idealism from other varieties, such as Berkeley's subjective and Kant's transcendental idealism (Losonsky, 2006). Thus, from the outset, it is clear that any attempt to reduce idealism to a cluster of generalizations would be ill-informed and misleading. A better strategy would be to strive to understand the differences, and to assist us in this task, Beiser's analysis will be invaluable throughout this chapter.

On idea-ism and idealism

One of the longest-standing philosophical conundrums has been the problem of how to reconcile appearances with reality. This predicament was introduced in Chapter 3 as the Two-World Assumption (see Figure 3.2). The sceptics challenged the naïve realist view of direct apprehension of objects and undermined all knowledge founded on experience and the human senses. The British empiricists responded with a new form of empiricism – idea-ism. In our efforts to maintain this important distinction between idea-ism (in epistemology) and idealism (in metaphysics), and to make it clear for the reader which philosophers were metaphysical realists and which were metaphysical idealists, we must first reiterate a few points about how the two approaches differ.

The preceding chapter explained that idea-ism is an epistemic term used to denote the views of those philosophers who held that human beings can only know ideas or sense data. Locke, Berkeley, Hume, and Kant were included among the thinkers described as idea-ists. It has also been suggested that out of the four, only Berkeley was a metaphysical idealist because only he rejected the existence of matter. Locke was an atomist and materialist, Hume turned sceptical, and Kant – as will become clear in this chapter – was a metaphysical realist about things. In addition to Berkeley, we ought to mention another seventeenth-century idealist, Gottfield Leibniz. Leibniz was a mathematician and a rationalist philosopher known, among other things, for discovering calculus independent of Isaac Newton. His idealist picture of the world differed from Plato and Berkeley's in that for him, all reality was comprised of spiritual entities, namely God and soul-like substances he called *monads*. The monads were immaterial, eternal, nonspatial entities responsible for all corporeal phenomena (Burnham, 2015). All else, including space and time, was – according to Leibniz – illusion. On the level of metaphysics, Berkeley and Leibniz's views are therefore fundamentally different from those of the other empiricists.

The one philosopher we have yet to locate on the materialist–immaterialist continuum is Plato. The ontological separation of objects of thought from the visible objects of the senses – a distinction that leads to 'the familiar dualism between appearance or phenomena and reality, between physical things and ideas' (Rockmore, 2011: 5) – began with Plato. According to the Platonic outlook, the everyday world as it 'appeared' to man was imperfect and flawed. But there was also a perfect realm of *forms* or *ideas*, and it is here that *truths* were to be found. Everything in the universe was categorized as either belonging to material and thus imperfect objects, or immaterial and thus perfect objects that he called *forms*. The kind of *forms* Plato had in mind were mathematical and geometric objects, which of course were not tangible or visible but abstract entities. Significantly, these were not just mere thoughts; Plato believed that these perfect forms *exist* in this ideal world of pure *forms* – a world that is 'eternal, immaterial, and more real than this one' (Solomon & Higgins, 2010: 121). In this respect, we can employ the term 'realism' to refer to the mind-independent universals or abstract objects (forms) that exist and are 'real' in this perfect realm. In order not to confuse this form of realism with other forms, such as Aristotle's empiricism, the term to be used is *Platonic realism*. In the wider context of our discussion on metaphysics and ontology in Chapter 1, there are different objects that can be argued to be onto-logically real, and to Plato these were not the imperfect objects of perception but *forms* or *ideas*. Figure 4.1 should make this point clear.

Two key observations ought to be made about Plato's philosophy concerning metaphysics. First, following Plato, we can have *objective knowledge* of reality, but what reality is, in Platonic terms, has very little to do with appearances and mate-rial objects observable in nature. In other words, what is *real* and *true* are only *forms*, with geometry and mathematics leading the way. Since these forms enjoy a mind-independent existence, we can speak of *Platonic realism*, and indeed a type of Platonic objectivism. Second, Plato did not suggest that nature did not exist – his argument was that 'we cannot find instances of pure properties among physical things' (Crombie, 2013: 50). Any absolute truths were to be found in the perfect

IMMATERIAL	Forms (e.g., circularity)
	Math objects (e.g., a circle)
MATERIAL	Physical objects (e.g., a wheel)
	Images (e.g., a picture of a wheel)

Figure 4.1 Plato's distinction between material and immaterial objects
Image adapted from Anglin (1994: 58).

realm of forms by reason, but that was not to say that material things – although held as imperfect – did not exist. And so we can say that Plato was not an idealist in the sense that Berkeley and Leibniz were.

Kant's transcendental idealism

Kant was not a subjectivist; he fought against the dogmatic variety of idealist philosophers. According to Kant, the proponents of empirical[1] or material idealism (i.e., idealism about matter) were either dogmatic idealists, such as Leibniz, who claimed that the existence of objects in space external to us is 'false and impossible', or they were sceptical idealists, such as Descartes, who held that the existence of objects in space external to us is 'doubtful and indemonstrable' (Beiser, 2002: 53). While the first group of philosophers denied the existence of external objects, the second were sceptical about appearances, though not going so far as to reject reality altogether. Kant's main target was the dogmatic sceptics, but he also rejected the notion of apprehending things as they are directly.

In contrast to direct realism – the idea that the way objects appear to us is how they really are in themselves – Kant's formulation of transcendental idealism states that appearances must be distinguished from things-in-themselves because 'objects do not have the properties they are perceived to have' (Beiser, 2002: 52). We may recall Figure 3.2 in Chapter 3, where we distinguished between the external realm of objects and events and the internal realm of ideas and experience. Kant's position is that of an idea-ist. The transcendental idealist, contrary to the direct realist, denies the possibility of knowing objects directly as they are in themselves through appearances. In other words, the object before us 'appears' to be a cat, but we cannot know what the object *really* is based on this appearance. We have epistemic access only to the object's appearance, not the object as it truly is. Importantly, the subject, seen as a problem or an obstacle that carries unwanted biases and sensory distortions (as argued by the sceptics), plays a fundamental role in the process; the subject is what makes knowledge possible (Braver, 2007). Transcendental idealism can therefore be understood in the following terms:

> The fundamental distinction between transcendental idealism and empirical idealism, Kant argues, is that the transcendental idealist affirms, while the empirical idealist doubts or denies, the existence of objects outside us *in the empirical sense*. In other words, material idealism holds that the empirical world either could be or is an illusion; but transcendental idealism affirms that it is real. Or, in more Kantian terms, the transcendental idealist maintains that these objects are appearances (*Erscheinungen*); but the empirical idealist holds that they are, or at least could be, an illusion (*Schein*). (Beiser, 2002: 53)

To reiterate the main point, whereas dogmatic or empirical idealism is an *immaterialist* doctrine, transcendental idealism, despite the confusing terminology, is not a subjectivist philosophy and is to be categorized as (weak) metaphysical realism. Ontologically, Kant's idealism is not equivalent to that of Berkeley or Leibniz. With Kant the external world exists, but our knowledge of it is limited to the appearances available to our senses, which we grasp cognitively as phenomena. Kant and the later German idealists battled with their dogmatic predecessors. Leibniz, for whom representations had no external causes, was the key villain in Kant's writings, Beiser tells us. In this respect Kant and some of his followers saw the main task of transcendental idealism as to 'explain the external world' (Beiser, 2002: 219). It would be a mistake to group all idealists into a single family of sub-jectivists or solipsists, or to place them into a paradigm box. To better understand Kant's position, it is necessary to open his casket of terminological gems.

Kant distinguished between *appearances*, or how objects appear to us, and *phe-nomena*, our cognitive grasp of these appearances. Holzhey and Mudroch explain that 'appearance was whatever preceded the use of the understanding, while expe-rience was held to be the cognition that arises when the understanding compares different appearances' (2005: 49). They further clarify that Kant did not associate phenomena with appearances but rather with experience (i.e., phenomena are internal objects of experience). Accordingly, the study of phenomena is not the study of external objects or things-in-themselves; it is the study of what appears in consciousness. Similarly to the idea-ists, with Kant we can only know the con-tent of our mind. Thus, the term 'phenomenon' (pl. phenomena) refers to what is perceivable by the human senses and is grasped cognitively. A fundamental pillar of Kant's philosophy is embedded in the view that the study of phenomena can-not tell us truths about the external objects in the world, only about our cognitive experience. This distinction became pivotal in the phenomenological tradition, and it is this distinction that was erased by the logical positivists and realists.

Aside from appearances and phenomena, Kant introduced the notion of the *thing-in-itself*. [2] The thing-in-itself and its appearance are somewhat related, but there is an important difference to bear in mind here. Schrader and Schrader wrote some time ago that 'the thing in itself is given in its appearances; it *is* the object which appears' (1949: 30). Beiser further elucidates that Kant insisted that appearances were indeed 'appearances *of* something, namely, things-in-themselves' (2002: 49). We perceive not only ideas (as Berkeley would argue) but also things that exist inde-pendent of us – 'it is just that we do not perceive them as they are in themselves but only as they appear to us' (2002: 49). To put it crudely, we can understand the notion of the *thing-in-itself* as that which produces or causes the appearance. Our senses always perceive only appearance, not the thing-in-itself whose appearance we perceive. In Kant's view, the thing-in-itself is not accessible to us. All that we have epistemic access to are appearances, internally grasped as phenomena. Dilworth puts it more bluntly in noting that 'phenomena exist in the mind, while things in them-selves are outside the mind' (2013: 54). An example may be useful here. If we were to apply Kant's concepts to, say, a person gazing at a tree, we could say that what the person is perceiving by her senses is an appearance that resembles a tree. What she sees is how the thing-in-itself manifests in the appearance of a tree. The important, epistemic part is that she does not perceive the tree directly as it is; instead, she is cognitively organizing the sense data of its appearance, which Kant called phenomena.

Kant's terminology

Thing-in-itself - that which causes the appearance.

Appearance - that which appears to the senses.

Phenomenon - cognitive grasp of appearances.

Noumena - epistemological 'beings of intellect'.

Kant did not fully agree with the formulation of innate ideas introduced earlier by Plato and Descartes, substituting these instead with (still *a priori*) 12 *categories of understanding*: unity, plurality, totality, reality, negation, limitation, inherence/ subsistence, causality/dependence, community, possibility, existence, necessity, and *forms of intuition*: space (i.e., external intuition limited to external phenomena alone) and time (i.e., the form of the internal sense) (Kant, 2012 [1781]). What is striking in Kant's philosophy is that space and time are not to be understood as something real, objective, and empirical but as *a priori* intuitions in the mind. This means that the things-in-themselves are not inherently spatio-temporal objects, rather space and time are the mind's way of organizing and cognizing external reality. In a way, human beings are born with a mind 'pre-programmed', so to speak, with time and space recognition – thus *a priori*. Moreover, we do not make sense of appearances on their own: we need *categories of understanding* and *forms of intuition* in order to organize appearances into something meaningful, and this 'something' is *phenomena*. The mind, therefore, is actively engaged in processing sensations to give us phenomena. This is a radical departure from Locke's (passive) notion of the mind as simply 'recording' information – his notion of the *tabula rasa*. The *ideal* in transcendental idealism is the 'subjective' or the 'mental'.

The last term we must acknowledge are Kant's *noumena*. Kant used the concept of noumenon (pl. noumena) to explain an aspect of reality that exists mind-independent of the observer, and also as part of the phenomena human beings experience. Noumena are 'thought entities' or 'objects of pure understanding' that are conceivable by the mind but beyond the reach of experience. Whereas phenomena are the objects of empirical knowledge, noumena are 'such that they cannot be empirically or otherwise known' (Dilworth, 2013: 54). In this light they have been described as 'beings of intellect' that can be conceived but not perceived, such as God, cosmos, and soul (Priest, 1995: 82). If we were to contrast noumena with things-in-themselves, noumena can be further delineated as rational and epistemological entities, and things-in-themselves as mind-independent ontological entities (Dilworth, 2013).

Scholars tend to disagree on what precisely should be included in the noumenal realm. Some philosophical commentators understand Kant's *noumena* to be synonymous with the *thing-in-itself* and extend these to theoretical entities such as atoms, electrons, genes, molecules, and radio waves (e.g., Hung, 2014). Others see noumena as strictly epistemic entities.[3] According to the latter view, atoms must be grasped cognitively as phenomena. Priest states on this matter that 'theoretical entities, such as photons and electromagnetic radiation, to the extent that Kant could make sense of such notions at all (which does not seem very great) are phenomena' (1995: 83). We shall not attempt to resolve this problem here, as both terms – noumena and things-in-themselves – have been used interchangeably, even by Kant himself (Rockmore, 2011). Nevertheless, it pays to take advantage of the available distinctions and ponder the consequences. Figure 4.2 is an attempt to represent Kant's concepts visually.

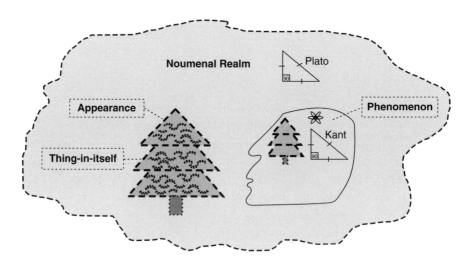

Figure 4.2 Noumena, phenomena, appearances, and things-in-themselves

It is worthwhile recalling that, in Kant's opinion, mathematical truths were not *a priori*. To arrive at mathematical knowledge, Kant argued that a certain type of cognition was necessary (Holzhey & Mudroch, 2005). In the philosophy of Plato and the early rationalists, mathematics belonged to the noumenal realm or the perfect world of *forms*. In Kant's philosophy, however, mathematical numbers are phenomenal, synthetic *a priori*. This distinction is noted in Figure 4.2. As remarked by Kline (1982), the mathematics of Kant is the product of man's mind: mathematical truths are no longer inherent in the universe, nor is the universe mathematically structured, as had been held by the Pythagoreans, Plato, and Descartes.

Overall, Kant is not an easy philosopher to understand, and his work has been interpreted in many, at times conflicting, ways. Beiser (2002) offers a convincing argument showing that Kant strove to combat subjectivism and in fact embraced realism and naturalism. Others, such as Braver, see Kant as a philosophical figure who radically undermined realism by offering a 'coherent, powerful alternative account of reality, subjectivity, and knowledge' (2002: 33) – a philosopher for whom realism was 'an obscure dogma' (2002: 34). We shall not attempt to determine the extent to which Kant was a realist or a subjectivist here, for that largely depends on one's angle of vision. However, if we return to the philosophical skeleton in Chapter 1, we can certainly appreciate that Kant was a (weak) metaphysical realist, that is, a realist of the weak variety. After all, Kant did admit 'the reality of something besides mere representation' (Beiser, 2002: 52). In Chapter 5, we shall further see that realism comes in many shapes and forms.

The departure from subjectivism in German idealism: Absolute/objective idealism

Beiser's (2002) analysis shows that German idealism came out of a critique of subjectivism, urging us not to think of the developments as the *culmination* of the Cartesian tradition, but more accurately as its *nemesis*. Kant in particular took issue with Cartesian scepticism about the empirical reality of human experience, which drove him to 'prove the empirical reality of the external world', as Beiser tells us (2002: 24). Seen from this vantage point, German idealism is best understood as 'the story about the growing reaction against subjectivism' and the increasing efforts 'to break out of that circle' (2002: 2).

Philosophers after Immanuel Kant have been concerned mainly with two issues: how is it possible to *know* the external world and account for the *reality* of it. All German idealists, including Kant, therefore developed the principle of *subject–object identity*, which denotes the relationship between the observer and the observed. However, objects also had to enjoy independence from the human mind, i.e., a separate existence. This distinction between that which is mental (ideas in the mind) and that which is physical (all that is external to mind) is called *dualism*. Broadly speaking, German idealism is an attempt to reconcile these two key issues, and can be formulated in the following question: *How is it possible to explain the possibility of knowledge according to the idealist principles and yet to account for the reality of the external world?* (Beiser, 2002: 14). To paraphrase, the German idealists were striving to solve the problem of the Two-World Assumption (depicted in Figure 3.2, Chapter 3).

Post-Kantian idealism was concerned with proving the reality of the external world. Whether in the form of the universal structure of space, the thing-in-itself, the single universal substance, or the eternal archetypes, for the German idealists external reality 'had to exist independent of the consciousness of the empirical and individual subject; and it had to be as certain as self-knowledge itself' (Beiser, 2002: 3). To emphasize this important point, German idealism did not seek to advance the doctrine of subjectivism (i.e., that the subject is only in possession of her own ideas), rather it was devoted to realism and naturalism. In this regard,

- In absolute or objective idealism, the *'ideal'* is the *archetypical*, *intelligible*, and *structural* (as opposed to the subjective, mental, or spiritual). It is something *impersonal*, *neutral*, or *indifferent*. Reality no longer depends on the self-conscious subject.
- The *subjective* is absorbed into the absolute in absolute idealism.
- The forms of experience are 'self-subsistent and transcend both the subject and object [...] while subjective idealism *attaches* the forms of experience to the transcendental subject, which is their source and precondition, objective idealism *detaches* them from that subject, making them hold for the realm of pure being as such' (2002: 11).
- Absolute idealism sees both the 'subjective' and 'objective' 'as equal instances of the archetypical' (2002: 12). The *subject* is only an embodiment or appearance of the absolute, and is held 'as the very culmination of nature and history' (2002: 13).
- The absolute cannot be said to exist independent of the knowing subject as there is no dualism between the 'subject's knowing the absolute and the absolute itself'. Hegel, for example, talks of self-actualization of God and the 'Absolute Spirit'.
- The absolute cannot be contrasted with anything else.

Figure 4.3 Absolute or objective idealism

Source: Content distilled and adapted from Beiser (2002).

Beiser's project sets out to debunk the myth of idealism as a radical form of subjectivism, and he shows that many post-Kantian idealists disputed the concept of the *absolute* as something subjective or mental. He further explains:

> The post-Kantian idealists understood the absolute in transcendental terms as the fundamental condition of the possibility of experience; as such, they refused to define it as either subjective or objective; rather, they argued that both subjectivity and objectivity fall within experience, so that these concepts cannot be applied to the absolute except on pain of circularity. (Beiser, 2002: 5)

This way the notion of the *absolute* is beyond the possibility of it being described as either subjective or objective 'since such terms limit what is meant to be unlimited' (2002: 6). To fully appreciate the subtle yet significant differences among the proponents of German idealism, one has to read Beiser's (2002) impressive 700-page volume, irreducible to a few paragraphs. There were three main groups in Germany associated with absolute idealism, with over a dozen of thinkers spread between them: one was located in Jena (with Hülsen, von Berger, Smidt, Rist, Bohlendorff, and Herbart), one in Frankfurt and Homburg (with Hölderlin, Hegel, von Sinclair, and Zwilling), and a third in Jena and Berlin, comprising the key romantic philosophers (with Schlegel, Schelling, and Novalis). Absolute idealism was different from Kant and Fichte's transcendental or *critical idealism*, Hume and Descartes's *sceptical idealism*, and Berkeley and Leibniz's *dogmatic idealism*. There is no definition or generally accepted meaning of *absolute idealism*. The best way to grasp it is to understand what was meant by the term 'absolute'. Beiser explains that the 'absolute' can be understood as the 'unconditioned', the 'infinite', or the 'in-itself' (2002: 351). Furthermore, the most distinctive feature of absolute idealism was *monism* – the thesis that there is only one universe, or a single substance, or one being. This eliminates any dualism between mind and matter and between idea and reality. All is part of the single reality; all is a manifestation of the archetypical or rational form – the absolute (Beiser, 2002). A brief summary of absolute/objective idealism is offered in Figure 4.3.

From idealism to phenomenology:
On Kant and Husserl

The primacy of *experience*, and the sustained interest in it, gave rise to a 'new' philosophical orientation known as *phenomenology*. We place the word 'new' in quotation marks to emphasize the difference in opinion on whether phenomenology is to be seen as an entirely novel philosophical orientation or a continuation of Kantian thought. Within this contested space, we can discern between (1) the view of those commentators who take phenomenology to be a movement that originated in the twentieth century, and is accredited largely to the work of Edmund Husserl – typically depicted as the father of phenomenology – and (2) the belief that the foundations of phenomenology were laid down by Kant. We have seen in the previous sections that Kant differentiated appearances and things-in-themselves from the cognitive processes of the mind. Thus, appearances are organized in the mind as *phenomena*. Rockmore (2011) argues that Kant was among the first philosophers to embrace a phenomenological approach to epistemology and to work out a claim 'for knowledge based on the "construction" of phenomena as distinguished from appearances' (Rockmore, 2007: 1). Particularly in his later writings, Kant adopted a constructivist outlook whereby the subject is actively involved in constructing knowledge. Rockmore identifies several phenomenological figures, including Husserl, Hegel, Heidegger, and Merleau-Ponty, as reacting to Kant's philosophy in developing their own phenomenological theories. The experiencing, cognitive subject became central to their phenomenology.

One of the areas where idealism and phenomenology overlapped was the rejection of direct realism. Both idealism and phenomenology opposed the notion of direct apprehension of the external world, arguing instead that knowledge had to be grounded in experience and located in the mind. Sparrow reasons that phenomenology can be understood as an 'elaborate recapitulation of transcendental idealism', as opposed to a distinct philosophical position, and adds that many of Husserl's 'descendants have struggled to distance themselves from his idealism' (2014: 185). Moran and Mooney (2002) further comment that Heidegger, too, thought that Husserl's phenomenology was just another form of idealist philosophy. Reading Cerbone, we learn that Husserl's view of phenomenology was that it 'ultimately establishes the truth of transcendental idealism' (2006: 36). We will not attempt to settle the dispute here, and will comment only to the extent of showing that Husserl can be understood as both a realist and an idealist.

There are notable differences between the phenomenology of Kant and Husserl. The most fundamental issue on which Husserl disagreed with Kant was the treatment of things-in-themselves as 'something beyond the bounds of sense' (Cerbone, 2006: 36). On this point, Husserl did not follow Kant's idealist–constructivist footsteps, as is apparent in his determination to return 'back to the "things themselves"'(Husserl, 2001 [1900/1901]: 168). The departure from Kantian idealism in Husserl's philosophy is thus marked by the return to a real world. Whereas Kant's phenomena were the mind's way of making sense of appearances (not necessarily representing things-in-themselves), Husserl's phenomena *are* the things as they appear. Phenomena cease to be merely mental states and become 'worldly things', endowing phenomenology with the task to 'provide a clear, undistorted description of the ways things appear' (Smith, 2015: para. 11). Phenomenology, then, becomes the science that studies appearances, concerned with the structure of appearing or the *how* of appearing (Moran, 2002). Husserl himself envisioned phenomenology as a discipline whose 'objects' are conscious phenomena (Cerbone, 2006).

The critics of phenomenology are quick to argue that despite the Husserlian promise to return 'back to the things themselves', phenomenology fails to reveal truths about the material world. Sparrow, for instance, comments that phenomenology does not 'get us to the noumenal, it instead keeps us chained to the phenomenal, where we have been all along' (2014: 1). Also in Sparrow's opinion, Husserl continued the tradition of transcendental idealism. Sparrow finds support in Zahavi's (2003) assertion that, according to Husserlian phenomenology, the world exists, but not completely independent of the mind:

> The world is not something that simply exists. The world appears, and the structure of this appearance is conditioned and made possible by subjectivity. It is in this context that Husserl would say that it is absurd to speak of the existence of an absolutely mind-independent world, that is, of a world that exists apart from any possible experiential and conceptual perspective. For Husserl, this notion is simply contradictory. (Zahavi, 2003: 52)

Zahavi makes it clear that although Husserl strove for pure essential knowledge, such knowledge had to include subjectivity, for there can be no knowledge without the interpreting mind. He states, 'Husserl claims that we need to return to the things themselves, that is, to base our theories on that which shows itself and actually appears, rather than make do with empty and idle talk' (2003: 52). But 'if we wish to truly understand what physical objects are, we will eventually have to turn to the subjectivity that experiences these objects, for it is only there that they show themselves as what they are' (2003: 52). Reality can only be understood through conscious acts and 'subjectivity is a condition of possibility of appearance or manifestation' (Zahavi, 2003: 52).

Accordingly, Sparrow declares that – as with the doctrine of idealism – the phenomenological focus is on what is experienced by the experiencing subject.

Our knowledge, even if claimed by Husserl to be certain and pure, does not leave the realm of the mind. For this reason, Sparrow purports that phenomenology is not a realist alternative to the Kantian programme because 'it leaves its practitioners gesturing toward the outside without ever actually stepping out of the house' (Sparrow, 2014: 1). Realism through phenomenology, as he sees it, is impossible, and phenomenology can only align itself with anti-realism.

In order to digest these claims, a quick debrief seems necessary to re-orient ourselves within the ideas seen so far in our exploration of epistemological and methodological issues. Firstly, it is important to distinguish between *scientific realism* and other varieties of realism (as that is the premise of Chapter 5, all we shall say for now is that Husserl was not a scientific realist). Secondly, Husserl's phenomenology was certainly not empiricism or direct realism – he was not motivated by the study of external objects to reveal the truths about nature. Indeed, he discarded such knowledge as naïve. Husserl strove to examine our *seeing* of the world, the way objects appear in consciousness, which would group him together with the other idea-ists. However, Husserl was also a metaphysical realist, for whom objects in the world were indeed real. Phenomenology does not claim that all that exists are appearances, i.e., it does not advocate *immaterialism* or Berkeley's idealism: the phenomena are the things themselves (Moran, 2002). Hence, phenomenology is a form of indirect or metaphysical realism that seeks to transcend the everyday 'taken-for-granted' existence of the world around us, which Husserl called the 'naturalistic attitude' (Smith, 2013a: 231). And thirdly, it is valuable to note that Husserl felt strongly about objectivity and truth, as evidenced in his *Logical Investigations* (Husserl, 2001 [1900/1901]), and also about the intersubjectivity of people's collective experience of things – 'a form of objectivity gained through subjectivity' – as described by Smith (2013a: 74). The following explanation by Smith further helps to clarify Husserl's philosophical stance:

> When I see that raven on the fence, I experience it as there for others also to see if they so look. In Husserl's terms, the object of my perception is 'constituted' as 'there for everyone.' [...] Husserl emphasizes the close tie between objectivity and intersubjectivity in this phenomenological feature of experience, beginning with everyday perception. An object in my surroundings - the raven on the fence, the sailboat on the ocean - is objective in that it exists and is what it is regardless of whether I or anyone else is perceiving it, or thinking about it, or interacting with it. (Here we assume that Husserl is not an idealist, a point of disagreement among Husserl interpreters.) An object is intersubjective, however, insofar as it is available to intentional acts of consciousness by different subjects, by me and you and others. (2013a: 218)

As to the problem of appearances, Husserl was aware of the limits of perception and the fact that one may come across unlimited appearances of external things. As argued and shown by his predecessors, an object, such as a piece of rock, can be perceived from different angles, suggesting that we never have a 'complete' perceptual experience. Cerbone (2006) further clarifies that an object may appear smaller or larger in our vision (e.g., by moving it closer or further away); it may reveal a multitude of angles (e.g., by rotating it in our hand); it may even appear, say, reddish-looking under red light; and it may disappear completely from our vision when there is no light. Husserl argued that in our experience of the things in the world, we can find their *essential* features. In other words, we can get beyond appearances and discover the essences of the objects in question. To achieve this task, we have to employ the method of *phenomenological reduction,* also known as *phenomenological epoché* (Cerbone, 2006). This demands that the phenomenologist must suspend any previous beliefs and *bracket* all the preconceived ideas held about the object. Phenomenological reduction also extends to suspending any 'specific theses about the existence of the world, including theses from the natural sciences, theology, even logic' (Smith, 2013a: 232). In Husserl's view, only in this way could one move past the naïve assumptions commonly held about the world and uncover the real *essences* of phenomena.

Phenomenology, therefore, as envisaged by Husserl, studies the structures of conscious *experience* as they manifest in our mind. It is necessary to emphasize that the task of phenomenology is not to provide descriptive accounts of objects as they truly are in nature, but to study how objects appear in consciousness. This means that phenomenology is only interested in experience from the first-person point of view (Smith, 2013b). There are many varieties of experiences that can be considered for phenomenological research. Apart from perceptual experiences (e.g., seeing), Smith notes other types, such as *thought, imagination, action, emotion, intention, desire,* and *volition*. All experiences can be further categorized as either active (dancing, running, swimming) or relatively passive (seeing, hearing). To help us better understand the differences, Smith (2013b: section 2, para. 10) gives the following examples:

- *I see* that fishing boat off the coast as dusk descends over the Pacific.
- *I hear* that helicopter whirring overhead as it approaches the hospital.
- *I am thinking* that phenomenology differs from psychology.
- *I wish* that warm rain from Mexico were falling like last week.
- *I imagine* a fearsome creature like that in my nightmare.
- *I intend* to finish my writing by noon.
- *I walk* carefully around the broken glass on the sidewalk.
- *I stroke* a backhand cross-court with that certain underspin.
- *I am searching* for the words to make my point in conversation.

Each of the statements above can be understood as a 'simple form of phenomenological description', and can be contrasted with 'rich phenomenological description' (Smith, 2013b). The former describes the content of experience or what an experience is about, and Husserl called statements falling within that category *noema* (pl. noemata); the latter points to a person's reflections on forms of consciousness. Smith points out that the task of phenomenology, contrary to some philosophers' belief, is not limited to 'what it is like to have sensory experiences, thereby describing the qualitative characters or sensory "qualia" of seeing red and the like' (2013a: 229). Husserl's programme was more ambitious: he strove for *rich* phenomenological descriptions. Using the example of a tree, Figure 4.4 shows that the goal of phenomenology is not to describe the object of perception, as was advocated by the direct or naïve realist in Chapter 3, but instead to arrive at a description of how the object is experienced in consciousness. Hence, we are not speaking about merely describing sense data that are perceived (size, shape, colour), nor of our previous knowledge of, and assumptions acquired about, the object ('that tree' in Figure 4.4). All of this knowledge must be 'bracketed' and suspended (*epoché*) so that a rich phenomenological description – as it arises in experience – can be given. In the words of Smith, 'that is the point of bracketing: put in parentheses the presumed existence of the object, the tree that is presumably before me and affecting my eyes; attend instead to the meaning or sense through which that tree is represented in my experience' (Smith, 2013a: 235).

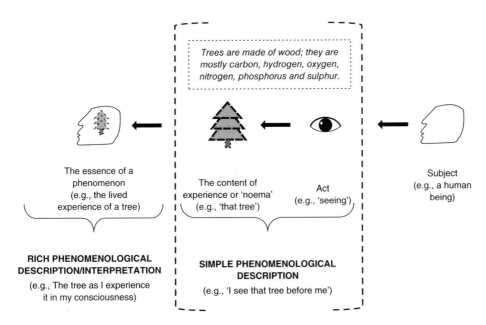

Figure 4.4 Phenomenology illustrated

We may consider a different example, say, a painting passed down in a family from parent to child over several generations. Here, too, a phenomenological inquiry would not be concerned with descriptions of the painting's size, the type and quality of canvas, the technical names for the colours used, or one's ability to accurately identify the objects painted. Rather, it would be motivated by how the painting is experienced by a subject in consciousness. To put it in different terms, there is a shift in focus from 'I see that painting on the wall … ' to 'My pure experience of this painting is … '. What can be noted with this example is the possibility of rich description to reveal a more profound, deeper experience that may not have so much to do with the object itself as with what it symbolizes for the beholder in the context of the family tradition. This last point allows us to discern between two approaches to phenomenology: whereas Husserl (as well as Merleau-Ponty) was interested in *describing* phenomena as they appear in consciousness – *descriptive phenomenology* – the hermeneutically inclined philosophers, such as Heidegger and Gadamer, related lived experience to wider contexts (social, political, historical, cultural), in what became known as *hermeneutic phenomenology*. Continuing with the example of the painting, we can pose an important question that will help us understand the difference between Husserl's phenomenology and the hermeneutic approaches: should the object in question be considered 'art', and how, in fact, do we arrive at the essence of art? The hermeneutic solution to this riddle will become clear in the following section. For the time being, we may get a foretaste from Heidegger:

> What art is, Heidegger says, can be derived from the art work. On the other hand, what the work is can be learned only from the essence of art. (Kockelmans, 1985: 100)

From phenomenology to hermeneutics

To segue from phenomenology to hermeneutics, we need only note the names of Martin Heidegger (1889–1976) and Hans-Georg Gadamer (1900–2002). Fundamentally, phenomenology and hermeneutic phenomenology endeavour to achieve different outcomes; they are philosophically and methodologically diverse theses. Husserl's phenomenology gives us essences of consciousness that are bracketed from the everyday world, with a promise of returning to the things themselves; Heidegger and Gadamer take us on a hermeneutic journey of understanding through social, cultural, and historical 'neighbourhoods'. If in Husserlian phenomenology the task is to suspend all existing beliefs, judgements, and previous knowledge as a secure path to essential understandings given in consciousness, Heidegger and Gadamer argue the opposite, proclaiming that all understanding is social, cultural, and historical, and that it cannot be conveniently bracketed away. Heidegger rejects Husserl's presuppositionless knowledge and develops hermeneutic phenomenology that is rooted in a 'historically mediated circle-of-understanding that is constitutive of existence' (Dahlstrom, 2014: 54). Gadamer further reinforces that all understanding is 'embedded in a context of tradition and that it is impossible ever to fully transcend this situation of embeddedness' (Schleibler, 2000: 2). There have also been other intellectuals who contributed to the expansion of phenomenology beyond its original vision. Hannah Arendt, for example, emphasized 'human plurality' over 'human similarity' (associated with the natural, social, and normative dimensions), and held that meaning is 'intersubjective and context-dependent instead of objective and generalizable' (Vasterling, 2014: 84). Here we shall mostly focus on Heidegger, but maintain the awareness that other phenomenological approaches exist with a multitude of angles and foci.

Heidegger's hermeneutic phenomenology is anti- or non-Husserlian because of its departure from performing a *descriptive* function and its aim to replace Husserl's vision of phenomenology as 'the science of the essence of consciousness' (Smith, 2013a) with a renewed ontological emphasis. Heidegger's phenomenology took a hermeneutic and ontological turn by shifting the focus to human life and *being* – the possibility of *being* and *self-understanding* (e.g., Heidegger, 1962, 1988) – and with it, to a much larger question of how phenomenological consciousness is possible. This question, as Figal and Espinet elucidate, is about 'the very possibility of phenomenology itself [...] Phenomenological consciousness, understood in this way, is an integral possibility of life itself; it is the very possibility of human life for understanding' (2014: 497). So construed, phenomenological inquiry becomes an inquiry into the meaning of being and 'the fundamental structures of human existence, which Heidegger calls "*Dasein*" (existence)' (Moran & Mooney, 2002: 247).

The main philosophical difference between the phenomenology of Husserl and the subsequent hermeneutic varieties is most clearly demonstrated in a process (of understanding) that has come to be known as the *hermeneutic circle*. The hermeneutic circle 'describes how, in the process of understanding and interpretation, part and whole are related in a circular way: in order to understand the whole, it is necessary to understand the parts, while to understand the parts it is necessary to have some comprehension of the whole' (Hoy, 1982: vii). In contrast to Husserl's presuppositionless philosophy, where the mind is bracketed from all previous knowledge, hermeneutic phenomenology sees social, cultural, and historical situatedness as necessary for the development of understanding/s. In other words, the hermeneutic circle becomes the 'very forestructure of existence', and the role of an inquiry is not to find a way out of the circle but to come 'into it the right way' (Dahlstrom, 2014: 54). In the eyes of Heidegger, understanding was to develop 'through a circling back and forth between presumption and surprise', and this is what in the literature is commonly called the 'hermeneutic circle' (Moran, 2002: 18). Figure 4.5 shows the movement between a part and the whole by drawing on our previous example of a painting. To be able to say that an object is a work of art, as opposed to non-art, we must have an understanding of what art is. Put differently, 'we come to know what the art work is from the essence of art' (Kockelmans, 1985: 100). Notice also that whereas Husserl would bracket all previous knowledge and turn to consciousness to find out the *essence* of art, in the hermeneutic circle the *essence* is derived from the individual parts, such as other available artworks. There is no absolute or objective truth about what is or is not art, rather such knowledge is constituted socially and culturally.

With respect to the origins of the hermeneutic circle, Ramberg and Gjesdal (2014) note that it can be traced to the works of Spinoza, Ast, and Schleiermacher, where it represented the relation between text and tradition, or the text as a whole

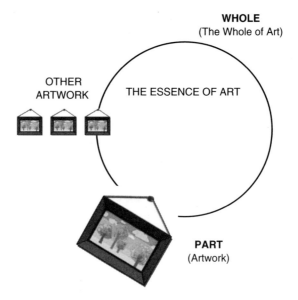

Figure 4.5 The Hermeneutic Circle

This figure shows the movement between the part and the whole in a circle. We can only know what Artwork is from the essence of art or the Whole of Art; what art is, is inferred from the Artwork and also other artworks (see Kockelmans, 1985: 100).

and its individual parts. There are two key points to be made with regard to its use in phenomenology: (1) the *hermeneutic circle* is not a phenomenological invention, and (2) the way Heidegger used it in his work differed completely from its previous uses. Heidegger approached it not merely as a philological tool but also as performing an existential role: he saw it as 'the interplay between our self-understanding and our understanding the world' (Ramberg & Gjesdal, 2014: para. 33). In this respect, Heidegger's use of hermeneutics is not methodological or purely linguistically oriented (i.e., understanding speech or texts), instead it denotes a mode of being that is characteristic of *Dasein* (Ramberg & Gjesdal, 2014). Hermeneutic phenomenology, including the hermeneutic circle, was further advanced by Gadamer (1976, 2004 [1960]), who underscored the role that tradition, history, and language play in processes of understanding.

We will bring this inquiry to a close here and not delve in any more depth into the methodological aspects of hermeneutic phenomenology. There are many books that explicitly cover the problematics of the hermeneutic circle; in qualitative research the ones that stand out are Schwandt (2015) and Alvesson and Sköldberg (2000). In terms of orienting Heidegger within the philosophical skeleton we outlined in Chapter 1, he is a realist concerning rocks and trees and natural entities. In the words of Dreyfus, he 'holds a subtle and plausible position beyond metaphysical realism and anti-realism. Nature is whatever it is and has whatever causal properties it has independently of us' (1991: 39). We can also add that Heidegger supports a pluralist thesis about truth, i.e., not *a* correct interpretation but *many* correct descriptions of reality. On this, Dreyfus states that 'for Heidegger, as finite beings capable of discovering truth, we work out many perspectives – many lexicons – and thus reveal many ways things as they are in themselves [sic]. And just because we can reveal things from many perspectives, no single perspective can be *the* right one' (1991: 40). There are no finite interpretations.

Hermeneutics

Hermeneutics has its origins in Ancient Greece, particularly in Plato's writings, where the spirit or *daemon* Eros is described as *Hermeneuon* and associated with the transmission of messages between gods and humans (Gonzalez, 2015). There are other Ancient Greek terms which are associated with our contemporary use of the word 'hermeneutics'; these include: *hermeneuein* or *hermeneusai* and *hermeneia* (all designating an activity), *hermenes* (designating the individual responsible for this activity), and *hermeneutike* (the discipline that studies this activity). Gonzales further clarifies that, despite popular belief, hermeneutics in Classical Greece was not so much about 'interpretation' as it was about 'communication' – in particular *oral* communication. Hermeneutics was also present throughout the Middle Ages in debates about the interpretation of the Holy Scriptures. It became a 'science of interpretation' with Baruch Spinoza (1632–1677) and Giambattista Vico (1668–1744). Spinoza had proposed a scientific method for interpreting the Bible, and Vico a method for interpreting ancient cultures (Amoroso, 2015). Hermeneutics thrived particularly during the Protestant Reformation, when biblical literature was subjected to critical hermeneutical inquiry in order to clarify the true meaning of scripture. Ferguson (2006: 75) highlights that 'what rapidly emerged from a sustained consideration of the difficulties of translation and contextualization was the realization that *no* text could, in fact, "speak for itself"'. Past events and experiences could yield numerous interpretations, and 'every text, like the reality to which it was thought to refer, remained undetermined in relation to its immanent meaning' (2006: 75). In the early 1800s, with Friedrich Schleiermacher (1786–1834) and Friedrich Ast (1778–1841), hermeneutics became 'romantic hermeneutics', closely related to the interpretation of ancient philosophical texts (Scholtz, 2015).

Wilhelm Dilthey (1833–1911) was one of the most influential philosophers within the hermeneutic tradition. Dilthey's overall significance was his ability to 'brin[g] into prominence the role of collective and historical processes in the development of all modern self-understanding and self-interpretation' (Ferguson, 2006: 76). But Dilthey did not share the same outlook as the aforementioned hermeneutic phenomenologists Heidegger or Gadamer. He strove for objectivity and reliability in interpretation. According to Wachterhauser, 'Dilthey argued that the historian could achieve "objective validity" in her results through an act of "empathy" (*sich hineinfühlen*) whereby the historian pulled herself out of her own immersion in history and transposed herself into the lives of others' (1986: 18). Furthermore, Dilthey's conception of a historian followed 'along Cartesian lines as someone who can free herself from the influence of her own historical context in order to reconstruct and represent the past as it actually was' (1986: 19). This notion of an inquirer capable of transcending her own history was challenged by both Heidegger and Gadamer. Given this context, we can describe Dilthey's hermeneutics as the science of correct understanding.

The attempt to objectively portray historical social facts became the programme of positivist and realist philosophers. Bevir (1994) tells us that the positivist accounts of objective historical knowledge were based on the method of verification. Interpretations were decoded into observational statements which could be determined to be either *true* or *false*; this way 'an interpretation is true if it consists of observational statements which are true' (1994: 330). Here it may be valuable to recall our discussion in Chapter 2 on the verificationist programme by the logical positivists, and the postpositivist alternative proposed by Karl Popper who advocated the method of falsification. In this respect the falsificationists, as Bevir notes, would disregard the notion of true interpretation, because the fact of having any number of positive observations does not warrant *truth*. Thus the postpositivists rejected the 'true or false' approach to confirming truth and replaced it with a falsificationist 'not-false or false' substitute. The idea of a given past was rejected by hermeneutic thinkers and critical theorists such as Gadamer, Foucault, and Derrida.

This brings us to an important point about hermeneutics and its role in qualitative research. It would make little sense to place hermeneutics on a continuum and juxtapose it with objectivism and realism. In this regard, hermeneutics is not inherently an anti-objectivist or anti-realist or anti-positivist project simply because it deals with 'interpretation' and 'understanding'. It would indeed be limiting, to say the least, if we were to attach it to carefully articulated paradigms and isolate it from other philosophical stances. There is no general or univocal hermeneutics, only a tradition with different tendencies, which can play out across a range of paradigms. To demonstrate this point, we can contrast between *hermeneutic realism* and *hermeneutic idea-ism*.

Hermeneutic realism and hermeneutic idea-ism

Hermeneutic realism is underpinned by the notion of 'correct interpretation', which states that there can be only one *truthful* account of an event, text, or object, and the role of the researcher, and indeed the purpose of an inquiry, is to make it known. In the words of Mailloux (1989: 5), '*hermeneutic realism* argues that meaning-full texts exist independent of interpretation', and that 'meanings are discovered, not created'. Furthermore, 'the facts of the text exists objectively, before any hermeneutic work by readers or critics, and therefore correct interpretations are those that correspond to the autonomous facts of the text' (1989: 5). The interpreter assumes a *passive* role – working towards the goal of making the 'correct interpretation [...] spea[k] itself' (1989: 6).

The opposing view, which we will call *hermeneutic idea-ism*, asserts that interpretation is not to be discovered in the text, object, or event, rather it is entangled within the interpreter, whereby the researcher plays an active role in the process of meaning-making. Interpretation may vary from person to person and according to their different frames of reference. Idea-ism, as previously defined, is the epistemic thesis which states that we can only know our ideas about objects, as opposed to objects directly as they are. To draw a link between the concepts of *idea-ism* and hermeneutics, we could say that the way in which idea-ism manifests in hermeneutics is through the inseparable tie between the interpreter and what is being interpreted – the social fact – such that the only certainty we can have are the ideas we hold about a social fact.[4] In contrast to hermeneutic realism, according to which an objective interpretation is to be found within a text or event, hermeneutic idea-ism attaches interpretation to the interpreter and various reference frames. Under hermeneutic idea-ism there are no objective and mind-independent facts, only interpreted and mind-dependent facts. Mailloux uses different terminology to make the same points. He employs the expression *hermeneutic idealism* (with an L) to explain that 'interpretation always creates the signifying text', and that 'meaning is made, not found' (1989: 6). In addition, he notes that 'textual facts are never prior to or independent of the hermeneutic activity of readers and critics'. Finally, hermeneutic realism is a 'build-up' model of interpretation whereas hermeneutic idealism is a 'build-down' one (Mailloux, 1989). Given the effort we have put into distinguishing idealism from idea-ism, we shall employ the term 'idea-ism' as a replacement for idealism. Idealism denies the existence of things – including social facts. Idea-ism, however, maintains contact with reality; what we do not have access to is the direct truth about events. The difference between hermeneutic realism and hermeneutic idea-ism is portrayed in Figure 4.6.

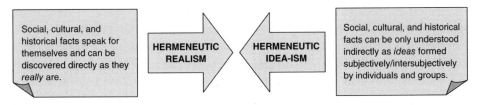

Figure 4.6   The Hermeneutic Continuum: Hermeneutic Realism and Hermeneutic Idea-ism

Hermeneutic realism is based on objective interpretation. Reichertz (2004) traces objective hermeneutics to a German sociologist, Ulrich Oevermann, and his colleagues (Oevermann et al., 1979), explaining that this particular type of hermeneutic analytical procedure emerged as a response to criticism of the quantitatively focused form of sociological measurement, which was prevalent at that time in North America. According to Reichertz, objective hermeneutics continues to be a very popular approach to qualitative research in German-speaking countries. In the discipline of discourse analysis, Titscher, Meyer, Wodak and Vetter (2000) provide a detailed account of *objective hermeneutics* both as a method of text analysis and as a methodology. They explain that objective hermeneutics understands meanings 'as an objective social structure that emerges interactively' (2000: 199); the goal is to 'render visible objective structures of interactions' (2000: 200). Emilio Betti (1890–1968) and Eric D. Hirsch (b. 1928) are other examples of thinkers who have promoted and defended objective hermeneutics. In the case of Betti, text and speech are taken as 'objectified representations of human intentions', and the purpose of an inquiry is to bring about 'the true and only meaning of the text' (Ramberg & Gjesdal, 2014: para. 45). Hirsch takes a normative approach to establishing objective knowledge (see, for example, Hirsch, 1967).

In our discussion of hermeneutic realism, we shall also note the objective turn in hermeneutic phenomenology represented mainly by Paul Ricoeur (2008) and Gunter Figal (2010). Ricoeur, despite opposing the idea of definitive or absolute historical knowledge and the notion of uninterpreted facts to be 'discovered', held that it was possible to arrive at objective historical knowledge – knowledge worthy of the adjective 'true' (Dauenhauer & Pellauer, 2014). Figal's hermeneutic phenomenology has been described as 'a most radical return to the objective as its own foundational principle of the self-givenness of things' (Figal & Espinet, 2014: 506).[5] Overall, it is clear that there are numerous thinkers and approaches that can be observed within the realist variety of hermeneutics.

On the other hand, hermeneutic idea-ism typically manifests as social constructionism, relativism, or pluralism. Social constructionism, simply put, asserts that our knowledge is socially constructed. We will examine social constructionism in Chapter 6, contrasting between the philosophies of Kenneth Gergen and John Searle to show that realist and idea-ist varieties are also relevant when it comes to social ontology. Relativism says that knowledge is relative to certain *relativizers*, such as paradigms, social classes, species, and historical epochs (Nola, 1988). Krausz (2010b) calls these *reference frames* (i.e., conceptual frameworks, systems of beliefs, practices, linguistic frameworks, languages, codes, norms, cultures, tribes, communities, countries, societies, traditions, historical periods, religions, races and genders, and also groups and individuals). From a relativist point of view, whether something is determined as true, moral, or beautiful is relative to a frame of reference. This means that there is no absolute standard that exists above the reference frames which we can consult. For the relativist, 'it is not possible for any cognizer, including the sociologist, to escape her local context and judge from some "context-free," "super-cultural" or context-independent perspective' (Siegel, 2004: 760). Bloor similarly asserts that 'to be a relativist is to deny that there is such a thing as absolute knowledge and absolute truth' (2011: 436).

Pluralism (also known as multiplism) is a thesis that states there can be multiple correct interpretations. As explained by Krausz, 'the multiplist affirms that admissibility may be understood in such multivalent terms as reasonableness, appropriateness, aptness, or the like' (2002: 2). Multiplists hold, for example, that a cultural entity (a) 'need not exhibit only one set of nonopposing properties', (b) that 'the identity conditions of an object of interpretation are themselves affected by interpretive practices', and (c) that 'the identities [of cultural objects] are relative to their historical situatedness' (2002: 2). In a nutshell, the pluralists or multiplists believe that there can be many, equally valid truths. Examples of multiplists/pluralists include Margolis (2002), Mohanty (2002), and perhaps most famously, Nelson Goodman – known for his notion of multiple worlds, advanced in his text *Ways of Worldmaking* (Goodman, 1978). Feagin (2002) emphasizes that objects can have multiple identities because they may move from one socio-cultural setting to another over time, and also because interpretation has to do with the personal identity of the interpreter.

Summary and implications for qualitative research

In this chapter we maintained the distinction between idealism and idea-ism, and outlined the remaining philosophers to complete the list of the key idealists: Plato, Leibniz, Berkeley, and Kant. This exercise has not only allowed us to appreciate the philosophical responses to the Two-World Assumption problem, it has also added an additional layer of understanding to phenomenology. While most texts portray Edmund Husserl as the originator of the phenomenological movement, the analysis of Rockmore (2011) suggests that phenomenology can be traced to the work of Kant, who, like Husserl, was concerned with the cognitive construction of phenomena in the mind.

With respect to the realism–idea-ism distinction, we have carried this theme into hermeneutics, differentiating between hermeneutic realism and hermeneutic idea-ism. We must reiterate that idea-ism is not idealism, and that qualitative inquiry embedded in idea-ist philosophy is perfectly compatible with metaphysical realism. The world exists, and so do other human beings, trees and rocks. Significantly, this also applies to social facts, such as historical events, US dollars, tourists, and all other social and cultural phenomena. To make this point clear, the Second World War is not something imagined in the researcher's head – the horrendous events did indeed take place. The issue at hand is epistemological and semantic in that idea-ism claims that interpretation cannot be divorced from the interpreter and the context.

In our exploration of the possibility of knowledge, rather than a single form of objectivism, we have come across several ways in which philosophers have conceived of objective knowledge. These notions vary with philosophical traditions, and also with what various scholars have held to be 'real' and 'knowable'. In scientific realism, objectivism aims to provide true descriptions of the world regardless of whether we speak of observable or unobservable entities (this problem will be addressed in more depth in Chapter 5). Platonic realism grants objective knowledge to mind-independent universals or abstract objects, which reside in a perfect realm of *forms* (or, in Kantian terms, the noumenal realm). In phenomenology, Husserl also strove for certitude and objectivity, but criticized any views of objectivism that denied or excluded subjectivity. Therefore his phenomenology 'would always approach objectivity as correlated to a corresponding subjectivity' (Moran, 2005: 50). Despite Husserl's approach as being best described by the term *intersubjectivity*, his essences of consciousness had an undeniable objective flavour – the 'treeness' of a tree holds for all subjects, and regardless of whether the tree falls and ceases to exist. With the later German objective idealists, the 'objective' transpires as the *absolute* or *archetypical*. Finally, objectivism in hermeneutics manifests as the discovery of *one* correct interpretation embedded in a text, event, artwork, or experience. A summary of the different notions of objectivism is offered in Figure 4.7.

Scientific–Realist Objectivism

We can obtain knowledge of a mind-independent external world, including physical and theoretical entities. Scientific realism erases any distinction between noumena and phenomena whereby both the physical and the theoretical are real things.

Platonic Objectivism

We can obtain true knowledge of the ideal, perfect world of *forms* but not the external and imperfect everyday world.

Objectivism in German Idealism of Hölderlin, Novalis, Schlegel, and Schelling

There are mind-independent forms of experience where 'the forms of experience are self-subsistent and transcend both the subject and object' (Beiser, 2002: 11).

Objectivism (Intersubjectivism) in Husserl's Phenomenology

We can have objective and direct knowledge of *essences* through immediate intuition. Phenomenology brings together the subjective and objective whereby 'objectivity is an achievement or production of subjectivity'; there can be no objectivity without subjectivity (Moran, 2002: 22).

Objective Hermeneutics

Objective hermeneutics is the science of correct interpretation – we can obtain correct interpretations and true meanings, to be found in the objects themselves (and also in texts, events, social phenomena, etc.).

Figure 4.7 Varieties of objectivism

In a nutshell, what we can learn from glancing through Figure 4.7 is that objectivism is not just a feature of scientific realism: varieties can be found across a range of philosophical movements, including idealism, phenomenology, and even hermeneutics. In Chapter 6, we will further see that objectivism is also present in social constructionism.

Phenomenology and hermeneutics

Our focus on phenomenology and hermeneutics was very limited in light of the vast number of intellectuals and approaches these doctrines comprise. Phenomenology comes in many varieties, and cannot be reduced to a common set of epistemic principles that are accepted and practised by all phenomenologists. Hence there would be little gain in making generic claims about phenomenology. A more fruitful strategy is for students and researchers to explore what individual philosophers have to say on various issues – be they ontological, epistemological, methodological, existential, or otherwise. It would also be a mistake to presume that all phenomenology can be reduced to a method or methodology.

Indeed, there is much more to phenomenology than our quick look at Husserl's phenomenological method of reduction and Heidegger and Gadamer's ideas about the hermeneutic circle might suggest. When the use of phenomenology is determined by the study's focus, many new possibilities open up:[6] Martin Heidegger (1889–1976), Hans-Georg Gadamer (1900–2002), and Paul Ricoeur (1930–2005) have something to say about hermeneutics, tradition, and interpretation; Jacques Derrida (1930–2004) on deconstruction; Maurice Merleau-Ponty (1908–1961) on embodiment; Jean-Paul Sartre (1905–1980) on freedom; Edith Stein (1891–1942) on empathy and Thomism; Adolf Reinach (1883–1917) on social acts, and together with Stein and Roman Ingarden (1893–1970) on realist phenomenology; Max Scheler (1874–1928) on the phenomenology of the person; Simone de Beauvoir on feminism (1908–1986); Emmanuel Levinas (1906–1995) on the Other (with a constructivist and hermeneutic undertone); and Alfred Schütz (1899–1959) on the phenomenology of the social world. The list could continue and include myriad other Polish, Czech, German, American, French, Canadian, and other phenomenologists – each making a contribution not to a homogeneous doctrine but to varied phenomenological terrains. Moreover, there many areas with which phenomenology intersects, such as existentialism, deconstruction, poststructuralism, critical theory, critical philosophy of race, phenomenological psychology, and literary criticism (on this see Luft & Overgaard, 2014). Phenomenology has also made manifold contributions to philosophy aside from the domains of ontology and epistemology. These include philosophy of mind, philosophy of language, moral philosophy, political philosophy, philosophy of mathematics, logic, philosophy of science, and philosophy of religion and theology. Last, but not least, Ferguson's (2006) phenomenological sociology provides insights into modern society through a process of social reduction – a phenomenology he describes as the 'ethnography of the present'.

With respect to hermeneutics, it is valuable to maintain an understanding that as with phenomenology its reach is much broader than what might be suggested by our mere scratching of the surface. A hermeneutics-inclined inquiry can be motivated by additional concerns, such as the role of structures, power, ideologies, and other influences that shape the ways in which meanings are manufactured and transmitted. In this regard, hermeneutics is not just a philosophical guiding principle or a methodological endeavour, it extends to a critical analysis of the 'hidden' and the 'taken for granted'. For example, in Habermas's (1987 [1968]) view hermeneutics ought to include critical theory of society – a view that resonates strongly with Foucault, Gadamer, and other critical theorists. In qualitative research and the area of education, critical hermeneutics has been advocated by Kincheloe (e.g., 2008) as a way of addressing issues of race, class, gender, and sexuality that often shape social phenomena.

Phenomenology and hermeneutics can be applied with degrees of complexity and offer a multitude of ways to enrich qualitative research. However, there is no consensus as to how hermeneutics or phenomenology must proceed in order to obtain knowledge in a hermeneutic or phenomenological fashion. The most fundamental question the researcher faces is not one of method, but a deeper philosophical problem of truth and interpretation. The choice of methods unfolds as a response to whether there is *a* correct interpretation or perhaps multiple ones. In other words, hermeneutics can be grounded in *realism* or *idea-ism*, and of course by other outlooks that fall within or between the two. The first will reject while the latter will demand that interpretation is always situated, context-dependent, and historical, and that there is no objective, acultural, ahistorical, context-free reading of social facts.

A final point to be noted is that there is nothing innately 'qualitative' about hermeneutics and phenomenology, if the term 'qualitative' is taken to mean 'anti-realist', 'anti-objectivist', and 'anti-reductionist'. As shown in this chapter, one can indeed engage in qualitative research that has realist and objectivist goals and use phenomenology and hermeneutics as the means of providing objectivity and truth. Qualitative scholars therefore ought to exercise vigilance in matters of philosophical and methodological choice.

Recommended reading

Alvesson, M. & Sköldberg, K. (2000) *Reflexive Methodology: New Vistas for Qualitative Research*. London: SAGE.

Baronov, D. (2004) *Conceptual Foundations of Social Research Methods*. Boulder, CO: Paradigm.

Bevir, M. (1994) Objectivity in history. *History and Theory*, 33(3): 328-44. doi:10.2307/2505477

Kockelmans, J.J. (1985) *Heidegger on Art and Art Works*. Dordrecht, The Netherlands: Martinus Nijhoff.

Luft, S. & Overgaard, S. (eds) (2014) *The Routledge Companion to Phenomenology*. Abingdon: Routledge.

Malpas, J. & Gander, H.-H. (eds) (2015) *The Routledge Companion to Hermeneutics*. Abingdon: Routledge.

Rockmore, T. (2007) *Kant and Idealism*. New Haven, CT: Yale University Press.

Rockmore, T. (2011) *Kant and Phenomenology*. Chicago, IL: University of Chicago Press.

Schwandt, T.A. (2015) *The SAGE Dictionary of Qualitative Inquiry* (4th edn). Thousand Oaks, CA: SAGE.
Smith, D.W. (2013) *Husserl* (2nd edn). Abingdon: Routledge.
Smith, D.W. (2013) Phenomenology. *Internet Encyclopedia of Philosophy*. Retrieved 15 May 2015 from http://plato.stanford.edu/entries/phenomenology
Stroud, B. (1980) Berkeley v. Locke on primary qualities. *Philosophy*, 55 (212): 149–66. doi:10.1017/S003181910004897X

Notes

1. Kant employed the term *empirical idealism* not to suggest that its adherents followed the doctrine of empiricism but because they denied the empirical world (Beiser, 2002).
2. In some literature, the *thing-in-itself* is used interchangeably with the term *noumena*, and it has been argued by philosophers that Kant himself used these two terms inconsistently in his writing. To keep things simple, here we maintain a strict distinction between the two.
3. The problem with extending *noumena* to such entities (e.g., atoms) or the *thing-in-itself* is that we no longer speak of something that belongs solely to the realm of reason but rather give it the status of ontological entity. Another way of putting this is that because atoms, electrons, and molecules are the fruits of empirical investigations and require the deployment of the human senses, they must fall into the same category as any other appearance.
4. It may be helpful to revisit this point after reading Chapter 6, which discusses social facts in more detail.
5. Figal's usage of the term *objective* is of a more nuanced variety. He does not suggest that what is understood as objective has to do with scientific methods of inquiry; instead, it denotes 'our receptiveness to whatever intelligibility an object may grant to us' (translator's introduction in Figal, 2010: xii).
6. For ease of understanding, the various phenomenological directions have been distilled from Moran and Mooney's *Phenomenology Reader* (2002), which provides an excellent overview of the diversity of phenomenological thought.

Five

Realism, its Varieties and Contenders

Realism is a difficult doctrine to pin down for there is far more to realism than the claim that reality exists. Rather than viewing realism as a single concept, it is more fruitfully understood as a large family of views which permeate several philosophical domains, including metaphysics and ontology, epistemology and methodology, and theories of meaning. The main purpose of this chapter is to facilitate a wider understanding of the various forms of realism as well as the degrees of commitment to ontological, epistemological, and semantic realism. Before we embark on this task, it would be useful to take stock of what has been noted in relation to reality and the existence of things so far.

In Chapter 2, we noted the urgency many Enlightenment-era philosophers felt to replace mystical interpretations and 'dubious' metaphysics with knowledge based either on observations and experiments (sciences) or formal deductions from definitions (mathematics) – all else was deemed scientifically meaningless (Rosenberg, 1999). Empiricism became associated with scientific knowledge, and sciences were ready to reach their final 'positive' stage, which Comte called positivism. Metaphysics, for its close association with the supernatural and inanimate agency, had lost its appeal, and philosophy became the philosophy of science. The logical positivists came to realize that mathematicians and philosophers did not possess a 'special faculty of insight into necessary truths' and that these were only 'necessary' and *a priori* because they were 'disguised or undisguised definitions and the logical consequences of definitions' (Rosenberg, 1999: 14). The logical positivists claimed that scientific knowledge could only be produced through observation, testing, and experiments. For them, theories that were not grounded in empirical work had no scientific significance. The postpositivist Popper saw a major weakness in the methods of positivism in that they lacked the ability to falsify theories. He criticized the method of verification and argued that scientific theories ought to be tested for their falsifiability. Contrary to inductivism, he proposed hypothetico-deductivism as a way of evaluating propositions.

The problem of unobservables is important. The point of contention between the positivists and the full-blown realists (i.e., scientific realists) stems from the empiricist attitude of doubt toward theoretical entities. Due to their rigid outlook, the various forms of empiricism (including logical positivism) have been catalogued as anti-realism, which is better termed anti-*scientific* realism – a point we will address later in this chapter. Although some commentators (such as Alvesson and Sköldberg) have suggested that 'modern positivism' is more flexible and perhaps on a par with scientific realism – stating that 'for modern positivism, what is observable also includes what is measurable or possible to register through some kind of instrument' (2000: 17) – it is necessary to stay attuned to the issue of what counts as observation and sufficient evidence. It is one thing to argue that with microscopes and telescopes we can now detect entities previously unavailable to our senses, but it is another to infer the existence of, for example, black holes. Black holes are not directly observable (not even by the latest telescopes), they can only be inferred from gravitational influences. Therefore we rely on some kind of hypothetico-deductivism and the methods advocated by the postpositivists. Thus, the distinction that sets apart the scientific realist and the anti-*scientific* realist lies in the observer-independent existence of both observable and theoretical/unobservable entities, and corresponding epistemological and semantic assumptions. For the scientific realists, black holes, dimensions, and quarks exist, and the theories in which these feature are true or close to being true.

We should also recapitulate what we have learned up to now about realism and appearances. Chapter 4 elaborated on *direct* or naïve realism – an older philosophical view of perception built upon the idea that we can perceive physical objects directly as they are through our senses. The direct realist thesis maintains that the objects we perceive have intrinsic properties and enjoy an objective, mind-independent existence. On the other hand, the competing view of *indirect* or *representational* realism (also called *inferential* or *causal* realism) holds that sense data are only representations or images of the world, grasped cognitively by the mind. The objects of the world are always mediated by our senses, and are therefore mind-dependent. Following the work of John Locke, direct realism has been 'saved' by distinguishing between (intrinsic) *primary* qualities of objects and (observer-relative) *secondary* properties, such as colour and texture.

In this chapter, we continue to explore the contemporary viewpoints on what can be said to exist and what can be known about it. The first part offers a conceptual schema based on the work of Robert Nola (1988), which will enable us to peel away the different layers of, and better understand, realism. The second part focuses on some of the nuanced realist and anti-*scientific* realist categories. Here, we will outline the key tenets of scientific realism, structural realism, constructive empiricism, internal realism, and surrealism. As anti-*scientific* realism accommodates any view that is not scientific realism, we will limit our discussion only to a selection of philosophical stances that are seminal in the philosophy of science. The closing sections explore the ways in which some of the discussed philosophies manifest in the social sciences, and how realism can be used in qualitative inquiry.

Unpacking realism

Realism comes in many flavours. In order to appreciate the various realistic out-looks, we have to explore its specific compartments. This way we can tackle it with regard to metaphysics/ontology, epistemology and methodology, as well as from a semantic point of view. This strategy is visually depicted in Figure 5.1. In the lower compartment, metaphysical and ontological realism, as detailed in Chapter 1, represents the claim that various categories of 'things' exist independent of the human mind. These can be tangible objects such as rocks and trees, or theoretical and unobservable entities such as electrons, but also numbers, structures, laws, and so forth. The weakest metaphysical /ontological claim is to acknowledge the

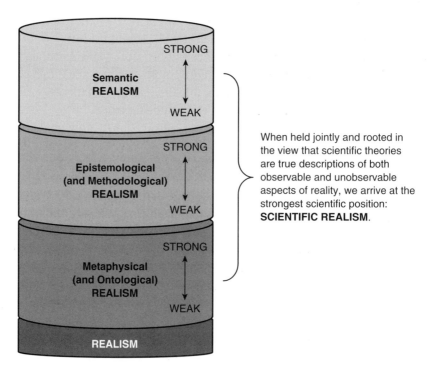

Figure 5.1 The Realist 'Barrel': Realism can be divided into distinct compartments: methodological realism reinforces the view that there are scientific methods for finding out how the independent world really is (ontological realism) and that it can be known (epistemological realism), and that language and sentences correspond to reality (semantic realism). In addition, there are degrees of commitment within each compartment, from *weak* to *strong*. When the barrel is full, so to speak, we arrive at *scientific realism*

existence of an external world out there. In Figure 1.3 (see Chapter 1), we have labelled this basic recognition of reality as *materialism* or *metaphysical realism* and contrasted it with *immaterialism* or *metaphysical idealism* and *solipsism*. The second compartment in Figure 5.1, epistemological realism, deals with knowledge – specifically the claim that we can know the world and its objects and phenomena. Methodological realism can be understood as the extension (or application) of epistemological realism. If epistemological realism purports that we can have secure knowledge of a mind-independent world, then there must be methods of obtaining its accurate representations. Methodological realism speaks to the ways in which we obtain knowledge, be they tools and scientific methods. The upper compartment, semantic realism, addresses the correspondence of sentences to reality (i.e., that the theoretical meaning of sentences is true).

In addition to marking the difference between metaphysical/ontological, epistemological, and semantic realisms, each of these domains contain stronger and weaker perspectives. For example, with regard to metaphysics, one can express a strong commitment to the existence of specific kinds of objects or hold a weaker position that *something* exists. Similarly, when it comes to epistemology, one can exert confidence about scientific theories or be reserved in making such judgements. And one, too, can have confidence in the truth of theories in general or perhaps in only some theories, when speaking of semantic realism. Important to note in Figure 5.1 is that the strongest views within each of the vertical layers of the barrel add to a philosophical position called *scientific realism* – the stoutest of scientific outlooks available. To fully appreciate the nuances within realism we shall further explore what Nola (1988) has to say on the matter.

Ontological, semantic, and epistemological realism

The notion of realism as a multi-faceted cluster of views is communicated most clearly by Robert Nola in his (1988) text *Relativism and Realism in Science*. Motivated by the writings of Hellman (1983), Nola's outline of the different realist stances in Table 5.1 provides the necessary ammunition for dispersing much of the confusion that has surrounded the realist debate. Nola distinguishes between ontological, semantic, and epistemological realism, and delineates the weaker and stronger positions within each domain. By providing these placeholders, not only is he able to show that there is a variety of realisms, he can also explain why some sociologists of science, for example, can be ontological realists (i.e., maintain that there is one common reality as far as objects and the external world are concerned), but at the same time remain epistemological or methodological relativists (i.e., giving no more importance to one theory or set of canons of reasoning over others) (Nola, 1988). In a similar fashion, qualitative researchers can appreciate that constructionists, constructivists, phenomenologists, critical theorists, idea-ists, and so forth are perfectly capable of accommodating metaphysical and ontological realism. It should be clear that it would be inaccurate to group them broadly with the relativists, the idealists, or worse, the solipsists.

Table 5.1 is structured vertically to differentiate between the forms or domains of realism (ontological, semantic, epistemological) and delineate the levels of commitment available. The first, ontological realism, speaks of the existence of mind-independent objects. By establishing the categories OR1, OR2, and OR3, Nola moves from generic ontic claims (OR1) towards specific articulation about what exists. OR1 is the weakest form of realism, sometimes associated with *fig-leaf realism*, which Devitt (1984: 23) sums up in the following statement: 'Something objectively exists independently of the mental'. It is mild enough, in Nola's view, to accommodate even the more extravagant[1] constructivist figures, such as Nelson Goodman. Goodman does not object to the existence of an external world but there is not much else that can be said about it (see, for example,

Table 5.1 Nola's Varieties of Realism (concepts derived from Nola, 1988: 4-10)

ONTOLOGICAL REALISM		SEMANTIC REALISM		EPISTEMOLOGICAL REALISM	
OR1	Something exists in a suitably mind-independent manner.	SR1	Some non-O* sentences have a truth-value.	ER1	It is reasonable to believe that (or there exists good evidence that, or it is known that, etc.) some non-O sentences have a truth-value.
OR2	There are individual objects which exist in a suitably mind-independent manner (and which are open to scientific investigation).	SR2	There is no defensible demarcation between O and non-O sentences in science generally such that only the former could be said to have truth-value.	ER2	There is good evidence that theory T is our best tested most comprehensive theory; T tells us that entities $E_1, E_2, ... E_n$ exist and that they are subject to laws $L_1, L_2, ..., L_n$ therefore it is reasonable to believe (a) that these entities exist and (b) that those laws are approximately true.
OR3	There are some kinds of objects (such as electrons, 'flu viruses, kauri trees, or galaxies) which exist in a suitably mind-independent manner (and which are open to scientific investigation).	SR3	(1) Terms in a mature science typically refer (i.e., they are referents). (2) The laws of a theory belonging to a mature science are typically approximately true.	ER3	It is possible that in the ideal limit of scientific investigation our final scientific theory is false.

*O = observational; non-O = non-observational

Note: ER3 is a strong version of epistemic realism, different from ER1 and ER2, that admits that even if all evidence for a theory is gathered, the theory may still be false. For more information see the thesis of underdetermination of scientific theory (e.g., http://plato.stanford.edu/entries/scientific-underdetermination/).

Goodman, 1978). By contrast, OR3 is the strongest ontological claim. To reject OR1 is to espouse a very strong non-realist stance; the standpoint Nola has in mind in OR1 is *subjective idealism*, the notion that only minds and their contents exist. We recall the distinction offered in Chapter 1, where the rejection of metaphysical realism was shown to lead to metaphysical idealism or solipsism. Social constructionism is commonly mistaken as a thesis that rejects OR1, although the vast majority of social constructionists are perfectly content to accept OR1 (some even OR2 and OR3).

Again referring to Table 5.1, OR2 and OR3 suggest that, in comparison to OR1 and a generic acceptance of 'something' to exist, there are individual *objects* and *kinds*. Objects are distinct entities and denote the existence of things (e.g., the object on the ground is rock-like); kinds refer to the specific features or properties objects actually have in common (e.g., this object on the ground is made of limestone). Holding on to OR3, we are no longer speaking of a general notion of 'something' existing (OR1), rather we are making a strong ontological claim that natural objects have objective similarities or certain properties in common, and that there are kinds of things as well as the objects that fall under a kind. OR3 is the type of commitment found in scientific realism. It is vital here to reiterate that to refute OR3 is not to refute all reality, only to claim that there are no mind-independent or naturally occurring *kinds* – or, as Nola explains, 'only the kinds that we construct as a result of our epistemic activities of classifying what objects there are' (1988: 5). Whereas the denial of all of OR1, OR2, and OR3 must lead to metaphysical idealism or solipsism, the rejection of only OR2 or OR3 (or both) still allows for various forms of weak realism. Hilary Putnam, whom we will discuss in the turn of a few pages, was a scientific realist (OR3) in his early career, but later became categorized as a weak realist (OR1) and even idealist after embracing *internal realism* and rejecting the idea of mind-independent reality. In his words, 'the mind and the world jointly make up the mind and the world. (Or, to make the metaphor even more Hegelian, the Universe makes up the Universe – with minds – collectively – playing a special role in the making up)' (Putnam, 1981: xi). To follow up on our critique of various conceptual models in the first chapter, the different realist outlooks outlined in Table 5.1, particularly with regard to metaphysics and ontology (OR1–OR3), exemplify the difficulty of trying to fit philosophical assumptions into rigid conceptual schemas. By revisiting Table 1.1 (see Chapter 1), for example, we can see that it fails to capture the subtler stances available to qualitative scholars.

Ontological realism tends to be misunderstood, and for this reason it is a good idea to consider further examples. Grinell's (1992) account of a working biologist comes to the rescue. In order for a biologist to study cells, she must first acknowledge that cells exist as external objects and can be studied scientifically. This implies a strong stance of ontological realism, as the scientist not only acknowledges the mere existence of external objects, she also accepts that they exist as a *kind*. When peering through a microscope, the biologist is looking for a specific example of something. She already has an understanding of what does and does not classify as a cell: in other words, that something either has or has not the properties of a *kind*. Therefore, a scientific realist would hold that cells exist as a kind, that we can have reliable knowledge about cells, and that when we speak about cells, the meaning corresponds to real structures that exist. By contrast, an anti-*scientific* realist (i.e., the rejection of OR3 but not necessarily OR1 and OR2) may respond that the notion of cells as a kind is a matter of convention. In the spirit of Kuhn's (1962) *Structure of Scientific Revolutions*, scientists learn to study objects in a certain way, and share agreed practices, principles, and methods. Paradigms, as explained in Chapter 1, are represented by such communities of scholars. Importantly, the anti-*scientific* realist may not wish to dispute that one could indeed see 'something' when looking through the microscope (OR1) and that what he sees are distinct entities (OR2) but maintain, nonetheless, that they become kinds (OR3) as a result of human activity – thus rejecting the notion of cells as true ontological entities.

Semantic realism tells us how to treat and interpret sentences (Anderson, 2002). These concern 'either the truth-values of sentences of a theory or the referents of terms of a theory' (Nola, 1988: 6). In the words of Psillos, if one is a semantic realist then she has a 'straightforward answer to the question: what is the world like, according to a given scientific theory?' (2005: 68). Put another way, the world *is*, as described by a scientific theory. The acceptance of semantic realism implies the acceptance of ontological realism, as statements are typically claims about mind-independent objects and kinds in the external world. However, when it comes to socially constructed phenomena, such as money and tourists, it is also possible to adopt semantic and epistemological realism but reject ontological realism. This problem will occupy us in the following chapter.

As shown in Table 5.1, Nola (1988) draws a distinction between observational sentences and terms (O) and non-observational sentences and terms (non-O). O sentences and terms have their meaning fixed prior to their use in a theory, whereas the meaning of non-O sentences and terms has yet to be secured in a theory. For instance, a limestone rock (OR3) can be described with regard to its observational features, i.e., it can be said to be 'grey', 'porous', and composed of specific 'minerals', all of which are terms imbued with already-established meaning. Nola further brings in examples of weaker, stronger, and very strong versions of sematic realism (SR1, SR2, SR3) by contrasting the levels of commitment to truth-value in theories. By moving from SR1 and accepting SR2, we notice that sentences and theories about those phenomena that have not yet been proven to exist (and may never be), such as the subatomic particles *quarks*, have truth-value. In other words, the fact that subatomic particles cannot be observed and are purely theoretical entities does not prevent a moderate semantic realist from believing that the theories in which these entities feature have truth-values, that is, are either true or false. This means that scientific statements in physics about 'black holes' refer to something ontologically real; they refer to black holes that are believed to exist, although scientists may never get to directly see one. Lastly, accepting SR3 'requires that mature scientific theories have got it nearly right in that the non-O sentences not only have a truth value but also have high verisimilitude'[2] (Nola, 1988: 8). Many contemporary scientists, and physicists in particular, are cautious about making claims that theories and models capture reality *exactly*. Reality is at best *approximately* captured by scientific models.

Epistemological realism (see Table 5.1) is about the ability to know the external world. By introducing a range of epistemic operators – 'It is reasonable to believe that', 'There exists (good) evidence that', 'It is known that', 'It is certain that' – Nola (1988) furnishes us with additional varieties of epistemological realisms (ER1, ER2, ER3). Note that there is a difference in degree of strength and commitment between the ways in which ER1 and ER2 are formulated. While the former statement is rather cautious, the latter represents a strong version of epistemological realism. Perhaps surprisingly, ER3 is also a strong version of epistemological realism, explained by Nola as a 'mixed modal-epistemic claim about our application of the best canons of scientific method to ultimately yield a theory of the world' (1988: 9). It denotes the commitment of scientific realists who are in search of *truths*, while acknowledging that, on the way, it is possible that some theories are likely to be proven false. Karl Popper, whom we discussed in Chapter 2, was a proponent of the method of falsification, which was a fundamental component of his view of scientific knowledge. It was also Popper who proclaimed that the aim of science is greater verisimilitude (Popper, 1972).

Having established the varieties of realism in Table 5.1, we can ponder their implications for research. Committed scientific realists would score highly in all three domains of realism – ontological, epistemological, and semantic. Things and kinds exist, we can know them with certainty or near-certainty, and our theories refer to how things really are. There are also weaker ontological realists in the likes of social constructionists and internal realists, who, for example, are happy to commit to the existence of the external world, but not to specific *kinds*. In addition, there are advocates of social constructionism, such as John Searle, who is an avowed scientific realist as far as natural phenomena are concerned, yet an ontological relativist in respect of socially constructed facts (professors, presidents, money, citizenship, etc.). The logical positivists, too, are only weak realists in this respect, for they are committed only to observable entities. For them, atoms, electrons, and black holes are rejected on the premise of not being ontologically real because they are not observable. In this respect, we noted in Chapter 1 Laudan's remark that all positivists were methodological relativists and 'radical subjectivists about methodology and epistemology' (1996: 15). Even postpositivism,[3] he proclaims, was 'thoroughgoing epistemological relativism about science' (1996: 5). Furthermore, one can reject semantic realism, yet be an ontological realist about observable entities and not about unobservable entities. Van Fraassen, as we will see shortly, is a philosopher who comes close to this outlook with his *constructive empiricism*. And finally, Nola tells us that there are also some sociologists of science who may adhere to the notion of a single reality, but are apprehensive of the theory of scientific method or 'set of canons of reasoning that can justifiably be accepted above any other' (1988: 3). Here Nola identifies the Canadian philosopher Ian Hacking as a figure that illustrates the amalgamation of ontological realism and epistemic relativism.

With Nola's cataloguing system, we reach a new level of philosophical sophistication. The overall value of such a nuanced view of realism is in the ability to discern various philosophical stances and their beholders, often too intricate to be given generic treatment. The added benefit for qualitative researchers ultimately lies in the opportunity to think about and articulate what one can be a realist about and to what degree.

Scientific realism and the problem of unobservable entities

Apart from distinguishing between *direct* and *indirect* realism (see Chapter 3), we have considered two ways of obtaining knowledge about the external world: rationalism, whereby 'truths' are grasped about nature by employing reason; and empiricism, which builds theories from observation. Consequently, claims can be made about objects and kinds in nature – rocks, trees, animal species, or any other entities or phenomena – which can be either verified or falsified by empirical methods. With the aid of inventions and modern technology, we are now also able to detect objects at the microscopic level (e.g., cells) and very great distances away (e.g., exoplanets and galaxies as far as thirteen billion light-years away).[4] Problems arise, however, when we consider knowledge claims about phenomena that are beyond the reach of our senses, and not so easily, or not at all, observable. Albert Einstein's relativity and quantum theories raised important philosophical problems for the philosophers of the twentieth century, leaving scholars divided on the issue of whether or not the accuracy of theories that deal with unobservable entities should be treated in the same fashion as those that describe observable entities. We have seen that for the logical positivists these were not comparable; we could be grandly mistaken about the existence of subatomic particles and black holes, and any statements about these should not be regarded as scientific. With this came the issue of whether theories that describe unobservable entities should be regarded as *true* descriptions of reality. The answers to these questions divided academics into two camps: the *scientific realists* and the anti-*scientific* realists of various sorts.

Scientific realism

The notion of scientific realism is described as having originated in the twentieth century as part of the debates surrounding the philosophical foundations of physics (Scheibe & Falkenburg, 2001). The core beliefs shared by scientific realists are a progressive view of science and a belief that scientific knowledge extends to unobservable or inaccessible empirical manifestations (Leplin, 1984). Following Lyons and Clarke, to this we can add two additional claims commonly shared by the adherents of this doctrine: the aim of science at truth, and that 'we can justifiably believe that our successful scientific theories achieve, or at least approximate, this aim' (2002: ix). In practical terms, this would mean that a scientific realist believes in the existence of the Higgs boson elementary particle, which was purely theoretical in 1964 when proposed by a team of scientists (including Peter Higgs) basing themselves on the Standard Model of particle physics,[5] and also in the (approximate) truth of the theory. The Higgs boson has since been proven to exist (in 2013) by the European Organization for Nuclear Research (CERN).

A scientific realist thus believes in the existence of subatomic particles, black holes, the four-dimensional space–time continuum, and many of the features of quantum mechanics. Of course, this does not mean that all theoretical physicists should be classified as scientific realists: for example, there are as many as nine notions of quantum reality, which we will explore in Chapter 7. Nevertheless, scientific realism maintains that both observable and unobservable entities exist in a mind-independent manner, and the aim of science is to produce *true* theories of these (or near-true). To help us understand exactly what is at stake for scientific realists, Sankey (2008: 13–17) has drawn six core assertions:

1. The aim of science is to discover the truth about the world, and scientific progress consists of advancing toward that aim.
2. Scientific inquiry leads to genuine knowledge of both observable and unobservable aspects of the world.
3. Scientific discourse about theoretical entities is to be interpreted in a literal fashion as discourse which is genuinely committed to the existence of real unobservable entities.
4. The world investigated by science is an objective reality that exists independent of human thought.
5. Truth consists of the correspondence between a claim about the world and the way the world is (note, however, that there are scientific realists, such as Michael Devitt who do not follow the correspondence theory of truth: see Devitt, 1984, Chapter 4).
6. Theories or claims about the world are made true (or false) by the way things are in the mind-independent, objective reality investigated by science.

Nonetheless, Leplin writes that 'like the Equal Rights Movement, scientific realism is a majority position whose advocates are so divided as to appear a minority'(1984: 1). Therefore, to make matters more complicated, we can consider ten tenets that, as argued by Leplin, are characteristic of scientific claims, but which are not all (or even the majority) necessarily endorsed by any avowed realist:

1. The best current scientific theories are at least approximately true.
2. The central terms of the best current theories are genuinely referential.

3. The approximate truth of a scientific theory is a sufficient explanation of its predictive success.
4. The (approximate) truth of a scientific theory is the only possible explanation of its predictive success.
5. A scientific theory may be approximately true even if referentially unsuccessful.
6. The history of at least the mature sciences shows a progressive approximation to a true account of the physical world.
7. The theoretical claims of scientific theories are to be read literally, and so read are definitively true or false.
8. Scientific theories make genuine, existential claims.
9. The predictive success of a theory is evidence for the referential success of its central terms.
10. Science aims at a literally true account of the physical world, and its success is to be reckoned by its progress toward achieving this aim. (Leplin, 1984: 1-2)

By breaking scientific realism into ten principles, Leplin communicates the philosophical subtleties one can observe within the scientific realism community. With the benefit of Nola's (1988) scheme (see Table 5.1), we are equipped to deal with this heterogeneity within scientific realism. In Nola's model, this heterogeneity manifests as the stronger and weaker views within each of the ontological, semantic, and epistemological domains. The point, and perhaps the overall theme of this book, is that we must pay attention to such subtleties, otherwise we will fall into the trap of mediocre generalizations. In this regard, Sankey (2008: 12) joins Leplin in the call against oversimplification, warning that there is no simple thesis but instead a set of doctrines, or a 'family of closely related doctrines', which are not necessarily agreed upon by all scientific realists. Taking into account the views of Nola, Sankey, and Leplin, and referring to Leplin's ten points, we can appreciate the variety of views. The notion of 'approximate truth', for example, is a much weaker thesis about the function of scientific theories – though still imbued with commitment – than is the view of theories as 'literally true accounts' of the world. Or, regardless of the range of epistemic and semantic claims, most scientific realists agree that unobservable entities, such as electrons and black holes, are ontologically secure and objective. Given that scientific realism has been formulated as one of the core epistemic outlooks in Chapter 1, it is useful to offer a quick summary (see the textbox).

––––––––––––––––––––––––––– **Scientific realism** –––––––––––––––––––––––––––

Scientific realism, formulated as an epistemological outlook, claims that – as far as knowledge is concerned – we ought not to discriminate between the observable and unobservable aspects of the world. It regards both the objects and phenomena that we can observe and those that we cannot as equally fit for the task of scientific inquiry. The aim of scientific theory, then, is to generate true (or at least approximately true) descriptions of a mind-independent world.

Anti-*scientific* realisms

So far we have established that realism comes in varieties, and that in its strongest form it manifests as scientific realism. The term 'anti-*scientific* realism' can be used to mark the weaker realist positions noted in Table 5.1, however it is also common to see references to its shortened version 'anti-realism'. As Braver notes, 'most writers on the topic agree that, as the name suggests, anti-realism is defined in contrast to realism: anti-realism is *not* whatever realism *is'* (2007: 13). Given our newly-gained understanding that there is not only one realist stance but many, it is necessary to remain vigilant about what different thinkers oppose when they employ the term.

Continental philosophers opposed to scientific realism (e.g., Hegel, Heidegger, Nietzsche, Foucault, Husserl, Kierkegaard, Deleuze, Gadamer, and Merleau-Ponty) feature regularly in the literature on qualitative research methods, and because the vast majority of books in this area tend to cover the hermeneutical and phenomenological responses as well as the critical theorists, in this section, we will focus only on the types of stances that may be less known by qualitative scholars. Therefore, we will not concentrate so much on the alternative philosophies that have rejected realism outright (or most of its parts), focusing instead on the views that object only to the strongest realist thesis. To maintain clarity of thought, the term we will continue to apply is 'anti-*scientific* realism'. The aim of the following sections is not to give a thorough account of each philosophical position but to outline the basic tenets. In addition to the philosophical assumptions enlisted in existing paradigmatic matrices (e.g., Figure 1.1, Chapter 1), these alternatives to scientific realism further highlight the range of philosophical assumptions available to researchers.

Structural realism

It has been explained that scientific realism does not discriminate between observable and unobservable entities, and that it treats both as genuine objects of scientific inquiry. Furthermore, its aim is to tell us truly or approximately-truly how the world really is. John Worrall (1989) proposed a different outlook from standard (or scientific) realism, which he called *structural realism*. Structural realism is different in that it is limited to the structural and mathematical content of theories (Ladyman, 2014). It makes claims about the structure of the natural world. There is no ontological and semantic commitment to accounting for things as they 'truly are'; all that can be known about the world is 'structure'. Fundamentally, the 'structural' in *structural realism* is to be understood in terms of the relations between elements – expressed in mathematical equations.

It is useful to consider structural realism in light of debates about the success of science and the linear notion of scientific progress, challenged, for example, in Kuhn's (1962) seminal text *The Structure of Scientific Revolutions* (according to which a given worldview or a scientific paradigm is replaced by a new one without any need for continuity). Worrall supports the claims of discontinuity in scientific theories, but argues that 'most of the mathematical content of superseded mature theories has been retained in the successor theories, and that this retention marks an important non-empirical continuity in science' (Psillos, 2005: 140). In other words, there is a continuity when it comes to mathematical equations (i.e., continuity at the formal mathematical level) but not at the level of description, mechanisms, and underlying causes.

The structural realist 'insists that it is a mistake to think that we can ever "understand" the *nature* of the basic furniture of the universe' (Worrall, 1989: 122). In contrast to the view of the scientific realist that scientific theories furnish us with *true* explanations of the world, the structural realist's response would go something like this: 'in view of the theory's enormous empirical success, the structure of the universe is (probably) something like quantum mechanical' (1989: 123). Hence the claims of structural realists are vastly more moderate than those of scientific realists. In the science of mathematics, for example, Bokulich and Bokulich (2011) note that *structure* denotes the relations captured in theory's equations. The authors further explain that there is a shift from a commitment to the existence of phenomena (e.g., electrons) toward the reality of the relations between phenomena. Therefore there is not much to be said either about the ontological status of 'electrons' or epistemic objectivity. The common epistemic and ontic features of structural realism (abbreviated as ESR and OSR) are summarized by French and Ladyman (2011: 27) as follows:

1. ESR and OSR both involve a commitment to the claim that science is progressive and cumulative and that the growth in our structural knowledge of the world goes beyond a knowledge of empirical regularities.
2. ESR and OSR both depart from standard scientific realism in rejecting the term-by-term reference of theories, and hence standard referential semantics, and any account of approximate truth based on it.
3. According to both OSR and ESR, scientific theories do not give us knowledge of the intrinsic natures of unobservable individual objects. (To this, we may add that they do give us knowledge of the structures in which the alleged objects are said to stand.)[6]

Continuing with the topic of structural realism, Grover Maxwell (1962) argued that the line between observables and unobservables (i.e., observational and theoretical entities) is diffuse, accidental, and largely dependent on available instruments. In his view, any attempt to separate the two of these has no ontological significance: '[T]here is, in principle, a continuous series beginning with looking through a vacuum and containing these as members: looking through a window-pane, looking through glasses, looking through binoculars, looking through a low-power microscope, looking through a high-power microscope, etc., in the order given' (1962: 7).

To be clear, Maxwell did not attempt to dispute realism; he merely did not see the difference to be as significant as others claimed it was. Ladyman explains that he meant to 'vindicate and not to revise the ontological commitments of scientific realism' (2014: section 3.2, para. 3), and that what he sought to accomplish was to make scientific realism compatible with *concept empiricism*.[7] As with the structural realists, to Maxwell, the knowledge of entities that are unobservable was limited to their structural properties, but there was 'no a priori or philosophical criteria for separating the observable from the unobservable' (Maxwell, 1962: 11). This leads Ladyman to remark that Maxwell's is the 'purest structuralism possible, for the notion of structure employed refers to the higher-order properties of a theory, those that are only expressible in purely formal terms' (2014: section 3.2, para. 2).

Bas van Fraassen's constructive empiricism

Empiricism took a 'constructive' turn with Bas van Fraassen. The key difference between scientific realism and *constructive empiricism* is that scientific realism aims at *true* depictions of reality – regardless of whether or not its features are observable – while constructive empiricism is more cautious about unobservable phenomena (Monton & Mohler, 2012): 'It says that the aim of science is not truth as such but only empirical adequacy, that is, truth with respect to the observable phenomena' (van Fraassen, 1989: 192).

Van Fraassen maintained that there ought to be a distinction between *observables* and *unobservables*, a position that earned him the label of anti-realist. According to his understanding, scientific realism demanded that 'scientific theory construction aims to give us a literally true story of what the world is like, and that acceptance of a scientific theory involves the belief that it is true' (van Fraassen, 1999: 322). Yet he saw a vast difference between studying, say, the Moon, and objects of nature that are not observable. To make his point about the problem with unobservables, he deployed a simple analogy. Van Fraassen compared subatomic particles (e.g., electrons) in a cloud chamber to a vapour trail left in the sky by a passing jet. Because one sees both the jet and the vapour, one sees the cause (the jet moving through the air) and the effect (the vapour). However, the same does not hold for unobservable particles. Theoretical physicists may observe some effects, but not their cause. Van Fraassen compared this to looking to the sky and seeing only the vapour but not the jet, leaving us to wonder what may have caused the vapour. Similarly, when observing micro-particles, 'while the particle is detected by means of the cloud chamber, and the detection is based on observation, it is clearly not a case of the particle being observed' (van Fraassen, 1980: 17). This is the basis for one of his main arguments: that observable evidence is not sufficient for determining the *truth* of theories about unobservables. The best we can hope for, as Bird (2004: 321) explains of van Fraassen, 'is a theory which is *empirically adequate* – one which generates true predictions about observables'. Theories may give us satisfying answers as to how things work and yet not be 'true' accounts of reality. Formulating the ideas of constructive empiricism more carefully, Kocklemans asserts that 'a theory is empirically adequate if and only if such a theory has at least one model into which all the actual (and not just the actually observed) phenomena fit' (1993: 132). Monton and Mohler further comment on the (solely) explanatory power of theories held by constructive empiricists:

> Indeed, one can recognize the explanatory power of a theory without taking it to be true. Van Fraassen points out that theories can explain well even if they are false. Newton's theory of gravitation explains the motion of the planets and the tides, 'Huygens's theory explained the diffraction of light, Rutherford's theory of the atom explained the scattering of alpha particles, Bohr's theory explained the hydrogen spectrum, Lorentz's theory explained clock retardation.' But none of these theories is now thought to be true. (Monton & Mohler, 2012: section 2.5, para. 3)

Following the long tradition of empiricism, we can say that van Fraassen remains dubious about the unobservable aspects of the world and is not prepared to fully commit to realist ontology and epistemology. Nonetheless, constructive empiricism is a semantically realist thesis; it is in agreement with scientific realism about the idea that terms refer to objects. It is also worth noting that van Fraassen raises objections against scientific realism as well as logical empiricism. As Hacking (1983: 51) explains, van Fraassen does not subscribe to the method of verificationism; in this respect, he is 'anti-cause', and downplays the explanatory power of scientific theories. Hacking comments that 'against the logical positivists, van Fraassen says that theories are to be taken literally. There is no other way to take them! Against the realist he says that we need not believe theories to be true' (1983: 50). Given that scientific realism aims at giving us true knowledge of the world as it really is about both its observable and unobservable aspects, van Fraassen is epistemologically and ontologically *weak*. He sees the role of scientific theories to be prediction, control, research, and sheer enjoyment (Hacking, 1983).

Of course, scientific realists committed to the existence of unobservable entities would disagree with van Fraassen's treatment of scientific realism, such as Devitt, who has, in fact, described it as 'agnostic' (1984: 142). In Devitt's view, due to the continual improvement of technologies, it has become possible to make more and more objects visible, and we have 'good inductive grounds for supposing that there exist objects which we cannot now see' (1984: 143). The more we learn about the unobservable world, then, 'the more we will be able to explain about the observed world' (1984: 143).

Surrealism

The notion of empirical adequacy is also advocated in Leplin's (1987, 1997) *surrealism* or 'surrogate realism'. This thesis addresses the problem of the success of scientific theories, claiming that theories are successful because they are empirically adequate. It is a much weaker thesis than scientific realism, which takes scientific theories to be true and accurate representations. Ontologically, surrealism does not deny that there may be deeper structures and governing laws, but it goes no further than that. In epistemology, it rejects the claim that scientific theories are truly representative. In the words of Leplin, 'the best that can be said for any representation is that the actual structure produces the observable effects that it would produce were that representation true of it. The explanation of the success of any theory, however great and exceptionless, is that the actual structure of the world operates at the experiential level as if the theory represented it correctly' (1997: 26). According to surrealism, then, it cannot be decided whether the theories that represent the deeper structures of reality are true. Leplin's surrealism seems compatible with moderate ontological realism (in that it allows for the existence of structures, governing laws, and facts), but incompatible with epistemic realism (in that we cannot know the truth of theoretical statements). Leplin puts it as follows: 'Surrealism tries to strike a middle ground between the success it would explain and the realism it would supplant' (1997: 27). The 'surrogates' for truth are empirical adequacy and the reliability of theories, but these are not meant to be interpreted as a replacement for the notion of 'truth'. Truth, in Leplin's view, is '*not* achievable (except, perhaps, by unknowing happenstance)' (1997: 28).

Internal realism

It would be a major omission not to at least briefly note the American philosopher and mathematician Hilary Putnam, whose philosophical position has evolved over his scholarly career from *metaphysical realism* to *internal realism* to pragmatist-inclined *direct realism*. Baghramian (2009) comments that the early Putnam was a scientific and metaphysical realist for whom scientific statements were either true or false descriptions of reality. Later, he developed the more nuanced stance of *internal realism*, whereby objects were no longer representation-independent. Towards the end of his career he became an advocate of *direct realism*, which can be understood as a modified theory of perception. He rejected the subject–object divide, arguing instead for immediate knowledge of the external world by our senses. Putnam's philosophical journey is interesting and perhaps capricious from a philosophical point of view and considering the radical change in his thought. He started as a *scientific realist* and accepted the notion of mind-independent, objective reality; in the 1970s he modified his outlook to accommodate *internal realism,* where any talk of a world that was independent of a human's mind seemed absurd; and he finally embraced 'natural' or direct realism in the 1990s (Baghramian, 2013; Braver, 2007). It is necessary to point out here that despite his evolving philosophy, in all stages of his work Putnam remained a realist about the external world (he used the term 'natural realist'). As he explains:

> A natural realist, in my sense, does hold that the objects of (normal, 'veridical') perception are 'external' things, and, more generally, aspects of 'external' reality. [...] [S]uccessful perception is *sensing* of aspects of the reality 'out there' and not a mere affectation of a person's subjectivity by those aspects. (1999: 10)

It is clear that Putnam did not deny that the external world exists, indeed he maintained that it is knowable. He did, nevertheless, came to challenge the notion of mind-independence. Because of this 'loss' of objective knowledge, some critics take internal realism to be an idealist doctrine. Sankey, for example, writes that 'for the internalist, the way the world is is not something that is independent of what we think. Rather, the way the world is depends on our being justified in thinking that it is a certain way' (2008: 115). Others have compared Putnam's philosophy to transcendental idealism (Brown, 1988), and yet others to transcendental nominalism[8] (Hacking, 1983). Hacking's summary of Putnam's view is perhaps the most apt:

> Putnam's internal realism comes to this: Within my system of thought I refer to various objects, and say things about those objects, some true, some false. However, I can never get outside my system of thought, and maintain some basis for reference which is not part of my own system of classification and naming. That is precisely empirical realism and transcendental nominalism. (1983: 109)

Putnam's ideas, although not widely popular, are kept alive by a handful of philosophers. One of the contemporary defenders of internal realism is Gábor Forrai (2001: 8), who describes it in terms of three key commitments: (1) the world is dependent on the human mind; (2) truth is not completely independent of verification; and (3) the world can be approached through many conceptual schemes. Forrai, like Putnam, maintains that the external world exists independent of our mind as far as causal relationships are concerned (e.g., it rains regardless of whether we think it does), but is determined structurally by human beings. The kinds, categories, and organization of the world are dependent on the mind, imposed by the mind. In epistemology and semantics, Forrai seems to be a pluralist – allowing many conceptual schemes, and hence, many interpretations of the world. Overall, there is a lot more that could be said about Putnam's philosophy (and indeed of all the thinkers noted in this section), but due to the limited space available, qualitative researchers interested in the thesis of internal realism may need to follow up with additional reading on Putnam and Forrai.

Instrumentalism

Instrumentalism is the philosophical thesis that eliminates *truth* as a necessary component of scientific theory. The instrumentalists hold that a scientific theory should be evaluated in terms of its usefulness or convenience, downplaying its epistemic significance. As Fuller remarks, they 'ground the rationality of the scientific enterprise on something other than search for underlying causal mechanisms, such as the reliable generation of empirical regularities' (1993: 147). Ladyman (2002) gives an example of early instrumentalism by referring to Copernicus's heliocentric model of the planets and the publication of his *On the Revolutions of the Celestial Spheres* in 1543. During that time the Catholic Church followed the Ptolemaic system, in which the Earth was a still centre of the universe. Copernicus's model of a Sun-centred solar system was far too radical for this time, and his ideas were deemed heretical and banned for the centuries to come. Instrumentalism comes into play in Andreas Osiander's preface to the first publication of the book, where, in anticipation of tensions and criticisms on the part of the Church, he stated that the model was a 'convenient assumption' and needed to be regarded only as 'a mathematical fiction' (Ladyman, 2002: 17). Ladyman points to Osiander's caveat, in its suggestion that scientific theories do not have to be true descriptions of the world but convenient 'fictions' (that model the observables), as an example of an early instrumentalist statement.

Instrumentalism as a competing philosophical view to scientific realism was developed largely by Pierre Duhem (1861–1916), a French philosopher of science. Duhem (1969) distinguished between explanatory and representative theories, and argued that physical theories can be only regarded as *representative*. For a physical theory to be explanatory, it would have to succumb to metaphysics and lose its autonomy (Ariew, 2013). To fully grasp what Duhem was suggesting, we need to understand that he fundamentally rejected the notion of science as being in the business of explaining phenomena or accurately describing reality. In this regard, Psillos clarifies that 'for Duhem the very idea of looking behind the "veil of appearances" belongs to the realm of metaphysics' and that 'science is concerned only with experiences, and as such it is not an explanation' (1999: 26). In this way, the scientific theories in physics, for example, do not 'explain' phenomena, instead they ought to be treated as a system of propositions that aim to 'represent' experimental laws. Therefore physics 'aims only to embed descriptions of the phenomena in a mathematical framework' (Psillos, 2005: 27). Following the instrumentalist outlook, there may be different theories and mathematical systems capable of representing experience (e.g., Newton's law of universal gravitation and Einstein's theory of General Relativity; the Ptolemaic model and the Copernican system, etc.) that are more or less convenient or *empirically adequate*. The scientific realist, of course, would say that they are either true or false explanations. In other words, the Ptolemaic model is wrong and the Copernican system is true. The difference between instrumentalism and scientific realism is illustrated in Figure 5.2.

Finally, instrumentalism can further be subdivided into two additional varieties: *eliminative* and *non-eliminative* instrumentalism. Eliminative instrumentalism is the stronger view that purports theories do not represent 'anything "deeper" than experience, because, ultimately, there is nothing deeper than experience to

Figure 5.2 Instrumentalism vs Scientific Realism (adapted from Psillos, 1999)

represent' (Psillos, 2005: 15). Following our earlier distinction between the varieties of realism in Table 5.1, this view lacks any commitment to the existence of unobservable entities – hence weak ontological realism. Ernst Mach's (1919: x) conception of the nature of science as 'economy of thought' is a prime example of this thesis. The *non-eliminative* variety, to which Duhem and the contemporary instrumentalists subscribe, is at least moderately realist. Psillos explains that 'one does not need to assume that there is an unobservable reality behind the phenomena, nor that science aims to describe it, in order to do science and to do it successfully' (2005: 15). Consequently, instrumentalists treat unobservable entities and phenomena, such as electrons and black holes, as *instruments* 'whose value consists in their ability successfully to predict what can be observed, rather than in their description of the fundamental structure of reality' (Ladyman, 2002: 266). A number of theoretical physicists, such as Bohr and Heisenberg, were instrumentalists, as we will see in the following chapter. As far as realism is concerned, Psillos describes Duhem-inspired instrumentalism as a 'realist-enough position' (2005: 35), based on Duhem's acceptance of the ability of science to reveal 'real relations among unobservable entities', and his belief in the scientific enterprise as progressing toward showing us that 'the world is as the theory says it is'. At the same time, he adds the following caveat: 'There is no reason to suppose that we shall ever attain such a perfect theory' (2005: 35).

Instrumentalism, pragmatism and realism in the social sciences

Instrumentalism and pragmatism are closely related responses to scientific realism, initially developed by an American philosopher, John Dewey (1859–1952), whose philosophy will preoccupy us in this section. Charles Sanders Peirce (1839–1914) and William James (1842–1910) are the other two figures credited with establishing the philosophical tradition of pragmatism. Dewey was an immensely prolific thinker whose scholarly contributions surpass our sole focus on the philosophy of science and the concerns of ontology, epistemology, and semantics. His influence extends to moral and political philosophy, social and political theory, education, ethics, aesthetics, and religion. We will only examine the ways in which instrumentalism and pragmatism feature in his work.

A fundamental pillar on which Dewey's philosophy is erected is the objection to the notion of knowledge as 'truth'. In *Logic: The Theory of Inquiry*, Dewey states that 'knowledge, as an abstract term, is a name for the product of competent inquiries. Apart from this relation, its meaning is so empty that any content or filling may be arbitrarily poured in' (1938: 8). In his opinion, the theories produced by scientists were to be seen, instead, as 'arising from an active adaptation of the human organism to its environment' (Field, 2015: para. 1). Knowledge is not a passive process whereby the human mind is a Lockean 'blank canvas', rather it is an active process, with human beings taking centre stage, actively grasping and cognitively organizing the world. As Field explains:

> On this view, inquiry should not be understood as consisting of a mind passively observing the world and drawing from this ideas that if true correspond to reality, but rather as a process which initiates with a check or obstacle to successful human action, proceeds to active manipulation of the environment to test hypotheses, and issues in a re-adaptation of organism to environment that allows once again for human action to proceed. (2015: para. 1)

Knowledge, therefore, is intrinsically human, practical, and transformative, and ought to be considered as an instrument for solving problems. This epistemic vision, as well as Dewey's distinctive view of philosophy, are well captured in Eldridge's (1998) statement that Dewey's pragmatist philosophy is a philosophy which does not deal with the problem of philosophers, but rather should be cultivated by philosophers to deal with the problems of humans. Put another way, Dewey's philosophy is a civic philosophy and a tool for solving human problems. Knowledge and 'truth', when viewed in this light, are notably different from the (narrow) realist and positivist conceptions of scientific knowledge as an objective, true description of reality. It follows that, for the pragmatist, it is impossible to disentangle the experience of human beings from the social and natural environment they inhabit. In fact, this is precisely what pragmatism seeks to avoid.

Locating Dewey's philosophical allegiances on an ontological level is a more challenging task, and as with Hilary Putnam his evolving thought is best appreciated chronologically. Dewey can be described both as an idealist and a weak realist. He did not challenge the existence of the external world and its objects, nor did he believe that the human mind could determine what there is. However, he rejected the realist view of mind-independent, objective knowledge, and as argued by Hildebrand, 'could not accept New Realism's insistence upon the stark and absolute independence of things from thoughts' (2003: 19). As we have seen in the previous chapters, the denial of a mind-independent world is a philosophy grounded in idealism. The early Dewey, we are told by Field (2015), was committed to neo-Kantian idealism and influenced by a German-trained Hegelian philosopher, George Sylvester Morris, but the latter Dewey was more interested in experimental methods and scientifically based naturalism. It was during his time at the University of Chicago that he finally replaced idealism with 'an empirically based theory of knowledge that was in concert with the then developing American school of thought known as pragmatism' (Field, 2015: section 1, para. 5).

Apart from the trio of Dewey, James, and Peirce, pragmatism has featured in the philosophy of numerous minds, including George H. Mead, Jane Addams, Alain L. Locke, F.C.S. Schiller, C.I. Lewis, W.V. Quine, Hilary Putnam, Jürgen Habermas, Richard Rorty, and others (for a comprehensive overview see Shook & Margolis, 2006). A list as varied as this one would suggest it to be a wasteful attempt to reduce pragmatism to a single paradigm. Pragmatist thought traverses various philosophical domains (e.g., realism, relativism, pluralism, idealism, absolute idealism, and rationalism), traditions, and movements (e.g., philosophical hermeneutics, critical theory, feminism). Pragmatism is first and foremost to be understood in a much broader sense as a North American philosophical tradition that flourished during the twentieth century, and which 'supplemented, consolidated, and expanded the focus from hermeneutics and phenomenology' (Brinkmann et al., 2014: 23). In this respect, it had a profound influence on the establishment of sociology as a discipline in North America and on the developments of the Chicago School. Brinkmann et al. note that the Chicago sociologists were interested in the practical and empirical side of sociological inquiry, and were 'keen to get out and study social life directly, often by use of participant observation' (2014: 25). Thus, making sense of pragmatism in its breadth and scope requires that researchers be familiar with its historical contexts as well as its various proponents.

Pragmatist approaches are generally popular in the social sciences, and hence among qualitatively minded scholars and in mixed-method research (e.g., Tashakkori & Teddlie, 2010). Creswell, for instance, acknowledges that there are different forms of pragmatism, but suggests that its use in qualitative research rests in employing multiple methods and sources of data collection, a focus on practical implications, and an emphasis on 'conducting research that best addresses the research problem' (2013: 29). Patton further describes pragmatism in terms of 'methodological appropriateness' whereby methods are judged appropriate to different situations and interests (2002: 72). In addition, Brinkmann et al. (2014) see pragmatism as useful in explorative qualitative studies and compatible with Glaser and Strauss's *The Discovery of Grounded Theory* (1967).[9] And finally, but not exhaustively, pragmatism has been also explained as the philosophical foundation for *action research* (Levin & Greenwood, 2011). As to the question of how 'best' to implement pragmatism, following Dewey's line of thought there is no 'best', only degrees of usefulness. Taken as an approach to research, pragmatism cannot belong to only a single tradition; it is open to multiple strategies, methodologies, and methods, the choices of which are driven by the research problem.

Realism and critical realism in the social sciences

Besides the kinds of realisms that centred around the discourse on natural phenomena, there are other varieties more suitable for social scientists, such as *critical realism*, advocated by Roy Bhaskar (1997) and others (e.g., Archer et al., 1998). Critical realism treats social realities, social facts, and social structures as real and mind-independent – in a sense, as *a priori* to human agency. Agency, however, remains necessary for the continued maintenance and alteration of existing structures. Critical realism is a varied doctrine in that it draws on a number of approaches: 'In its emphasis on underlying patterns, critical realism shares some tangential points with hermeneutics and critical theory; in its searching for some kind of scientific laws, and in its view of the commonality of social science and natural science research, it shares ground with positivism' (Alvesson & Sköldberg, 2000: 16).

Critical realism offered specifically as a philosophical perspective for qualitative researchers has been tackled, for instance by Maxwell (2012), who distances himself from Bhakasar's reading of critical realism, and presents it as a combination of realist ontology (described as the belief in a mind-independent real world) and a constructivist epistemology (described as the view that knowledge is individually constructed and lacking objectivity). Furthermore, critical realists treat not only physical objects but also ideas, meanings, concepts and intentions as equally real. This way, mental phenomena, Maxwell argues, are 'inextricably involved in the causal processes that produce behaviour and social phenomena' (2012: 16). In the following chapter we will explore the topic of social ontology in order to better understand the possibility of social reality (not just the claim that something is socially constructed), and to show that for some analytical philosophers, such as John Searle, social and natural facts are not one and the same. They are not, and ought not, to be treated as equal. In fact we will see that Searle makes the opposite argument to Maxwell and other critical realists: that social facts are ontologically relative but epistemically objective.

Summary and implications for qualitative research

This chapter sought to highlight the differences between positivism, postpositivism, and scientific realism. It has been argued that scientific realism is the strongest philosophical stance, the one which allows us to know the world as it *truly* is, even its unobservable and theoretical aspects. Although positivism and postpositivism enjoyed popularity for a large part of the twentieth century, increasing doubt about both approaches eventually led to their downfall. The verificationist programme promoted by the positivists, and the falsification methods offered by the postpositivists as a better solution to scientific knowledge, were not able to withstand the critical attacks. One of the reasons for this, Laudan points out, was that verificationism and falsificationism were simultaneously too permissive and too restrictive: on the one hand 'they countenanced *as scientific* many claims that palpably were not', and on the other 'they denied scientific status to many claims that were patently scientific' (1996: 23). Eventually, positivism and postpositivism became too limiting to account for scientific knowledge. In the words of Laudan, 'the verificationists had to deny the scientific status of all universal scientific theories, while the Popperians had to deny the scientificity of singular existential claims – for instance, that there are black holes' (1996: 23).

Despite the fact that Popper was a rationalist and a realist, and although some (e.g., Leplin, 2007) see him as a scientific realist (mainly due to his realist conception of scientific goals), the temporariness and uncertainty of scientific theories – stripping them of any glimpse of absolute certitude – coupled with the substitution of *truth* with the notion of *verisimilitude* render his view of scientific theories as somewhat unstable. For this reason, the *strong* scientific realists find the method of falsificationism difficult to reconcile with scientific realism. We recall that for Popper science is 'not the search for universal or objective truth, but a method, a set of logical procedures for the constructions or testing of hypotheses, a process of "trial and error"' (Smith, 1998: 108). It has been suggested that an elegant solution to understanding Popper within the realist framework can be found in Nola's (1988) distinction between the different domains of realism and their stronger and weaker varieties. By Nola's scheme, Popper remains a realist, but is not the strongest contender for realism. Table 5.1 makes it easier to grasp that one can be a realist in a multitude of ways. The strongest in the realist conviction are not the positivists or the postpositivists, but scientific realists. To underscore the extent to which scientific realists think of positivism as an inferior doctrine, we only need to consider what Musgrave has to say on the matter:

> We think poorly of a person who 'explains' why the light goes on when we press the switch by saying "it is just a lucky accident". And we should think equally poorly of the positivist who says the same thing of science's (novel) predictive success. (1988: 240)

The common thread in all the philosophical positions noted in this chapter, apart perhaps from Hilary Putnam's *internal realism*, is that they all conform to a form of realism. It is important to emphasize that anti-*scientific* realism is not to be confused with immaterialism or idealism. The way in which the term 'anti-*scientific* realism' has been employed here, as is typical in the philosophy of science (often called simply 'anti-realism'), is to capture various objections to scientific realism that have to do with truth correspondence, the existence of unobservable and theoretical entities, the aim of science, and so forth.

One question is whether we have to be realists about everything, some things, or perhaps nothing at all. The philosophical viewpoints covered thus far should be of some help. To deny reality altogether and hold that it is only one's mind that exists is a commitment to the doctrine of *solipsism*. To deny the possibility of knowing anything is to invoke *scepticism*. To argue that all that exists are ideas or sense data would classify us as *idealists*. The acknowledgement of the external world in its most basic sense is an appeal to materialism or metaphysical realism. If we accept specific kinds and entities, we claim allegiance to strong ontological realism. As for the question, then, of whether we have to believe in anything at all, it would appear that we do, unless we are prepared to defend our views as idealists or solipsists. On this, Vernes argues that we need to adopt the doctrine of materialism if we are to believe in the existence of others and 'provide a reasonable explanation of experience' (2000: 97). Sokal and Bricmont make a similar point when they state that 'unless one is a solipsist or a radical sceptic – which nobody really is – one has to be a realist about *something*: about objects in everyday life, or about the past, dinosaurs, stars, viruses, whatever' (2004: 37). But being a realist about something – and this is a key point – does not place one in a rigid paradigm box. This chapter has demonstrated that there are different domains, degrees of commitment, and subtle varieties of realism. This means that scholars are free to weave intricate and sophisticated philosophical patterns that best reflect their views – views that may indeed change over time, as we have seen with Hilary Putnam.

Using realism in qualitative research

Realism can feature in qualitative inquiry in numerous ways. It is most often found in the discourse surrounding philosophical assumptions, such as in Table 5.1 (in this chapter) and Table 1.1 (in Chapter 1). In this respect, this book concentrates solely on epistemic and metaphysical concerns, as heralded by its title. However, realism can also be embedded in one's research design all the way down – extending to methodological and methods-related decisions, to informing the research question, to deliberating the study's value to various stakeholders. Those qualitative scholars leaning towards a *strong* realist conception of research, but unsure of how to implement scientific realism in their own praxis, may find Pawson and Tilley's (1997) insights of much practical value. The authors demonstrate the ways in which qualitative methods (in particular, structured, unstructured, and what they term the 'realist interview') can be used in Realistic Evaluation research. Realistic Evaluation research is popular among practitioners and policy makers, and is mostly used in exploratory case studies and realist sample surveys to develop theories. The objective of realist inquiry, Pawson and Tilley note, is 'to explain social "regularities", "rates", "associations", "outcomes", "patterns"' (1997: 71). Notably, what lies at the heart of their realist approach is explanation and causation. As a way of contrasting it with other methodologies, consider, say, phenomenological studies that seek to describe essences of phenomena. Phenomenology and other inductive approaches are descriptive (i.e., they describe phenomena) as opposed to explanatory research that aims at understanding relationships, causes and effects. The basic logic of realist explanation is articulated in the textbox below.

Pawson and Tilley's (1997: 71) articulation of the logic of realist explanation

The basic task of social inquiry is to explain interesting, puzzling, socially significant regularities (R). Explanation takes the form of positing some underlying mechanisms (M) which generates the regularity and thus consists of propositions about how the interplay between structure and agency has constituted the regularity. Within realist investigation there is also an investigation of how the workings of such mechanisms are contingent and conditional, and thus only fired in particular local, historical or institutional contexts (C).

We can see in the definition provided by Pawson and Tilley above that, in a similar fashion to that of critical realism, Realist Evaluation takes into account both agency and structure, whereby individuals have the freedom to make choices but are, nonetheless, impacted by wider collective social constraints. Moreover, the notion of 'contexts' injects a sense of hermeneutic sensibility into their realist approach, as causes for various social problems do not apply universally and in all scenarios; rather, they are context-specific.

To conclude, in this chapter we have explored realism with regard to ontology, epistemology and semantics, and offered some additional alternatives that qualitative researchers can draw upon when (in)forming their philosophical assumptions about what there is, what can be known about it, and whether the statements and propositions truly describe the world as it is. Much of the terrain covered thus far has concentrated on natural phenomena and natural facts, yet these are not the same, some would argue, as social phenomena and social facts. In order to avoid making muddled arguments about reality, it is necessary to differentiate between that which is natural and that which is social. Chapter 6 is dedicated precisely to this task.

Recommended reading

Devitt, M. (1984) *Realism and Truth*. Oxford: Blackwell.
Emmel, N. (2013) *Sampling and Choosing Cases in Qualitative Research: A Realist Approach*. London: SAGE.
Ladyman, J. (2002) *Understanding Philosophy of Science*. London: Taylor & Francis.
Laudan, L. (1996) *Beyond Positivism and Relativism: Theory, Method, and Evidence*. Cumnor Hill: Westview.
Nola, R. (ed.) (1988) *Relativism and Realism in Science*. Dordrecht, The Netherlands: Kluwer Academic.

Pawson, R. & Tilley, N. (1997) *Realistic Evaluation*. London: SAGE.

Stroll, A. (2000) *Twentieth-Century Analytic Philosophy*. New York: Columbia University Press.

Wrigley, A. (2007) Realism and anti-realism about mental illness. *Philosophical Papers*, 36 (3): 371-97.

Notes

1. Extravagant in that Goodman claimed that multiple worlds exist – and not just in a semantic sense!
2. Verisimilitude is a term used by Karl Popper; it means close proximity to truth, good approximation to truth, or being near to the truth (see Popper, 1972, 1999b).
3. Here Laudan (1996) lists figures such as Kuhn, Feyerabend, Wittgenstein, Goodman, Rorty, and the late Quine as postpositivist philosophers.
4. Strictly speaking, with the help of telescopes we can only *infer* the existence of exoplanets and distant galaxies because of the gravitational effects. Gravity deflects light passing through galaxies – a phenomenon called gravitational lensing. See, for example, www.nasa.gov/press/2014/october/nasa-s-hubble-finds-extremely-distant-galaxy-through-cosmic-magnifying-glass
5. A quick summary of the Standard Model can be found on the website of the European Organization for Nuclear Research: http://home.web.cern.ch/about/physics/standard-model
6. As pointed out by Robert Nola after reading an early draft of this chapter.
7. Concept empiricism is the view that concepts derive from experience, that is, that they are grounded in perception. This idea can be traced to the work of Aristotle, Locke, and Hume. Aristotle argued that there 'is no idea without an image'; Locke and Hume's notion of ideas was of 'abstracted or copied forms of impression' (see Prinz, 2010: 184).
8. Nominalism, as used by Hacking, means that one does not have to deny external reality as existing independently, only that it is 'naturally and intrinsically sorted in any particular way, independent of how we think about it' (Hacking, 1983: 108).
9. The authors argue that grounded theory was 'one of the first self-denoted and systematically described qualitative methodologies – in which the purpose is to create workable scientific knowledge that can be applied to daily life situations' (Brinkmann et al., 2014: 24).

PART III
Intangible Realities

We have sought for firm ground and found none. The deeper we penetrate, the more restless becomes the universe, and the vaguer and cloudier.

(Max Born, *The Restless Universe*, 1951)

Six

Social Ontology

Thus far, our exploration has focused largely on the philosophical problems concerning knowledge and the reality of the external world. Whether it was the early Greeks, the medieval scholastics, the Enlightenment thinkers, or the relatively recent doctrines of positivism, postpositivism, idealism, and scientific realism, much of the philosophical inquiry over the centuries concentrated on mathematics and physical objects observable in nature. In this chapter, we will depart from the discourse on the physical, natural, and tangible world, and move to examining socially and culturally constituted realities. The philosophical problems tackled up to this point should serve us well in this venture, for we now have the necessary tools to discern the differences between the study of that which is *natural* and that which is *social*. We also are now familiar with materialism and immaterialism or metaphysical realism and idealism, direct and indirect realism, and importantly, the epistemic thesis of idea-ism. Without a clear understanding of how empiricism and realism, for example, transpired in the processes of knowledge production in the natural sciences, we would only be able to make vague and muddled claims about social phenomena.

To eliminate any confusion, this chapter does not deal with Karl Marx's (1918–1883) social ontology (i.e., the categories of labour, freedom, individuals, relations, and justice) and the critique of political economy, nor with Max Weber's (1864–1920) political theory of authority, Émile Durkheim's (1858–1917) notion of social facts,[1] critical theory, or neo-Marxist accounts of contemporary social realities. Rather, the premise of this chapter is purely ontological and epistemic: it deals with the possibility of social reality, as opposed to the 'additional theoretical concerns' that were separated out in our summary of core philosophical concerns in Chapter 1 (Figure 1.3, Tier 4). While the latter undoubtedly shapes how humans relate to one another and social life in general, this is not the focus point in this chapter. We simply wish to examine, in Searle's words, 'how is it possible in a universe consisting entirely of physical particles in fields of force that there can be such things as consciousness, intentionality, free will, language, society, ethics, aesthetics, and political obligations?' (2010: 3). In other words, our purpose here is mainly philosophical.

Apart from outlining the basic elements of social ontology, the more profound argument put forward here is for social ontology to be recognized as one of the key concerns in qualitative research. It is contended that, at a fundamental level, *all* qualitative inquiry deals with socially constructed realities. Social constructionism has carried a stigma due to misinformed ideas about its claims, in particular a widespread belief that all proponents of constructionism stand united in a philosophical view that has been variously labelled as idealism, subjectivism, and even solipsism. In order to correct this misconception and demonstrate some of the key differences between streams of constructionism, we will draw a contrast between the views of John Searle and Kenneth J. Gergen, who are both vocal about the constructed nature of certain aspects of the world and among the more prominent contemporary contributors to the literature on constructionism.[2] Along the way, we will address the problem of objectivity and scrutinize the extent to which social facts can be said to exist objectively or relatively, and whether they can be epistemically objective.

Articulating the need for social ontology in qualitative research

Qualitative researchers find themselves having to navigate problems of philosophy of science, and in so doing, have organized various philosophical stances into convenient schemas. Most models, however, fail to distinguish the differences between the ontological and epistemological problems inherent in the study of the natural world, and the issues relevant to the study of social realities. The problem before us can be formulated as follows: not only are there views about atoms, rocks, and trees, which may or may not exist and be known in light of the views discussed in the previous chapters, there are also social facts, which form a different ontological category. Therefore, in regard to ontology and metaphysics, as part of their efforts to articulate philosophical assumptions, qualitative scholars ought to concentrate more on the neglected domain of social ontology. Why? Because qualitative research is not so much concerned with understanding physical objects as it is with social reality and social phenomena.

Searle (2010) conceives of social ontology as a much broader philosophical project, and suggests that there is a need for a new branch of philosophy, which he terms *The Philosophy of Society* (2010: 5). This new direction, he explains, shifts the focus away from social and political philosophy or philosophy of social science and moves it to the study of the nature of human society itself. In his words, it seeks to understand 'the mode of existence of social entities such as governments, families, cocktail parties, summer vacations, trade unions, baseball games, and passports' (2010: 5). The 'Philosophy of Society' should thus become a philosophy *for* the social sciences, as opposed to a philosophy *of* the social sciences (Searle, 2010). Formulated in this way, our inquiry will take us beyond the questions of whether something is or is not constructed and into the realm of how it is possible for social facts – such as 'US dollar banknote', 'sustainability', 'blogger', 'tourism', or 'university professor'– to exist.

In a broader sense, the project of social ontology, despite its contemporary formulation and strictly philosophical undertone in the hands of Searle, finds its origin to varying degrees in the key figures of sociology (Marx, Weber, Durkheim, Mannheim, Sheler, and others), and was formulated, in theoretical terms, by Berger and Luckmann (1966). Many of the ideas advocated by Searle are compatible with those of Berger and Luckmann, although Searle's analysis aims to explicate the possibility of social reality at a much more fundamental level. For instance, Berger and Luckmann argue that 'consciousness is always intentional; it always intends or is directed towards objects', and that we can never understand consciousness in 'some putative substratum' but rather as consciousness of something, whether the object of consciousness is an external object or 'an element of an inward subjective reality' (1966: 34). They note that the realities of everyday life are *intersubjective* – they are shared and construed with others. The sociology of knowledge is therefore focused on 'what is "real" for the members of a society' and 'must concern itself with the social construction of reality' (1966: 27). Searle then moves the discourse from *what is real or constructed* to the more profound question of *how it is possible* that something like a piece of paper can become a 'social fact' and enable a person to be transported by airplane to another country and pampered and looked after on the way. We are, of course, talking about a 'boarding pass'.

We could make a bold claim and argue that it would be irrational for anyone not to accept that social realities are constructed. Unlike the natural world and the kinds of objects that can be claimed to exist independent of our minds, social realities are the product of socializing individuals. This simple recognition makes social reality fundamentally different from physical reality. Social reality hinges on the cognitive faculties of human beings, who possess the ability to assign meanings to people, objects, events, and experiences, and recognize these as collectively meaningful. Social reality comes into existence, so to speak, as the result of the relationships and behaviour among socializing human agents. Up to this level of argumentation, it should be possible for scholars of any philosophical orientation to agree on these basic tenets. This leads to the key point that the claim of social reality as constructed by humans is a claim rooted in rational thought: it would be irrational to think otherwise. We can even go so far as to argue that at this basic level of understanding social reality, we are all social constructionists.

Complications arise when this point is misunderstood. In addition to this 'baseline' notion of constructed social realities, various philosophers have extended the theory of social construction to the natural sciences (e.g., Gergen, 1998a,

1998b, 2001, 2009; Golinski, 2005; Goodman, 1978; von Glasersfeld, 1984a, 1984b; Watzlawik, 1984) and argued that scientific facts, in addition to social facts, are also constructed. In other words, we can observe different varieties and degrees of commitment to social constructionist thought. Others have commented on this being problematic (e.g., Gubrium & Holstein, 2008; Pernecky, 2012, 2014), with Kukla (2000) going to great lengths to distinguish between *scientific facts* (facts produced by the natural sciences), *social facts* (facts produced by the social sciences), *everyday facts* (facts that lie outside science), and *noumenal facts* (facts about the world which are inaccessible to us). It is by one's acceptance, denial, or combination of these facts that we can obtain what Kukla terms *very strong constructivism, strong constructivism* and *weak constructivism.*[3] When this point is missed, any scholar who asserts that social reality is constructed is generally (and mistakenly) discarded as belonging to the *very strong* or extreme variety of constructionists. A very strong social constructionist may indeed deny mind-independent reality and thus approach idealism, but they would also be a rarity.

Therefore, claiming that social realities are constructed does not make one a *sui generis* social constructionist. Instead, we must be careful to discern between (1) the baseline or weak constructionist claim that social realities are constructed (but not natural objects and scientific facts!) and the quest to formulate, in philosophical terms, how social reality is possible (e.g., Searle); (2) strong constructionism, whereby both social and physical objects are claimed to be socially constructed; and (3) the extreme or very strong social constructionist stance that rejects mind-independent reality – namely, idealism. By maintaining this distinction, we avoid the trap of simplistic generalizations. With this hurdle cleared, we can now proceed to exploring in more detail what is or is not real for various writers on social constructionism.

Constructionism and realism

There has been abundant confusion about constructionist perspectives, making it challenging for constructionism to be accepted as a legitimate way of explaining social reality and social phenomena. A large part of this misunderstanding has to do with ill-informed ideas about what is or is not claimed as 'real' under various constructionist outlooks. As noted above, this problem has been addressed elsewhere, and suffice to say that a large number of contemporary constructionists are at least *weak realists* (i.e., metaphysical realists), in the sense that they do not dispute the existence of the external world. Constructionism, apart from the extreme variety which does not concern us here, does not deny the existence of physical objects, nor do constructionists believe that we live in a dreamworld. In the words of Gergen, social constructionists 'do not say, "There is nothing" or "There is no reality" […] to be sure, something happens, but in describing it you will inevitably rely on some tradition of sense making' (2009: 4). This important point has been acknowledged in a number of scholarly works (see, for example, Burr, 1998, 2003; Gergen, 2001; Patomäki & Wright, 2000; Slife & Williams, 1995; Weinberg, 2008). Constructionism is not a thesis of immaterialism (see Figure 1.3 in Chapter 1), and as asserted by Crotty, 'those who contrast "constructionism" and "realism" are wide of the mark' (1998: 64).

What *some*, but not all, constructionists are not prepared to commit to are the definitive claims one can find in scientific realism and empiricism. This view is best demonstrated by Gergen, who asserts that constructionism 'is ontologically mute' and that 'whatever is, simply is' (1994: 72). Moreover, 'there is no foundational description to be made about an "out there" as opposed to an "in here," about experience or material' (1994: 72). Other constructionist writers, such as Burr (1998: 23), have argued that there are different meanings of the term *reality*, and that these are not consistently grounded in the same assumptions. They can vary depending on what we mean when we speak of reality: the *reality (truth)* versus *falsehood* dimension, the *reality (materiality)* versus *illusion* dimension, and the *reality (essence)* versus *construction* dimension. Unless we rise above such dichotomies, Burr argues, it is difficult to talk about a world that is both socially constructed and real at the same time.

We shall not attempt to dissect these any further here; we will simply state that social constructionism is founded upon the claim that *social realities* are constructed – which is not the same as to proclaim that the existence of external objects is not real. Material objects are part of socially constructed worlds, but 'once we attempt to articulate "what there is," [...] we enter the world of discourse. At that moment the process of construction commences, and this effort is inextricably woven into processes of social interchange and into history and culture' (Gergen, 1994: 72). Put differently, rocks and trees are not hallucinations, but our understanding of what these are is socially constructed.

Recognizing that there are varieties of social constructionism, here we must also note the realist thinkers. Searle (1996: 10), in his work *The Construction of Social Reality*, makes the existence of external reality explicit by stating that 'the sheer existence of the physical object in front of me does not depend on any attitudes we may take toward it'. Elsewhere, he maintains that 'the real, observer-independent world does not give a damn about us', and that things such as tectonic plates or hydrogen atoms 'do not become something different' when observed and interpreted by humans (Searle, 2006b: 81). Hence, both Gergen (a strong constructionist) and Searle (a very weak constructionist/scientific realist) agree on the existence of things. However, notice that Searle accepts scientific facts such as tectonic plates and hydrogen atoms. While Gergen is a metaphysical realist about the external world (i.e., there is something 'out there'), Searle is a full-blown scientific realist who accepts scientific facts produced by the natural sciences. We will contrast these two philosophers later in this chapter. For now, it is sufficient to establish that there is a distinction to be observed between Searle and Gergen.

The implication for qualitative research is that constructionism is not necessarily rooted in relativistic or idealist/immaterialist philosophy, and therefore it would be inaccurate to categorize only according to one paradigmatic conception. Social constructionists can accommodate not only metaphysical realism, as is the case for strong constructionists, but also scientific realism and epistemic objectivism, which include weak constructionists, such as Searle. The point being made here is that one can be a realist about the chemical composition of water and global warming, but not about professors and tourists. And at the very least, one can be a realist about external objects, but without committing to objective knowledge about what these are, such as Gergen.

How is social reality possible?

The nationality of Michael Jackson, a US dollar banknote, a boarding pass, a holiday, a blogger, and sustainability are all examples of socially constructed social facts (Searle, 2010). Their existence is contingent on a sufficient amount of people granting them this recognition. Consider a person in a remote village, say in a rainforest still untouched by modernity, who does not understand the concept of nationality, has never used money, and has seen some noisy objects in the air without being able to make much sense of them. For this person, these social facts would not exist in his worldview. The words 'nationality', 'banknote', and 'boarding pass' would be meaningless to him. If this example is not sufficiently convincing to demonstrate the constructed nature of social facts, we can use another which draws on some historical facts. Consider a government deciding that days in a month should be named after natural elements such as plants or animals rather than numbered. As far-fetched as this may seem, this was indeed the case during the French Revolution. The republicans rebelled against the old regimes and the Holy Scriptures and created a new calendar they felt was more representative of the values of the 'new' France. In the period between 1793 and 1805, a person could be born in the 10th hour of the day of Rose in the month of Blossom (for an interesting read, see Ozouf, 1988). Any attempt to guess the time of year this might represent is futile unless we are familiar with additional vital details. The days were divided into ten instead of twenty-four hours, the year started on the autumnal equinox (22, 23, or 24 September) instead of 1 January, and weeks lasted ten rather than seven days. In addition, the first day of the month of Blossom, for example, fell on what we call 20 or 21 April. This second example marvellously demonstrates the nature of social facts. If we were to try to rely on social facts that are not relevant in our current social reality, we would not get too far: one only needs to attempt to convince a customs officer that one was born in the month of Blossom on the day of Rose. Our social realities are socially constructed, and even though we take them for granted, all social facts are constructed, relative, and intersubjective.

Unpacking Searle's social ontology

To put it very simply, social reality exists because we believe that it exists. Searle's (1996, 2010) project seeks to demystify this remarkable feature of cognizing human beings and provide an analytic philosophical explanation. There are several concepts he deploys to explain social ontology, and although it is necessary to read his works to fully grasp them (see the recommended reading at the end of this chapter), here we will make an attempt to crudely cover at least the most important ones.

Status Function: Humans ascribe meaning to objects, events, and people, and this meaning is shared and accepted collectively. 'Status function' is a term Searle uses to capture the aspect of social reality that enables us to 'impose functions on objects and people where the objects and the people cannot perform the functions solely in virtue of their physical structure' (Searle, 2010: 7). For instance, one could not perform the function of being a tourist, a professor, or the president of the United States of America if there was no collective agreement on, and recognition of, such a status. One could indeed declare oneself to be a president, but this is not enough for it to become a social fact – it lacks collective intentionality. Status functions are therefore imperative because they 'are the glue that holds society together – they are created by collective intentionality and they function by carrying deontic powers' (Searle, 2010: 9). An important aspect of status functions is that they are not 'intrinsic to the physics of any phenomenon but are assigned from outside by conscious observers and users' (Searle, 1996: 14). In other words, there is nothing inherent in a piece of paper that determines that it is money. It becomes money when it is accepted and perceived as money. Status functions are thus observer-relative.

Collective Intentionality: In explaining status functions, we have already noted three additional concepts: collective intentionality, deontic powers, and social facts. Collective intentionality can be described as the 'collective acceptance or recognition of the object or person as having [a particular] status' (Searle, 2010: 8). Collective intentionality is different from individual intentionality in that we are no longer speaking about 'I believe' and 'I want', but about 'we believe' and 'we want' – it is a way of carrying out 'cooperative planning and acting' (2010: 43). For example, it is due to collective intentionality that a piece of paper is a banknote and that Barack Obama is the president of the United States of America.

Deontic Powers: Status functions carry what Searle calls deontic powers. Deontic power is what enables someone to use a piece of paper which we call a banknote to purchase things. Deontic power is what allows a person who is collectively recognized as the president of the United States of America to send people to war. And deontic power is what permits certain people whom we recognize as nurses to take our blood. Hence, the term captures obligations, duties, rights, permissions, requirements, authorizations, entitlements, and so forth (Searle, 2010: 9). Significantly, deontic powers 'provide reasons for action that are independent of the preexisting desires of the agent in question. They create, in short, desire-independent reasons for action' (Searle, 2014: 18). In our day-to-day lives, we are entangled in a wide range of deontic powers that can be further categorized as either 'positive' (i.e., we have certain rights) or 'negative' (i.e., we also have obligations). For example, a university student has the right to a fair assessment of assignments and to use the library, but also the obligation to attend classes and complete assignments; a professor has the duty to deliver lectures, as well as the right to get paid.

Social Facts: Social facts denote the sharing of intentional states, such as beliefs and intentions (Searle, 1996). 'US dollar banknote', 'professor', 'student', 'president of the United States', 'homework', 'sustainability', 'blogger', 'Afghan citizen' are all social facts. However, if an object is only accepted by one person as a US dollar banknote, that is not enough for it to become one. Rather, a fact must involve the 'collective intentionality of two or more animals' (Searle, 2014: 18) to be a social fact. With regard to the ontological status of social facts, *their existence is mind-dependent*; they can only exist if there is both collective intentionality and status functions. Contrary to objects such as rocks, trees, and galaxies, social facts do not come into existence in their own right through natural processes. Instead, they are created socially by the means of the cognitive faculties of individuals – that is, by collective intentionality. Examples of social facts are listed in Figure 6.1.

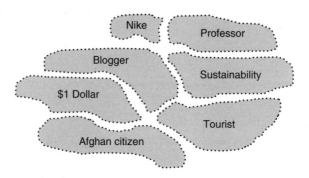

Figure 6.1 Examples of social facts

Institutional Facts: In addition to social facts, Searle also distinguishes institutional facts. To begin with a brainteaser, all institutional facts are social facts but not all social facts are institutional facts. What turns a social fact into an institutional fact is deontic power (Searle, 2014). For instance, Searle explains that it is a social fact that today is 16 October, but because this fact carries no deontic powers, it is not an institutional fact. Because there are no rights, duties, obligations, etc. (as far as we know) associated with this date, it is only a social fact. Christmas Day, on the other hand, is an institutional fact because it carries a deontology that introduces rights, obligations, and entitlements: it gives people the right to have a day off work, it obliges some people to go to church, etc. An easy way of establishing whether a social fact is an institutional fact, Searle (2014) tells us, is by considering whether there is a collectively accepted deontology associated with it. This also applies in situations where institutional facts may be created inadvertently or unconsciously. In his words, 'if treating someone in a certain way assigns that person a certain status, even though the participants may not be fully conscious of assigning this different status, and if the resulting status affects behaviour in a way that involves such things as obligations, rights, duties and responsibilities, then the participants in question have created a new institutional fact' (Searle, 2014: 24). A fundamental point about the interdependence of institutional facts and deontic powers is that there would be little point in socially creating the former without the latter. For example, calling a piece of paper 'money' without having the ability to do anything with it would not count as an institutional fact.

So far, we have established that social facts require collective intentionality, and that status functions are a key subset of social facts – ones that have been endowed with a collectively accepted status. And so objects, events, and people can be assigned status functions by a process called collective intentionality and become social facts. As little as two people can create a social fact. Whenever social facts carry deontic powers, they become institutional facts. Searle offers a summary of the key points (2014: 18):

1. All institutional facts are social facts, but not all social facts are institutional facts.
2. All institutional facts are status functions and all status functions are institutional facts. There is thus a complete equivalence between status functions and institutional facts.
3. Status functions are created, consciously or unconsciously, by a certain class of linguistic representations, speech acts that have the form of declarations where you make something the case by representing it as being the case. This special subclass of declarations I call status function declarations. All institutional facts (status functions) are both created in their initial existence and maintained in their continued existence by representations that have the logical form of status function declarations.
4. The point of doing this is to create power, and the power relations are invariably what I call deontic powers: rights, duties, obligations, etc., and these are distinctive in that for anyone who accepts the relevant status functions, the deontic powers provide reasons for action that are independent of the preexisting desires of the agent in question. They create, in short, desire-independent reasons for action.

There are two more important features of social reality which are further delineated by Searle. These include *brute facts* and *language*.

Brute Facts: What we have not yet taken into consideration are the material objects that exist in the external world, which inevitably feature as part of certain social and institutional facts. A boarding pass or money are not just ideas; they are created out of physical material. Searle calls such features of reality that exist independent of us brute facts (and variously also *intrinsic features* of the world). Brute facts are 'matters of brute physics and biology', whereas institutional facts are 'matters of culture and society' (Searle, 1996: 27). With regard to the ontological status of brute facts, they are independent of human institutions. Following Searle's views, it is a brute fact that there are sticks and rocks composed of molecules and atoms, but it is an institutional fact that there are baseball bats and sacred altars. A crude way to explain brute facts is to see them as the building blocks of some institutional facts (i.e., the institutional fact of money requires the brute facts of paper,[4] plastic, ink, and money-pressing machines).

Language: Lastly, social ontology is possible because of language. Language is not merely an element of social ontology – in Searle's view, it is necessary for institutional reality to exist. While he acknowledges that it is obvious that language is a social phenomenon used by all societies, his point is that of necessity. He proffers that 'language is not a component of social reality, so to speak, on all fours with money, property, marriage, or government. But rather, you cannot have money, property, marriage, or government without a linguistic component' (2006a: 41). Therefore, institutional facts can come into existence mainly due to humans' linguistic ability to give something a status which is not inherent in the object itself (e.g., a US dollar banknote). Language is also important in establishing deontic powers, whereby an agreed obligation to do something remains in place whether we actively think about it or not. For these reasons Searle proclaims that 'human societies require deontology, and the only way they can do this is by having language' (Searle, 2006d: 21). Many of these ideas were developed in Searle's earlier work on *speech acts* (see Searle, 1969).

To put Searle's taxonomy to use and render these ideas more digestible, consider again, the example of a boarding pass. To be allowed to board an 'airplane' as a 'tourist' and 'travel' to another 'destination', human beings have constructed an institutional fact that is collectively accepted and recognized as a 'boarding pass'. This, of course, is in addition to myriad other social and institutional facts, including the notions of tourism, travel, holiday, resort, hotel, passport, customs officer, business class, flight attendant, luggage, and so forth. The boarding pass is more than just an idea – it has a tangible form, made of paper and ink. We could also add that at the quantum level the boarding pass is made up of molecules, atoms, electrons, and other micro-particles. All of these are brute facts, whose existence does not depend on the observer, and which are ontologically real. When it comes to what the object signifies and how it is understood (its recognition as a boarding pass), we no longer speak of mind-independent brute facts but mind-dependent institutional facts. Without the specific meaning collectively intended for it, the piece of paper we have just described would cease to be a boarding pass. And therefore, its existence as a social fact is user-relative; it is contingent upon collective intentionality.

It is necessary to emphasize here that the boarding pass is not just a social fact. It is not merely something a couple of children may invent as part of a game one afternoon. The boarding pass is an institutional fact because of the deontic power it carries. It is directly linked to a range of rights, duties, obligations, and benefits. For example, it gives the owner the right to board an aircraft, to be seated in a seat

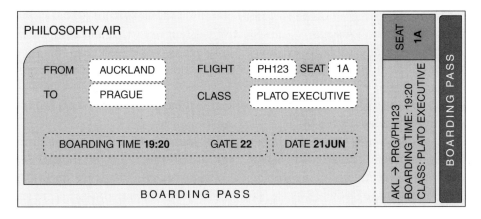

Figure 6.2 A boarding pass

marked '1A', to travel to another place (e.g., 'Prague' in Figure 6.2), and perhaps to watch a free movie. The holder of the boarding pass for flight 'PH123' has the obligation to be inside the aircraft before 19:20, to not smoke, and not endanger safety and health. She may also be entitled to additional privileges, such as the experience offered in the 'Plato Executive class'. The pilots and flight attendants, too, have responsibilities and duties, such as to serve meals and drinks and ensure the comfort of all passengers.

In summary, the existence or ontological status of the boarding pass is mind-dependent – thus observer-relative, and intersubjective. There would be no boarding passes without the collective acceptance and maintenance of the boarding pass as an institutional fact. Aside from its observer-relative features, it also includes brute facts, which are the material substances making up the boarding pass. But there is an additional twist that sets Searle apart from the stronger variety of social constructionists. He argues that social facts are *epistemically objective*. In other words, he proposes that socially constructed social and institutional facts can be known objectively.

Searle's epistemic objectivity

In all of his writing on social ontology, Searle tells us that social and institutional facts are *ontologically subjective* but *epistemically objective*. This philosophical attitude sets him apart from the anti-objectivists, epistemic relativists, and the strong variety of social constructionists. We have already established that, according to Searle, the human mind plays a crucial role in creating social facts: 'A feature is observer dependent if its very existence depends on the attitudes, thoughts, and intentionality of observers, users, creators, designers, buyers, sellers, and conscious intentional agents generally' (Searle, 2003: 196). And therefore people's shared attitudes (i.e., collective intentionality) are 'necessary to constitute something as money, movement, political parties, or final examinations' (Searle, 2010: 17). This means that we cannot speak of the objective existence of social and institutional facts, only of observer-relative existence. Nonetheless, Searle maintains that social facts are epistemically objective. He explains: 'It is not just a matter of my opinion, for example, that this piece of paper is a twenty-dollar bill; it is a matter of objective fact. But at the same time, these institutional facts exist only because of our subjective attitudes' (2010: 18).

In order for Searle to achieve the sense of objectivism he strives for, he distinguishes ontological objectivism, which typically affirms the mind-independent existence of objects, from epistemological objectivism, which claims knowledge about social facts to be objective. He clarifies by explaining that 'the statement that Vincent van Gogh died in France is epistemically objective, because its truth or falsity can be ascertained independently of the attitudes and opinions of observers' (2010: 18). On the other hand, an evaluative statement, such as 'Van Gogh was a better painter than Manet', Searle claims, is a subjective opinion. What Searle wishes to communicate is that the Olympic Games, a twenty-dollar banknote, communism, tourism, sustainability, boarding passes, and professors are epistemically objective facts – despite them all being constructed and their existence subject to collective agreement (i.e., they are ontologically relative) – because they are not matters of individual opinion. In a nutshell, we create social and institutional facts whose existence is relative to users, but once created, we can know them objectively. Hence, whether someone is a US citizen, a tourist, or a refugee, is ontologically relative, but constructions can be studied and known objectively.

Building on what we learnt in Chapter 4, we can say that Searle's epistemic objectivism is compatible with realist and objective hermeneutics: we can arrive at a true and accurate knowledge of events and texts, whereby social and cultural phenomena are believed to speak for themselves. Therefore all constructions, including historical events and the status functions ascribed to objects, people, and affairs, can be studied and known in an objective fashion. What Searle advocates is hermeneutic realism.

The problems with epistemically objective social facts

To claim the objectivity of social facts is to attract the critique of anti-realist and anti-objectivists, strong social constructionists, deconstructionists, and many a critical theorist. This claim has also been challenged within the traditions of phenomenology, hermeneutics, symbolic interactionism, and ethnography. Polanyi and Prosch, for example, proclaimed objectivity to be a 'false ideal' (1975: 31) and argued for 'personal, tacit assessments and evaluation of knowledge' (1975: 181). In Derrida's view, there are 'no absolute foundations for truth or knowledge: interpretative analysis is instead an open-ended and never ending task' (Baert et al., 2011: 477). We could go on and list the viewpoints of other anti-objectivists, such as Habermas, Foucault, Heidegger, and Gadamer, but there are already many books that perform this task well. In general, they demonstrate that the pluralists would claim that there is not one but multiple truths, the relativists that what is true is true only in one context but not necessarily in another, and the strong variety of social constructionists that there is nothing epistemically objective about social and institutional facts such as 'gender', 'race', and 'mental illness'.

Furthermore, not only have social and institutional facts been denied an epistemically objective status, they have also been argued to prejudice knowledge to begin with. In other words, scientific activities have been claimed to be influenced by social and institutional facts themselves – including race, colour, politics, sex, religion, and ideology. Therefore, knowledge does not come in pure or objective forms; what we can know is, in fact, influenced by other social and institutional facts. The critical theorists would demand that researchers fully engage with these messy entanglements and study 'truth' with caution. In qualitative research, issues of objectivity have been attacked on several fronts, and are well mapped in Denzin and Lincoln's edited volumes (1994, 1998, 2000, 2005, 2011b) and works such as *Interpretive Interactionism* (Denzin, 2001) and *Interpretive Ethnography* (Denzin, 1997). Much of the critique of epistemic objectivism rests on the counter-claim that knowledge is not free of power, politics, and various interests, and therefore, claims of epistemically objective social facts must be rejected.

To underscore some of the issues with epistemic objectivism as regards social and institutional facts, consider the notion of 'involuntary unemployment'. The problem of accurate description is highlighted by Douglas (2011), who draws on the work of Hausman and McPherson (2006). The term 'involuntary unemployment', Douglas explains, is usually intended to capture 'the situation of where one is out of work and cannot find employment' (2011: 524). However, there has been disagreement among economists as to whether such a situation actually ever exists. The protagonists of the view that it does not exist state that it is very rare that a person is in a situation without any work options whatsoever: the more likely scenario is that there *are* options, but the person may not wish to consider them because of their undesirability or low pay. It would thus be inaccurate to suggest that the unemployment is involuntary. What this example shows is that in light of certain social and institutional facts, it is problematic to provide an epistemically objective account. It would seem, instead, that the truth about 'involuntary unemployment' is discursive. To further engage with the issues at hand, we shall now invoke another example: *The Historikerstreit*.

The problem with 'objective' accounts of historical events: The *Historikerstreit*

The famous *Historikerstreit* was a public debate among German historians in the late twentieth century about the crimes of the Third Reich. This debate provides an excellent illustration of the problems inherent in claims that historical facts are objective. By focusing on the history of the Third Reich (an institutional fact, following Searle's taxonomy), Lorenz brings to the fore one of the biggest controversies among German historians – a controversy so profound that he calls it a 'postmodern spectacle' (1994: 302). In short, he explains that the historians Ernst Nolte and Andreas Hillgruber suggested a new historical perspective that would recast understandings of Nazi Germany and the Third Reich according to a global, comparative European perspective. They criticized other historians for their lack of scope, and Nolte in particular believed that the old picture of the Third Reich 'as the empire of pure evil' was out of date (1994: 299). As Lorenz points out, one of the consequences of Nolte's suggestions was that Hitler 'could no longer be treated by historians as an unsuccessful imitation of the German Bismark, but should be seen as the European "Anti-Lenin"' (1994: 300). In addition, Lorenz notes that the concentration camp system introduced by Hitler was reinterpreted by Nolte against the backdrop of the Russian Revolution and the fear of annihilation by the Bolsheviks. And because Bolshevism 'was a Jewish invention and the Soviet Union a state dominated by the Jews', Hitler's struggle against Bolshevism was identified with 'the struggle against the Jews' (1994: 345). The philosophers who opposed these new perspectives were led by Jürgen Habermas, Hans Mommsen, and Martin Broszat, who denounced them as the 'apologetic tendencies' of West German historians (1994: 343). Lorenz further comments on the view of Mommsen and Broszat (1994: 347):

> They regard the causal reduction of the Nazi crimes to Hitler's frame of mind and his fear of Bolshevism as a politically motivated effort to obscure the crucial role of this conservative 'Funktionseliten' in the Third Reich – and by the same move shifting the responsibility for the Third Reich to Communism. (1994: 347)

To this Nolte responded that these historians 'are misusing the Third Reich as an instrument for their leftist critique of today's society' (1994: 347). This episode shows that historical facts can be presented, interpreted, and thus constructed in different ways. Lorenz remarks that the *Historikerstreit* split many historians into two camps: at one end were the leftist supporters of Habermas's critique, at the other the more conservative rightist historians who supported Nolte and Hillgruber. The 'secure pillars' of historical science, including sources, facts, and historical method, were radically challenged. The result was two different interpretations of social facts. But there is yet another, and equally worrisome, layer of complexity to which we alluded earlier: the *Historikerstreit* demonstrates that social facts can be interpreted in one way by right-wing intellectuals and in another way by left-wing ones. Any notion of epistemic objectivity, therefore, is doubly lost.

Lorenz's ultimate motive is to use the *Historikerstreit* to go beyond objectivist and relativistic accounts of history and argue for what is essentially pluralism (he calls it *internal realism*). In his opinion, statements about historical facts (i.e., social facts) correspond to real events, but these events may be interpreted in multiple ways rather than there being just a single accurate account (objectivist) of them.

To the question 'What is actual, true, or real?', Lorenz says that the response 'is always dependent on and *internal* to the specific linguistic framework in which reality is described' (1994: 351). In other words, social facts can be made sense of according to different frameworks. In our books, however, this would make the veracity of social facts relative to the contexts within which they unfold. There are some historians who hold that there is no absolute certainty in history (e.g., McNeill, 1986), and as noted by Lorenz, there are also idealistic approaches to historical knowledge, such as Ankersmit's *narrative idealism* (Ankersmit, 1983) or White's *linguistic idealism* (White, 1987). Of course, none of these should be interpreted as fitting in with Searle's account of social ontology. To him, social facts are epistemically objective: researchers do not make up social facts, and they can study and report on them objectively. But as we have seen, objectivity about social facts is not unproblematic, and researchers ought to consider in what ways, precisely, it is possible to say that social facts are objective.

Further complications with objectivity about social facts

It is important to distinguish between different notions of objectivism. SAGE's *Key Concepts in Social Research* (Payne & Payne, 2004) summarizes objectivity in terms of researchers as neutral observers and maintaining a distance from what is being studied. Similarly, according to Slife and Williams, 'objective observation means that the scientist, as observer, stands on some "privileged" ground to make the observations. When made from these grounds, the observations have scientific credibility' (1995: 171). But there is also the view that 'objectivist epistemology holds that meaning, and therefore meaningful reality, exists as such apart from the operation of any consciousness' (Crotty, 1998: 8). And Boghossian (2006: 22), for instance, describes the classical picture of knowledge by discerning between three theses of objectivism:

1. *Objectivism about Facts*: The world which we seek to understand and know about is what it is largely independent of us and our beliefs about it. Even if thinking beings had never existed, the world would still have had many of the properties that it currently has.
2. *Objectivism about Justification*: Facts of the form (information E justifies belief B) are society-independent facts. In particular, whether or not some item of information justifies a given belief does not depend on the contingent needs and interests of any community.
3. *Objectivism about Rational Explanation*: Under the appropriate circumstances, our exposure to the evidence alone is capable of explaining why we believe what we believe.

These accounts of objectivity highlight that there are three broad ways of understanding 'objective facts': (1) objective facts as mind-independent and universally *true*; (2) objective facts as accurate accounts of events, and whose justification is value-neutral; and (3) objective facts as an appeal to reason and evidence. To return to our discussion of Searle's suggestion that social facts are epistemically objective, when applying the definitions offered by Boghossian the claim of epistemic objectivity do not go unchallenged. For instance, we can discard the first thesis, 'objectivism about facts', because if thinking beings had never existed, neither would social facts. Here we could also consider Crotty's (1998: 5) definition of objectivism as the epistemological view that 'things exist as meaningful entities independently of consciousness and experience', which would also suggest that social facts cannot be epistemically objective according to such characterizations of objectivity.

The problem of mind-independence has a specific meaning in the natural sciences and the kinds of truths available in, for example, the disciplines of mathematics and physics. The claim that $1 + 1 = 2$ is an epistemically objective fact of the mathematical variety, and that the Earth orbits the Sun of physics. With mathematically objective facts, there is always the assurance that anyone with sufficient cognitive abilities will arrive at the truth that $1 + 1 = 2$. Indeed, as we have seen in Chapter 2, this was the view held by the rationalists. Likewise, the epistemic accuracy of the claim that the Earth orbits the Sun may be verified by other intelligent beings as they approach the solar system. In both cases, epistemic objectivity is the kind of objectivism Boghossian has in mind when he speaks of 'objectivism about facts'. But we cannot make the same claim about social facts. Social facts are mind-dependent and have to be placed in contexts, 'decoded', and interpreted.

With regard to Boghossian's second thesis, 'objectivism about justification', we can appreciate Searle's views on epistemic objectivism, although it is worthwhile to proceed with caution. According to Searle, it is possible to have objective knowledge about (ontologically) relative social facts: the existence of presidents and money is observer-relative and demands collective intentionality, however we can study presidents and money and acquire objective knowledge about these. This way, we can know with certainty the past and present presidents in the United States of America, and that their currency is the US dollar. The same can be said about tourism, university professors, sustainability, and many other social facts. Searle's proposition is particularly attractive in respect of institutional facts and deontic powers, as we can study, say, tourism, in terms of duties, rights, obligations, and responsibilities.

Nevertheless, not all social facts are equal in their complexity, and some would argue that certain kinds of social facts *are* contingent on the needs and interests of communities.

Consider a British soldier fighting in the war against terrorism in Afghanistan. He can be a 'hero' in one context and an 'enemy' in another; the act of killing human beings can be 'commendable' in one context but 'murder' in another. The literature on relativism is abundant with examples such as this one. And so, in describing social facts objectively – especially those that involve people and actions – not all are necessarily epistemically objective in an absolute sense, rather they hold only in specific contexts, geographical locations, historical periods, and cultural beliefs. What can be claimed as true, therefore, is relative to a reference frame (Krausz, 2010a). Epistemic relativism tells us that there are no absolute epistemic facts, and especially 'there are no epistemic facts of the form: *S* is justified in believing that *p*. There are only facts of the form: *S* is justified in believing that *p* is relative to the system of epistemic rules that ascriber *A* accepts' (Lammenranta, 2008: 28). Last but not least, critical theorists would urge us to be vigilant, telling us that what is presented or justified as true and objective is always influenced by the needs and interests of specific groups. They too would be reluctant to accept objectivism about justification.

Boghossian's third thesis, 'objectivism about rational explanation', is no less problematic because 'evidence', as far as social facts are concerned, represents itself in and through consensus and collective intentionality. The evidence about social facts does not lie in objects themselves, as acknowledged by Searle in his notion of status functions. In other words, social facts do not exist by virtue of their physical composition. Of course, social facts may be recorded in documents, written accounts, photographs, cultural artefacts, survived tales, and oral history – all of which serve as 'evidence' for anthropologists, historians, and archaeologists. However, pluralists would argue that despite these records there can be more than one explanation of a given social fact. In addition, the sceptic would point out that given what we have learned about the *Historikerstreit*, historians (indeed, any researcher) are not necessarily to be trusted as 'neutral' observers in giving us true accounts of events.

In summary, social science scholars have a choice about where to place themselves as regards to objectivity and truth; they have a choice between the weaker and stronger forms of social constructionism. To help us understand the differences, the following section will briefly outline the core philosophical views held by John Searle, whom we can describe as a weak constructionist and realist, and Kenneth Gergen, whom we can categorize as a strong constructionist and pluralist. There are, of course, many other thinkers who have contributed to the development of social constructionism (for a comprehensive account, see Lock & Strong, 2010), but here we will focus only on two well-known contemporary constructionist figures to tease out some of the differences between the weaker and stronger varieties.

Weak and strong constructionism: Searle vs Gergen

John Searle (weak constructionism)

Searle's realism is apparent right from the start of his philosophical projects in the way he formulated his central questions. For instance, he asks, 'How can there be objective reality that exists in part by human agreement?' Or, 'How can it be a completely objective fact that the bits of paper in my pocket are money, if something is money only because we believe it is money?' (Searle, 1996: 2). His goal is not to offer a relativistic philosophy; rather, he is driven by a realist attempt to explain social reality. Searle is an *external realist* and a supporter of the correspondence theory of truth (i.e., statements and beliefs represent how things really are, and are therefore either *true* or *false*) (see Searle, 1996). He is also a *scientific realist* about natural phenomena and scientific facts, which he includes in his notion of brute facts. These, as defined earlier, are independent of human institutions, i.e., they are observer-independent. The statement 'the Sun is ninety-three million miles from the Earth' is, in Searle's view, an objective, brute fact (1996: 27). Also important to note here is that Searle is not a dualist. He abandons the long tradition of separating the mind from the body, in fact calling it the worst mistake in western philosophy (Searle, 2015). The view he vouches for is *direct realism*, whereby we have direct presentations of the world and its objects. As for dualism, he states that 'the mind is just a set of higher-level features of the brain, a set of features that are at once "mental" and "physical"' (Searle, 1996: 9).

In terms of his vision of social ontology, Searle holds that the 'basic unit of social ontology is not the social object but the Institutional Fact' (2014: 17). He makes it abundantly clear that his focus lies not with the analysis of social objects, but with social and institutional facts. In this regard, it is valuable to recall Lally's (1981) conceptual schema in Chapter 1 (see Figure 1.2), which discerns between the scholars interested in the *subject* and those motivated by understanding social structures and social facts, i.e., the *object*. According to Lally's schema, Searle is to be placed toward the *object* end of the subject–object continuum. He maintains that 'society has a logical (conceptual, propositional) structure that admits of, indeed requires, logical analysis' (Searle, 2010: 6), which elsewhere he calls 'the invisible structure of social reality' (Searle, 1996: 4). Searle's views are therefore close to, but not entirely compatible with, what Lally describes as *structural determinism* (Lally, 1981). Finally, in Searle's opinion, neither internal and phenomenological investigations nor external and behaviourist description are sufficient in explaining the possibility of socially constructed reality; there are underlying structures 'that make behaviour possible' (1996: 5), and this is precisely what he seeks to unravel.

Given this analysis of Searle's philosophy, it would be difficult to obtain a more realist reading of socially constructed reality than the one described above. In this regard, anyone who objects to the notion of a socially constructed reality on the (misinformed) premise of anti-realist claims is well off the mark. Realism and objectivism are fully present in the broader family of constructionist views about social reality. Nevertheless, there are some constructionists who are much more hesitant to commit to such realist readings, one of them being Kenneth Gergen.

Kenneth J. Gergen (strong constructionism)

Whereas Searle formulates his project in terms of analytical philosophy and envisages it as 'The Philosophy of Society' (2010: 5), Gergen's views are rooted in a discourse of a different kind. Gergen (2009) traces the origins of social construction to the concerns notable in *postmodernism,* in particular the rejection of modernism in western culture in all its aspects, including the importance of scientific truth, reason, objectivity, prediction, and control. According to Gergen, there are three lines of discourse central to constructionism: (1) the crisis of value neutrality (i.e., the impossibility of objectivity); (2) the assault on rationality (i.e., all rational arguments are ambiguous); and (3) the constructionist challenge to scientific truth, whereby science is seen as a man-made, social construction (building on the work of Berger & Luckmann, 1966; Fleck, 1979; Kuhn, 1962; Winch, 2008 [1958]). Hence, from the outset, we can see that Searle and Gergen differ in fundamental ways.

Gergen describes constructionism as a 'dialogue' or an 'invitation to a way of understanding' (2009: 29). He is a heartfelt (strong) constructionist who takes constructionism to be a critical, emancipatory, discursive, political, and liberating project. Inquiry embedded in Gergenian constructionism may therefore lead to scrutinizing common conventions and 'the taken-for-granted realities' (2009: 65). The goal of the various forms of speaking, writing, and representing is to 'challenge existing traditions of understanding, and offer new possibilities for action' (2009: 12). In this regard, constructionist researchers have goals alternative to prediction, control, and traditional rigorous methods. Gergen also speaks of *poetic activism* and *critical reflexivity.* Poetic activism is an invitation for 'the emergence of new forms of language and ways of interpreting the world'; critical reflexivity is 'the attempt to place one's premises into question, to suspend the "obvious", to listen to alternative framings of reality, and to grapple with the comparative outcomes of multiple standpoints' (2009: 12). And last but not least, 'truth', in Gergen's view, is something that can be 'both useful and potentially dangerous' (2009: 11). He replaces it with *doubt* – declaring that we must doubt 'everything we have accepted as real, true, right, necessary or essential' (2009: 12).

We will not find any of these concerns in the work of Searle as his interest is purely analytical. Nonetheless, there are some basic points on which Searle and Gergen agree, and we could say that both start as weak constructionists in their views about the constructed nature of social reality. They both agree that meaning is generated socially and culturally. Searle speaks of social facts, institutional facts, and brutal facts; Gergen talks of social convention, social utility, and practices of language and relationships that are 'bound within broader patterns of practice' (2009: 11). Gergen argues that without 'shared languages of description and explanations' the tradition of higher education, for example, which depends on a discourse of 'students', 'professors', 'curricula', and 'learning', would cease to exist in its present form (2009: 11). Searle similarly declares that human beings impose upon objects *status functions* that cannot be performed in virtue of the physical features of the object itself. For this reason, there must be 'collective *acceptance* or *recognition* of the object or person as having that status' (2010: 8). Hence, Searle and Gergen agree that social facts are the product of collective intentionality. Where they differ dramatically is their reading of what is/is not a social construction. For example, Gergen argues that *everything* is a matter of social convention:

> [E]verything we have learned about our world and ourselves – that gravity holds us to the earth, planes and birds both fly, cancer kills, or that the earth revolves around the sun – could be otherwise. There is nothing about 'what there is' that demands these particular accounts; we could use our language to construct alternative worlds in which there is no gravity or cancer, or in which persons and birds are equivalent, and the sun revolves around the world. [...] Not only does this suggest that there is no truth – words that truly map the world – but it also suggests that there is nothing we can hold on to, nothing solid on which we can rest our beliefs, nothing secure. (2009: 5)

Searle would object. To him, not *everything* is a matter of social construction, and importantly, epistemic objectivity or truth is available to us not only about natural facts but also about social and institutional facts. Searle would accept, perhaps, that people may use different terms to describe phenomena, but he would maintain that we live in a world of cause and effect, and consequently, that cancer kills, birds fly, and the Earth revolves around the Sun. In this respect, Searle is a realist and objectivist as far as epistemology is concerned. From the standpoint of Gergen[5] facts can always be constructed in different ways, and therefore objectivity, logic, and truth belong to tradition. All truth claims, he asserts, 'are specific to particular traditions – lodged in culture and history' (2009: 8). Thus, what Gergen denies, and Searle endorses, is the epistemically objective status of social and institutional facts. In addition, Gergen would likely disagree with Searle on the status of brute facts (for example, that hydrogen atoms have one electron and that molecules exist independent of our representations of them), and commit only to basic metaphysical realism, i.e., there is *something* there.

Summary and implications for qualitative research

We are entangled in a complex web of ideas about people, objects, and events – ideas that we accept as real. And yet if there were a virus that would make us forget almost everything we have learned to date, the social aspect of reality would cease to exist. Rocks and trees would still surround us, and so would other people, but the ideas we had once accepted and that were firmly embedded in our consciousness would be lost. Hence money, tourists, sustainability, holidays, citizenship, professors, bloggers, managers, Nike, boarding passes, presidents, and Christmas are social facts. We are not born with this knowledge *a priori*; rather, we acquire our knowledge of social facts *a posteriori*, and indeed play our part in their maintenance and constitution. They are embedded in our realities to such an extent that they shape our action, behaviour, practices, desires, rights, obligations, and relationships with other people. The intriguing part is that although the existence of entities like money and boarding passes is observer-relative, Searle would say we cannot simply wish them away. Social facts structure and determine our ways of being in the world.

This chapter was mainly concerned with social ontology and the constructed nature of social reality. It has been proposed that social ontology is not only an optional but also an inevitable part of qualitative research, and should feature prominently in the articulation of students' philosophical assumptions. The intention was not to sway researchers towards one particular form of philosophical view, such as relativism or realism, but to show that what qualitative scholars study are socially constructed social facts. This realization alone does not warrant that one must be a thoroughgoing subjectivist, relativist, or idealist. Indeed, it has been argued that there are stronger and weaker varieties of constructionism, and that it is possible to maintain a realist view. Conversely, it is also possible to conform to a relativist or pluralist view about social facts, including their epistemic status.

This chapter has corrected the misconceptions that equate social constructionism with subjectivism, solipsism, anti-realism, and relativism. To claim that social realities are constructed is not the same as to claim that rocks and trees do not exist. It has been shown that many constructionists are at least weak metaphysical realists, content to accept that we live in a material world. We must emphasize that constructionists are not subjectivists. The claim of constructionists is not that what exists exists only in a person's mind. Rather, constructionism is an intersubjectivist thesis, whereby constructions are constituted through a process that was explained as collective intentionality. From a social constructionist point of view, social reality is constructed collectively, and is possible only because of the interaction among agents and the processes outlined by Searle as status functions, collective intentionality, and deontic powers. Constructionism *is not* some kind of personal subjectivism. There has to be a level of acceptance and agreement among at least two agents for social and institutional facts to exist.

With regard to the choices before us, we can distinguish between epistemic objectivism about social facts and epistemic anti-objectivism about social facts (relativism and pluralism). These are contrasted in Figure 6.3. The first is representative of the weaker variety of social constructionism (e.g., Searle), the latter of the stronger claims to social constructionism (e.g., Gergen). Searle distances himself from any notions of strong constructionism by claiming that social facts, despite being ontologically relative, are epistemically objective; he says that we can have epistemic certainty. Hence, the kind of objectivism Searle most likely has in mind is 'truth' and 'accurate description'. The observant reader may implement what was learned in Chapter 4 and realize that Searle's weak constructionism is compatible with hermeneutic realism and hermeneutic objectivism. On the other hand, the stronger varieties of constructionism are compatible with the anti-realist and anti-objectivist philosophical stances. In terms of locating constructionism as

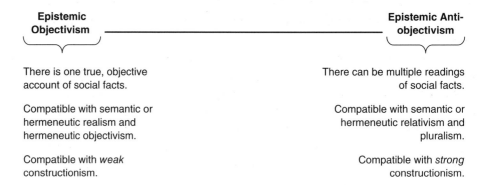

Figure 6.3 Epistemic objectivism and anti-objectivism about social facts

a theory of knowledge within the philosophical skeleton we erected in Chapter 1 (see Figure 1.3), constructionism is epistemologically most compatible with *idealism*. Constructionism studies the ideas human beings construct about things, places, and people through intersubjective processes. Importantly, constructionism is not direct realism, as meaning is imposed collectively by people in a process whereby things are assigned status functions and deontic power and become established as institutional facts. Therefore, we can only know the ideas people have/had about objects, events, and experiences. Nevertheless, such knowledge can be objective – as Searle would argue.

Searle's formulation of status functions and deontic powers is useful for understanding institutional facts in terms of rights, duties, desires, obligations, and so forth. It gives us an understanding of the existence of entities such as money, which enables us to purchase goods. His point is that we can and do have true and objective knowledge of institutional facts. This way, it is true that the Romans used gold coins as a form of currency, and it is also true that the US dollar banknote is used as money today. Epistemological realism about social facts is shared by other philosophers, including Nola and Sankey, who assert that 'science can make objective claims about the mind-dependent items investigated in the social sciences as well as the mind-independent items investigated in the natural and life sciences' (2007: 339). Realist readings of social facts have also been propagated by the Cambridge Social Ontology Group, collected in the text *Social Ontology and Modern Economics* (Pratten, 2015). However, as highlighted in this chapter there are challenges to objectivism, and qualitative researchers must ponder the extent to which social facts can be said to be objective – choosing, perhaps, between the positions in Figure 6.3.

It is also possible to arrive at additional varieties. For instance, we can accept objective knowledge about certain deontic powers and status functions, e.g., theories about economics and tourism, while rejecting semantic objectivism. This way we can study economic systems and tourists in terms of socially accepted rights, duties, and obligations, but when it comes to the semantic content of social facts, we can adopt semantic pluralism. By following this approach, it is no longer necessary to strip social facts of personal life histories, values, and morals that yield abundant versions of what it means to be an artist, teacher, tourist, patient, housekeeper, or manager. To make this final point clear, consider, for example, that tourism can be known objectively as a web of rights and obligations that have been socially accepted on a global scale (i.e., the deontic powers and status functions that come with passports, hotel receptionists, cruise-lines, boarding passes, and so forth). Yet when we attempt to answer the question 'What does it means to be a tourist?', we enter the realms of relativism and pluralism, because the answer is inevitably bound up with tradition, culture, geographical location, and personal experience – it is relative to a reference frame or context. Thus, researchers can find ways of accommodating both Searle and Gergen, to varying degrees, in their efforts to articulate more nuanced views about social reality.

In conclusion, the most rational explanation about social reality is that it is constructed. To claim that money, tourists, and the days of the week are social constructions is a view grounded in common sense. Those who disagree face the arduous task of providing an alternative account of social ontology. Understood as a philosophy *for* social science, social ontology is not a radical form of social constructionism – a point that has been laboured extensively in this chapter. Qualitative researchers can align their view with a realist or an objectivist stance, or with anti-realist and anti-objectivist philosophies. It is also possible to find a compromise between the two.

Recommended reading

Arbib, M.A. & Hesse, M.B. (1986) *The Construction of Reality*. Cambridge: Cambridge University Press.

Burr, V. (2003) *Social Constructionism* (2nd edn). New York: Routledge.

Gergen, K.J. (1994) *Realities and Relationships: Soundings in Social Construction*. Cambridge, MA: Harvard University Press.

Gergen, K.J. (2001) *Social Construction in Context*. London: SAGE.

Gergen, K.J. (2009) *An Invitation to Social Construction* (2nd edn). London: SAGE.

Gergen, K.J. (2009) *Relational Being: Beyond Self and Community*. New York: Oxford University Press.

Goodman, N. (1978) *Ways of Worldmaking*. Indianapolis, IN: Hacket.

Hacking, I. (1999) *The Social Construction of What?* Cambridge, MA: Harvard University Press.

Kukla, A. (2000) *Social Constructivism and the Philosophy of Science*. London: Routledge.

Lock, A. & Strong, T. (2010) *Social Constructionism: Sources and Stirrings in Theory and Practice*. Cambridge: Cambridge University Press.

(Continued)

(Continued)

Pratten, S. (ed.) (2015) *Social Ontology and Modern Economics*. Abingdon: Routledge.
Searle, J.R. (1996) *The Construction of Social Reality*. London: Penguin.
Searle, J.R. (2006) Social ontology: Some basic principles. *Anthropological Theory,* 6 (1): 12–29. doi:10.1177/1463499606061731
Searle, J.R. (2010) *Making the Social World*. New York: Oxford University Press.
Velody, I. & Williams, R. (1998) *The Politics of Constructionism*. London: SAGE.

Notes

1. It is important to stress that Searle does *not* use the term 'social facts' to build on the work of Émile Durkheim. On the contrary, Searle is rather critical of Durkheim's work. Furthermore, whereas Durkheim takes social facts to be essentially *coercive*, Searle sees them as *enabling* and *empowering* (for a detailed and clear contrast, see Searle, 2006c).
2. There is, of course, a much longer list of scholars who have contributed, directly or indirectly, to developments in constructionist thought, some of whom are listed in the recommended reading section at the end of this chapter.
3. Kukla, like Lincoln et al. (2011), uses the term constructi*vism* as opposed to constructionism.
4. Of course, one can argue that 'paper', too, is a social fact. These examples are used here (and by Searle) to demonstrate that besides its social component, some social facts are made of more fundamental 'building blocks' – matter.
5. To fully appreciate the arguments on both sides it is important to read Searle and Gergen's seminal texts, which are listed in the recommended reading section at the end of this chapter.

Seven

Quantum Reality: Contemporary Views of the Things-in-Themselves

It would be a major omission if, as part of our philosophical contemplations about what there is, we did not consider the progress made in physics towards understanding objects at the smallest possible level. For if we are to speak of reality in contemporary terms, a twenty-first century perspective must include at least a brief visit to the district of quantum reality. The preceding chapters raised some of the problems with appearances, phenomena, and noumena, and examined the different epistemic strategies available to secure empirical knowledge of the external world. We also distinguished between direct and indirect realism, and in Chapter 1 established the difference between *materialism* or *metaphysical realism* – the view that the external world exists independent of the human mind – and *immaterialism* or *metaphysical idealism*, which rejects the mind-independence thesis of objects. All this effort will serve us well in this chapter, where we will abridge the philosophical insights gained thus far and consider them alongside contemporary scientific views on, following Kant's terminology, what we will call the *thing-in-itself*.

In the pages to follow, our focus will shift toward a relatively neglected and mostly non-existent topic in qualitative research: quantum mechanics. To ease the mind of the apprehensive reader, the aim is not to explain quantum theory in its full breadth and scope but rather to concentrate on the broader philosophical implications of the quantum realm. It will be shown that as many as nine notions of quantum reality exist, capable of accommodating a wide range of philosophical views – from realism and rationalism to subjectivism, idealism, and pluralism. This chapter will point to important conundrums, as everything we take for granted on the phenomenal level of reality, including the law of cause and effect and our customary ways of thinking about objects, has to be abandoned when we enter the quantum world. If quantum mechanics – one of the most successful scientific theories to date – is taken as telling us how the world *really* is, then we face new philosophical questions. The implications for qualitative research come in the form of the realization that there is not only one way of thinking about reality, and that it would be naïve to think about it in a simplistic, direct way. This chapter will close by proposing that there are four notions of reality researchers may wish to consider when they establish their philosophical assumptions, and although social sciences, and thereby qualitative inquiry in general, deal with the phenomenal aspects of the world and with socially constructed realities, all of the layers are intertwined – inviting us to contemplate the extent to which things are *real*.

The things-in-themselves

The views then: The rationalist and empiricist legacies

Many of the views we hold about our world today were introduced more than two thousand years ago. The ancient Greek thinkers gave us the notion of *atoms*. They believed that the universe was composed of *void* interspersed with actual physical atoms, which were indivisible and considered to be the smallest components of reality. The doctrine of atomism[1] can be traced to the ideas of Leucippus, Democritus, Epicurus, and Lucretius, and marks the beginning of naturalist philosophy. It sought to explain the origins of everything purely in terms of the material interactions of bodies, and notably, without having to involve the notion of divine design (Berryman, 2011). In opposition to the atomistic outlook stood Platonism. We have already established that Plato viewed the universe as designed mathematically/geometrically and mathematical laws as the essence of reality (Kline, 1982). What we shall add to our pool of knowledge in this chapter is the Platonist conception of the actual structure and composition of the world, which will prepare us for exploring it at the quantum scale.

O'Leary (2010) explains that according to Plato, the universe was designed by a deity or God, the *demiurge,* who created the four elements of fire, water, earth, and air. These elements were made up of small bodies invisible to the human eye which consisted of perfect triangles: the 45-45-90 isoceles right triangle and the 30-60-90 triangle. The triangle thus was the basic building block of geometric solids that made up the universe. These were the tetrahedron (pyramid), which represented fire; the octahedron (eight triangular faces), which represented air; the hexahedron (cube), which represented earth; the icosahedron (20 triangular faces), which represented water; and finally the dodecahedron (12 pentagonal faces), which represented the cosmos (O'Leary, 2010). This notion of reality championed by Plato is notably different from the atomist one, according to which the universe was made of actual physical entities – the atoms.

Turning the clock forward, we may remark on the fact that it was only from the nineteenth century onwards that the discourse on atoms began to shift from spiritually intertwined metaphysics to epistemology (Chalmers, 2014). Eventually, the atom, stripped of any religious connotations, became an object of science. In Chapters 2 and 5, we saw the passionate debates between the empiricists and the scientific realists and the implications of those debates for the philosophy of science. The empiricists were of the view that atoms, or any theoretical entities, for that matter, were not a proper object of empirical science, and disregarded them as unworthy of scientific inquiry. It was scientific realism that embraced both observable and unobservable entities, treating them as equally legitimate for the pursuit of scientific knowledge. Scientific realists did not see atoms as any different from objects visible to the naked eye; indeed, according to Chalmers (2014: para. 2), 'many contemporary philosophers see the ultimate triumph of atomism as a victory for realism over positivism'. Furthermore, atomism was no longer a universal theory that explained everything (in the metaphysical sense), instead becoming mainly an epistemic concern within the fields of physics and chemistry.

The scientific achievements of the twentieth century are part of our recent history; they are the building blocks on which a newer – not solely philosophical but also scientific – understanding of reality was erected. With the progress of international research institutes such as CERN, researchers have discovered new particles such as the Higgs boson in 2012 and reaffirmed the Standard Model of particle physics, which is the most developed quantum theory about fundamental particles and fundamental forces. We also know that atoms are no longer the smallest particles knowable to mankind: the typology of the subatomic family now includes the categories of fermions (quarks and leptons), and bosons. Inevitably, the discoveries, experiments, and progress in physics must have philosophical implications. The following sections will explore the impact of quantum mechanics on the ontological and epistemological landscapes.

The views now: The 'return' to idealism and subjectivism?

From our previous discussions in Chapters 2 and 3, and taking into account the relatively recent popularity of positivism, postpositivism, and scientific realism, it would appear that idealism and subjectivism are philosophical doctrines of the past. They have been fought, ridiculed, and defeated to such an extent that not many researchers today would identify with them. The most obvious reason for this fall from grace is common sense. The notion of there existing *ideas* only, and not autonomous and mind-independent objects such as rocks and trees, goes against our customary beliefs. Common sense tells us that chairs, tables, bicycles, people, and planets are external objects whose state is not determined by our cognitive abilities. If we were to ask most people if rocks and trees really exist, the likely response would be 'Of course they do!', and they would point to a tree and a rock. Indeed, we can easily test whether or not these are mere ideas by attempting to walk through a tree or lifting a heavy rock. Yet despite our everyday experiences of a physical world and our common sense, idealism and subjectivism have not completely left the philosophical scene. Idealist and subjectivist readings of the world persist in our very attempts to decipher the building blocks of reality at their most fundamental level.

One could argue that idealism has come back with a vengeance because previous attempts to establish idealism as a viable response to scepticism were purely philosophical, whereas today, idealism is advocated by scientists. The kind of idealism we encounter in the twenty-first century is in a branch of science known as quantum mechanics, which is the study of physical entities at very small atomic and subatomic levels. We might say that quantum physics is the modern, scientific study of things-in-themselves. Quantum physics rests on quantum theory, which is the theoretical basis of modern physics. Herbert describes it as 'a method of representing quantum stuff mathematically: a model of the world executed in symbols. Whatever the math does on paper, the quantum stuff does in the outside world' (1985: 41). It is important to emphasize that the mathematics behind quantum mechanics is well understood and widely accepted. On the list of products, technology, and machinery that exist because of the mathematics of quantum mechanics are such objects as CDs, satellite antennas, navigation systems (GPS), and medical imaging systems (e.g., NMR, CT, PET). In addition, it is estimated that 25 per cent of the gross national product (in countries with advanced economies) comes from products that are affiliated to varying degrees with quantum physics (Lüth, 2012). In simple terms, the mathematics used in quantum theory yields reliable results – it 'works' – and some would purport that it represents how things *really* are at the quantum level. But mathematics is only a *way* of explaining, a type of language. It does not tell us what there *is* in ontological terms; it is not a bullet-proof direct representation of quantum phenomena. As a result, various interpretations have emerged as to what the mathematics associated with quantum theory means. Before we explore these in more detail, a quick outline of the key ideas underpinning quantum mechanics is necessary.

The quantum realm

Quantum mechanics asks us to abandon everything we have learned about the everyday world. Things just do not 'work' at the quantum scale in the same fashion. For example, one of the main puzzles of quantum mechanics has been the dichotomy of quantum entities, such as electrons, photons, and neutrinos, apparently behaving as both waves and particles. Thus, according to one theory – Maxwell's law of electromagnetism – an electron can be scientifically grasped as a *wave*, but according to Einstein's particle theory of light (after Pierre Gassendi and Thomas Hobbes), quantum objects seem to behave and are scientifically grasped as discrete *particles* (Davies & Brown, 1986). The particle-wave duality, one of the core ideas of quantum mechanics, has been demonstrated by the *double-slit experiment* (see, for example Davisson, 1928; Young, 1807), and more recently confirmed also by Australian researchers (Manning et al., 2015). Briefly explained, when particles are fired through a double slit, they behave like waves and create an inference pattern. As an example, consider firing tennis balls at a wall through a couple of narrow slits. What physicists have found is that the balls do not hit only the areas along the straight paths of the slits, but are distributed across the wall, in the same way a wave of water would reach the wall. The only difference is that the experiments used electrons rather than tennis balls. (See Figure 7.1 for an illustration.)

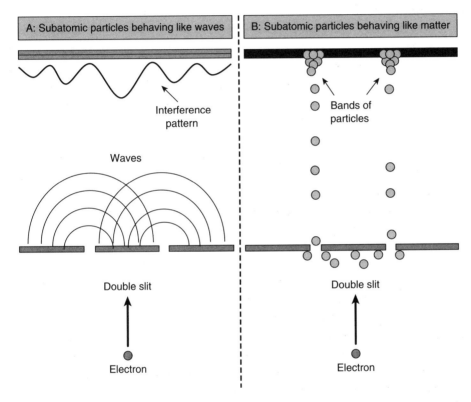

Figure 7.1 The workings of the particle-wave duality: Subatomic particles are known to have the properties of both waves and particles

The particle-wave duality has become one of the well-established facts of quantum mechanics. Max Born provided a statistical understanding of how such waves function and Erwin Schrödinger (1926) formulated the mathematical equation of the probability wave (for an easy to follow overview of quantum mechanics, see for example Davies & Brown, 1986; Greene, 2004). The atomists' notion that there are single particles that make up our reality has been proven incorrect, and replaced with an updated view according to which subatomic particles assume the properties of waves that can behave as particles, but only when observed. And this is where things take on a philosophically interesting turn.

Observing things into existence and the uncertainty principle

The Danish physicist Niels Bohr (1885–1962) received the Nobel Prize in Physics in 1922 for his contribution to quantum theory. He is considered to be one of the founders of modern atomic theory. According to Bohr, whether quantum objects behave like 'waves' or 'particles' depends on the nature of the experiment conducted and the setting in which it takes place. In other words, the properties of the scientific experiment itself influence what is observed during the experiment. The researcher is not merely an observer of quantum phenomena but an active participant in them. As explained by Davies and Brown (1986), researchers face the choice of measuring either the position or momentum of a particle, but it is not possible to determine the particle's specific values *prior* to the experiment. They clarify further that '[i]f we decide to measure the position, we end up with a particle-at-a-place. If we choose instead to measure the momentum, we get a particle-with-a-motion. In the former case, after the measurement is complete, the particle simply does not have a momentum, in the latter case it does not have a location' (Davies & Brown, 1986: 21). This finding led physicists like Niels Bohr to suggest the principle of *complementarity* that states quantum objects have both (or complementary) wave and particle properties, but it is not possible to measure these at the same time. This is also called the *uncertainty principle*, reflecting that we can neither measure nor be certain about both at the same time.

From a philosophical standpoint, the inability to determine with absolute certainty whether subatomic entities are waves or particles, coupled with the impossibility of knowing their state before measurement, creates a set of noteworthy problems. In quantum mechanics, we do not know with certainty what things are 'in-themselves' before the experiment, yet it is the experiment that determines what we observe. Put differently, we lose the certainty of objects possessing inherent properties and the possibility of knowing the intrinsic properties of things-in-themselves. Moreover, we are asked to give up the notion of mind-independence because the researcher and the research setting shape what is experienced at the quantum level. Therefore, quantum-speaking, our knowledge of what things-in-themselves *really* are is limited and speculative. The paradox of where to draw the line between the observer and that which is observed also preoccupied John Bell:

> The problem of measurement and the observer is the problem of where the measurement begins and ends, and where the observer begins and ends. Consider my spectacles, for example: if I take them off now, how far away must I put them before they are part of the object rather than part of the observer? There are problems like this all the way from the retina through the optic nerve to the brain and so on. I think, that – when you analyse this language that the physicists have fallen into, that physics is about the results of observations – you find that on analysis it evaporates, and nothing very clear is being said. (see the interview in Davies & Brown, 1986: 48)

To put these views in a wider philosophical perspective that reflects the discussions in the previous chapters, the problem of measurement implies that the researcher is not a distant observer, describing events truthfully as they are; she influences what manifests in the very act of observation. For this reason, we cannot speak of objectivity or mind-independence. Despite this not being something that necessarily holds in our everyday, phenomenal reality, for the time being it is the case within the quantum realm. The central issue facing scientists, then, is one of reconciliation, i.e., reconciling locality and Einstein's relativity with quantum mechanics. It would be a fatal mistake if researchers were to ignore quantum mechanics, for the ramifications are on par with the ignorance of direct realists. If the 'quantum world' lies beneath the phenomenal, visible, observable, and everyday world, and if we are to speak of things-in-themselves in their most fundamental state, we must take quantum mechanics into account. We cannot simply disregard what science says about reality beyond appearances. But by including quantum mechanics in the larger picture of reality, things become fuzzy, and we open the doors to strange phenomena.

Nonlocality and entanglement

According to quantum mechanics, things in the universe are thought to be interconnected in ways which we do not yet properly understand. The physicist John Bell mathematically proved that certain quantum phenomena cannot have a local cause. His theory, commonly referred to as Bell's theorem, asserts that reality must be nonlocal, i.e., that quantum objects have to be connected by nonlocal influences, and that these are faster than the speed of light (Herbert, 1985). Bell stated that with regard to the 'results of individual measurements, without changing the statistical predictions, there must be a mechanism whereby the setting of one measuring device can influence the reading of another instrument, however remote' (Bell, 1964; 2004: 20). This paradox of interlinked quantum states is possible because of another phenomenon called *entanglement*, a term coined by Erwin Schrödinger. Entangled particles, such as two electrons, behave as if they are instantaneously connected. In other words, entangled objects have an immediate effect on one another, regardless of how far apart they are. As Greene puts it, 'roughly speaking, even though the two particles are widely separated, quantum mechanics shows that whatever one particle does, the other will do too' (2004: 83). He further notes:

> This sounds totally bizarre. But there is now overwhelming evidence for this so-called quantum entanglement. If two photons are entangled, the successful measurement of either photon's spin about one axis 'forces' the other, distant photon to have the same spin about the same axis; the act of measuring one photon 'compels' the other, possibly distant photon to snap out of the haze of probability and take on a definite spin value - a value that precisely matches the spin of its distant companion. And that boggles the mind. (Greene, 2004: 115)

The implications of nonlocality and entanglement allow for a range of peculiar scenarios. For instance, the act of measuring a photon that was entangled during the Big Bang 14 billion years ago could potentially 'compel' its entangled counterpart to behave in the same fashion, even if the second particle is in another galaxy. This is because quantum objects are not influenced locally (e.g., impacted by immediate and empirically measurable causes), but instead are nonlocally causal and influenced by other 'hidden' variables. In the everyday, phenomenal world, we are accustomed to the laws of cause and effect, which are 'local' in the sense that if I were to push a book on the table in front of me, the force exerted by my hand against the book would cause the object to move, and consequently, if it went over the edge, the book would fall to the ground. According to quantum theory, however, an action somewhere else, even as far as another galaxy, can have an effect in our world and vice versa. What's more, the objects have instantaneous knowledge of each other. Herbert puts it this way: 'a non-local interaction links up one location with another without crossing space, without decay, and without delay. A non-local interaction is, in short, *unmediated, unmitigated,* and *immediate*' (Herbert, 1985: 214, emphasis in original).

The most intriguing issue about nonlocality and entanglement is not just the theorem itself. Bell proved 'conclusively that the world behind phenomena must be non-local' (Herbert, 1985: 230); in other words, Bell proved 'the existence of an invisible non-local reality' (1985: 231). Therefore, we are not speaking of a speculative theory, and indeed Bell's theorem has been proven in several experiments (e.g., Aspect et al., 1982; Freedman & Clauser, 1972). It also pays us to note that progress made in some of the newly emerging disciplines, such as quantum biology, is beginning to suggest that quantum mechanics is relevant to the world of larger objects. For example, Al-Khalili and McFadden (2014: 135) argue that the biochemical reactions in the astonishing speeds associated with photosynthesis and enzymes can be explained by a quantum mechanical process called *quantum tunnelling*. They state that 'discrete energy levels, wave–particle duality, coherence, entanglement and tunnelling aren't just interesting ideas relevant only to scientists working within rarefied physics laboratories' (2014: 295). Although it is possible that quantum theory may one day be superseded by another theory, Herbert asserts that Bell's theorem would survive and 'impose nonlocality on quantum theory's successor' because 'it makes contact with a general feature of reality itself' and 'foretells the shape of all future physical theories' (1985: 52). Overall, from the viewpoint of quantum mechanics, there is no guarantee for objects to exist mind-independently. In fact, they may not even have any definitive attributes, or what Locke called primary qualities:

No longer is it possible to think of the microworld in the terms Einstein, Podolsky and Rosen advocated. Rather we must think in terms of nonlocality, and/or we must renounce the very idea that individual objects possess discrete attributes. (Greenstein & Zajonc, 2006: 161)

The issues raised by nonlocality and entanglement weigh heavily on the philosophical mind. What Bell's theorem suggests is that the *thing-in-itself* is not necessarily a thing-in-itself but also an interconnected thing-elsewhere. If the 'atom's measured attributes are determined not just by events happening at the actual measurement site but by events arbitrarily distant' (Herbert, 1985: xiv), then whatever we think the thing-in-itself is, or whatever we believe the inherent properties of objects are, may be influenced by other events. Bell's theorem challenges the local–realist view, which maintains that all effects must have local causes, and that nothing can travel faster than the speed of light. As ill-conceived as the notion of nonlocality is to the local realists, Herbert points out that 'those who prefer their realities to be local have so far not been able to refute Bell's argument' (Herbert, 1985: 231). This still stands today.

Quantum realities

Albert Einstein and Niels Bohr represent two different views about observation, and more generally, about the scientific method. For Einstein the role of observation was to uncover the world as it *really* was, whereas for Bohr observation interfered with and influenced quantum reality. Broadly speaking, they anticipate two dominant philosophical outlooks in relation to quantum reality: on the one hand, there are the realist or neorealist thinkers, with figures such as Einstein, Schrödinger, Planck, and Louis de Broglie, and, on the other, the anti-realists, who have proposed alternative, nonrealist interpretations. (These outlooks are outlined in detail in Table 7.1.) Realist views are represented in this table under quantum reality #6 (i.e., neorealism); all the others can be understood as anti-realist stances.

The most noteworthy, and also the most influential, is the Copenhagen school, described by Jammer as a 'radical revision of traditional epistemology and even ontology' (1979: 55). The so-called Copenhagen interpretation denotes a set of views mainly advocated by, and associated with, Niels Bohr and Werner Heisenberg. It enjoyed great popularity in the twentieth century and was accepted as the 'official view among professional physicists' (Davies & Brown, 1986: 26). Roughly speaking, it states that 'in a certain sense the unmeasured atom is not real: its attributes are created or realized in the act of measurement' (Herbert, 1985: xiii). We can paraphrase and say that whatever manifests in an experiment is created by the experiment itself. It would be incorrect to typecast Bohr as a full-blown idealist;[2] nonetheless, if we accept the theory of quantum mechanics put forth by him and his colleagues, we open the door to different readings of quantum reality – the idealist variety in particular. Under this view, and in line with the Copenhagen interpretation, quantum objects exist in uncertain quantum states, and it is the scientific experiment itself that influences what eventually transpires during the experiment. This does not imply that the subatomic particles are imaginary entities – something does indeed manifest (e.g., an electron) – however, our knowledge of the *true* states of such entities (prior to experience) is not only dependent on but also *influenced* by the observer. This is why, according to the Copenhagen interpretation, there are no mind-independent objects. Consequently, *'on its own* an atom or electron or whatever cannot be said to "exist" in the full, common-sense, notion of the word' (Davies & Brown, 1986: 24, emphasis in original). In a sense, the atom is constructed into existence by the experiment.

This type of idealism is not the Berkeley kind, which would have us believe that only ideas exist. Instead we see here a version of Kantian idealism, according to which we play a part in constructing reality into existence. Saunders argues that there is abundant evidence to support the claim that Bohr's philosophy was 'committed if not to a Berkelerian idealism, then to anti-realism or to neo-Kantianism' (2005: 418). In his early days, Bohr shared the same outlook as Einstein, for whom empirical science was about the conceptual grasping of thought-independent reality. Later, though, Bohr came to appreciate the need to accommodate a new outlook, whereby reality was 'not independent of its being observed' (Held, 1995: 401). Whereas both Einstein and the early Bohr stood closer to the doctrine of realism, the later Bohr shifted towards an idealist conception of quantum particles. Held further comments that '[i]t is not true [for Bohr] that those observables we could determine have determinate values; only the observables we do determine have such values. Bohr thus meets the Kantian position that the real is only what we actually observe' (Held, 1995: 400).

Apart from quantum reality #6 (neorealism), Table 7.1 comprises predominantly anti-realist attitudes. John Wheeler, the proponent of quantum reality #2, for example, regarded the existence of conscious observers to be fundamental in

Table 7.1 Herbert's Eight Quantum Realities

Quantum Reality #1: *The Copenhagen interpretation, Part 1*	- There is *no deep reality*. - The world human beings perceive (i.e., the phenomenal world) is 'real enough'; however, 'it floats on a world that is not as real'; - 'Everyday phenomena are themselves built not out of phenomena but out of an utterly different kind of being'; - An anti-realist and cautiously sceptical stance about hidden realities; - 'Atoms are not things!', as proclaimed by Heisenberg; - Key proponents: Niels Bohr and Werner Heisenberg.
Quantum Reality #2: *The Copenhagen interpretation, Part 2*	- There is no reality in the absence of observation; - Observation creates reality; - What we see is real, but 'these phenomena are not really there in the absence of an observation'; - 'No elementary phenomenon is a real phenomenon until it is an observed phenomenon', as proclaimed by Wheeler; - Key proponent: John Wheeler.

The **Copenhagen interpretation** often refers to both QR #1 and QR #2 and the claims that there is no deep reality and that observation creates reality. The acceptance of the Copenhagen interpretation leads to the assertion that only phenomena are real, while the world that underlies all phenomena is not in the same sense - there is no deep reality.

Quantum Reality #3: *Reality is an undivided wholeness*	- The world is a seamless and interconnected whole – 'a new kind of togetherness undiminished by spatial and temporal separation'; - Reality is observer-created, whereby the observer is part of a larger whole; - There is no objective outside reality and us, objects and subjects are inseparable; - Key proponents: Walter Heitler, David Bohm.
Quantum Reality #4: *The many-worlds interpretation*	- There are many worlds; - Reality consists of 'a steadily increasing number of parallel universes'; - New universes 'spring into being, identical in every detail except for the single outcome that gave them birth'; - Key proponents: Hugh Everett, Bryce S. DeWitt, Paul Davies, David Deutsch.
Quantum Reality #5: *Quantum logic*	- To understand quantum events we have to think quantum-logically; - The world obeys a non-human kind of reasoning; - Human reasoning has to be abandoned and replaced with 'quantum logic'; - Quantum logic provides only a logical skeleton, not a complete quantitative picture of quantum phenomena; - Key proponents: David Finkelstein, John von Neumann, Garrett Birkhoff.
Quantum Reality #6: *Neorealism*	- As with (scientific) realism, the world is made of ordinary objects or entities that possess attributes of their own, whether they are observed or not; - The phenomenal and familiar everyday reality can be 'extended to the atomic realm and beyond'; - 'Atoms are things!'; - Described as the 'blackest heresy of establishment physics'; - Key proponents: Albert Einstein, Max Planck, Erwin Schrödinger, Louis de Broglie.
Quantum Reality #7: *Consciousness creates reality*	- Reality is created by consciousness; - Some proponents of QR#2 (observer-created reality) assert that 'only an apparatus endowed with consciousness is privileged to create reality; - The observer's consciousness plays an active role in creating reality; - Key proponents: Walter Heitler, Henry Pierce Stapp, Eugene Wigner, John von Neumann.
Quantum Reality #8: *Heisenberg's duplex word of potentials and actualities*	- The world consists of *potentials* and *actualities*; - There is 'no deep reality – nothing down there that's real in the same sense as the phenomenal facts are real'; - Observer-created reality is created out of *potentia* – 'raw material' or 'stuff' or 'tendencies'. These tendencies 'are continually on the move, growing, merging, and dying according to exact laws of motion discovered by Schrödinger'; - 'The unmeasured world is merely semireal, and achieves full reality status during the act of observation' – atoms and elementary particles are not real, but *potentials* or *possibilities* surface during the 'magic measurement act' as actual events. - Key proponent: Werner Heisenberg.

Source: Distilled and adapted from Herbert (1985: 15-29).

quantum mechanics, and is known for proclaiming, 'I cannot believe that nature has "built in", as if by a corps of Swiss watchmakers, any machinery, equation or mathematical formalism which rigidly relates physical events separated in time' (Davies & Brown, 1986: 60). Table 7.1 shows the views of other physicists, such as David Deutsch, who supports the 'many-universes' or 'many-worlds' interpretation of quantum mechanics which asserts that there are many parallel universes which may be infinite in number and which share the same space and time with us (see Davies & Brown, 1986). An even stronger anti-realist position is quantum reality #7 (consciousness creates reality), elucidated in John von Neumann's contention that 'the world is not objectively real but depends on the mind of the observer' (Herbert, 1985: 189). David Bohm's articulation of reality as *undivided wholeness* further tells us that the world is understood as one seamless whole. In *Wholeness and the Implicate Order*, Bohm emphasizes intertwined existence as an 'unbroken and undivided totality' or the *holomovement*, arguing that 'in certain cases, we can abstract particular aspects of the holomovement (e.g., light, electrons, sound, etc.), but more generally, all forms of the holomovement merge and are inseparable' (2002 [1980]: 191). Of course, there is an even more radical view – perhaps the strongest idealistic interpretation of quantum physics – purported by Amit Goswami, who in *The Self-Aware Universe* (1995) argues that all existence is consciousness. In his view, it is consciousness that creates the physical world in which we live.

It is important to emphasize here that not all physicists are anti-realists. Some scientists are neorealists, holding that atoms are 'things'. But it is equally important to add that this view was rejected by the founders of quantum theory, Bohr and Heisenberg, and is generally taken to be 'misguided and hopelessly naïve' (Herbert, 1985: 186). The physicist Brian Green is a contemporary advocate of quantum realism. He holds that String Theory[3] may be the key to uniting quantum mechanics and general relativity (presently incompatible), potentially providing 'a single explanatory framework capable of encompassing all forces and all matter' (Greene, 2003: 15). String Theory assumes a reductionist approach as everything in the universe is believed to be reducible to vibrating strands or strings.

There are also the pragmatists weary of the existing theories, whom we may describe as the physicists who do not follow the logic of quantum theory to the extreme, tacitly assuming that at some level 'quantum physics somehow "turns into" classical physics, in which the independent reality of tables, chairs and moons is never doubted' (Davies and Brown, 1986: 31). However, no unanimous agreement has been reached, and all the options listed in Table 7.1 are potentially viable explanations of quantum reality.

Quantum idealism and subjectivism

We obtain idealist readings of reality by denying the autonomous existence of quantum objects and by accepting the thesis of observer- or consciousness-created reality (represented in QR#1, QR#2, QR#3, QR#7, QR#8). As Herbert asserts, whether we like it or not, 'through their conscientious practice of quantum theory more than a few physicists have strayed within hailing distance of the idealist's dreamworld' (1985: 18). According to *quantum idealism*, there *appear* to be quantum objects, but these do not have a definitive place or motion – their existence is relative to the observer. The quantum realm exists independent of the mind, but we cannot speak of the objective existence of (quantum) things-in-themselves, only a kind of Kantian *noumenal* realm perhaps, or 'raw quantum material' in which objects are constituted by the observer. Since we can only know the latter, i.e., the observer-relative appearances, it is neither accurate to speak of the definitive existence of quantum particles, nor possible to obtain objective knowledge of their inherent states prior to observation. The mind always interferes with how reality represents itself to us. Herbert puts it as follows:

> [A]ll quons [Herbert's term for a generic quantum object] and their static attributes enjoy an absolute existence whether they are observed or not. Only a quon's dynamic attributes, including the major external attributes position and momentum, are mind-created. Thus all those entities 'which compose the mighty frame of the world' do certainly *exist* without the intervention of mind, but until someone actually looks at them, these entities possess no definite place or motion. (1985: 193)

In addition to quantum idealism, there is also a more recent subjectivist interpretation of quantum mechanics based on Bayesian probability. It could be added to Table 7.1 as Quantum Reality #9. According to this interpretation, the prior beliefs of an observer play a fundamental role in the ways quantum entities are experienced. Whereas traditional, realist scientific methods strive for objectivity and seek to remove all the bias from the experiment (including the subject), the proponents of what has been termed *QBism* (see Fuchs et al., 2014) have argued that quantum states represent people's beliefs, not the objective properties of physical systems. In other words, the phenomena quantum physicists report and describe are not objective states of quantum objects, rather they are constituted by prior beliefs and expectations. In this regard, Caves, Fuchs and Schack claim that all quantum states 'must be regarded as subjective' (2007: 257), and that 'even probabilities that appear to be given by physical law, as in quantum theory, are subjective' (2007: 260). Their subjectivist interpretation of quantum-mechanical probabilities challenges any objective accounts of probability. Hence probability is not an objective feature of events based on frequency; it is observer-relative and determined by the prior expectations and beliefs of the individual. Caves et al. further explain the role of the observer in quantum measurements:

> Since probabilities are an agent's subjective degrees of belief about the possible outcomes of a trial and quantum states are catalogues of probabilities for measurement outcomes, it follows that quantum states summarize an agent's degrees of belief about the potential outcomes of quantum measurements. This approach underlines the central role of the agent, or observer, in the very formulation of quantum mechanics. (2007: 263)

Of course, the QBists are no less passionate about their view than all the other proponents of the various interpretations of quantum reality. In the journal *Nature*, Mermin advocates for QBist approaches to be taken more seriously by physicists, and asserts that 'it is time to consider what other foundational puzzles can be resolved by restoring the balance between subject and object in physical science'

(2014: 423). QBism is only one of nine interpretations of quantum reality, and there are other theoretical perspectives as well which are beyond the scope of this book (e.g., String Theory). The views noted above and in Table 7.1 have been put before us by leading physicists and cover an immensely broad spectrum of philosophical beliefs. The various notions of quantum reality demonstrate that we are at an intriguing point in time in which all philosophical stances seem to be on the table. Although we have made much philosophical progress at the level of appearances and phenomena, nothing has been settled as far as quantum reality is concerned.

In a snapshot of contemporary beliefs among scientists, Schlosshauer, Kofler and Zeilinger (2013) report the findings of a poll collected during the Quantum Physics and the Nature of Reality conference in Austria in 2011. The results show that 48 per cent of respondents believed that physical objects do not have their properties well defined 'prior to and independent of measurement'; 68 per cent believed that Einstein's (realist) view of quantum mechanics is wrong; 27 per cent perceived Bohr's view of quantum mechanics as wrong; and an additional 3 per cent stated that it will eventually turn out to be wrong. When it comes to the role of the observer in experiments, 6 per cent maintained that the observer plays a distinguished physical role; 39 per cent that the observer is a complex quantum system; 55 per cent that the observer plays a fundamental role in the application of the formalism (mathematical formulations) but no distinguished physical role; and 21 per cent that the observer plays no fundamental role whatsoever. The Copenhagen interpretation of quantum mechanics received the most support (42 per cent), and Everett's *many-worlds* or *many-minds* interpretation was indicated as a favourite by 18 per cent of respondents. Despite the fact that the poll only consisted of 27 physicists, 3 mathematicians, and 5 philosophers,[4] it highlights the diversity of beliefs about (quantum) reality among scientists and academics, whom we might regard as the contemporary experts on things-in-themselves.

Summary and implications for qualitative research

Quantum mechanics may at first glance appear irrelevant and even too distant from the concerns of qualitative research, but when we consider that it underpins the appearances and phenomena to which we are accustomed, quantum reality must form an inevitable part of the ontological and epistemological landscape. The price of disregarding quantum mechanics completely is that it would yield only a superficial discourse on reality. If we accept that the objects we perceive in our everyday life are composed of subatomic particles, which in turn are subject to quantum behaviour, and if we take into account that quantum mechanics is one of the most successful theories to date, then it behoves us to include it in the overall metaphysical/ontological picture. Inevitably, quantum physics has a place in the formulation of philosophical assumptions. It introduces an additional layer of complexity to how we can think about what is or is not real. This way, we can be realists about the *noumenal* realm, like the older rationalists, who believed that the universal laws and axioms of mathematics were the *truths* upon which all reality is founded. Or we can be weak metaphysical realists and commit only to the existence of an unknowable quantum realm made up of tendencies, potentialities, and 'raw material' (as in QR#8). We can also be neorealists and vouch for the actual existence of atoms and electrons, or be realists about appearances and phenomena. And finally, some may extend realism to social facts, although the existence of social reality is observer-relative, as we established in Chapter 6. The different notions of reality are depicted in Figure 7.2.

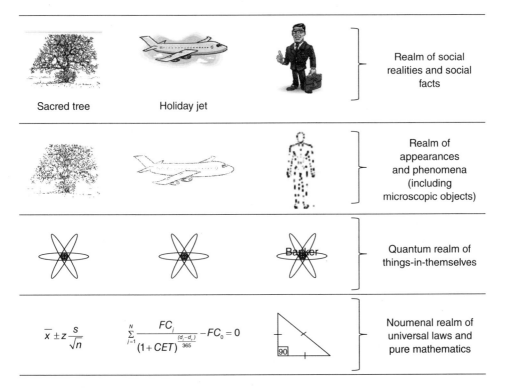

Figure 7.2 Different notions of reality

Figure 7.2 marks the distinction between various ontological foci. The first tier captures social realities and social facts. The ontological focus here lies on what is constituted socially, and extends to a range of social facts, including experiences, social phenomena, and social institutions. Examples include governments, tourists, bloggers, professors, sustainability, nationality, gender, ethnicity, currency, and all social roles. Common sense tells us that we are born into already existing social realities, but that does not make them universal or absolute. Therefore, whereas in the first tier it makes sense to talk of sacred trees, holiday jets, and bankers, which are socially constructed facts shared among agents in a society, the second tier represents appearances and phenomena, which we access through sense data and grasp cognitively. We may recall that in Chapter 6 we employed Searle's term *brute facts* to describe this aspect of reality, though Searle extended it to all scientific knowledge about the natural world.

The conflict between appearances and things-in-themselves has led some philosophers to espouse doubt about common sense. As we have seen in the previous chapters, these are the sceptics and the anti-realist thinkers. Goodman, for example, asserts that there is no faithful or exclusive representation of the way the world is, only many true descriptions. In his view, 'none of them tells us *the* way the world is, but each of them tells us *a* way the world is (1996: 10, emphasis in original). Putnam (1996) takes a more moderate stance by appealing to both realism and conceptual relativism. In his account, truth is determined by the choice of concepts. He declares, 'To require that all of these must be reducible to a single version is to make the mistake of supposing that "Which are the real objects?" is a question that makes sense *independently of our choice of concepts'* (1996: 25, emphasis in original). Conversely, from a scientific realist point of view, phenomena and appearances can be known in an objective fashion as stable manifestations of knowable reality. Objects in nature appear reliably regardless of what we think. As Sankey elucidates, scientific realism does not treat appearances with a sceptical shrug, rather it *corrects the explanation* of the appearances: 'science places the appearances within the context of a theoretical system, which corrects the common sense view' (2008: 25).

At a deeper level, we can consider the quantum realm, stepping down from the world of everyday macro and micro objects and entering the territory of quantum particles. This is the region of electrons, quarks, bosons, leptons, and other subatomic particles that make up reality. It is necessary to reiterate here that when we speak of things-in-themselves, we must also include the quantum 'stuff' that makes up appearances. Our picture of reality would be incomplete if we were to stop at appearances and exclude the theory of quantum mechanics because it does not correspond to our customary beliefs.

The last tier, called the noumenal realm in Figure 7.2, acknowledges the fact that we have the necessary knowledge to reliably make things based on the mathematics of quantum mechanics, such as CDs, DVDs, and flash memory. It recognizes that there might exist universal laws that govern the universe; the mathematical axioms of Plato, Descartes, and Kant; the laws of physics; and perhaps even quantum logic, noted in Table 7.1 as Quantum Reality #5. In contrast to the other tiers, this is an epistemic, logical, and purely rational province. Therefore, depending on one's philosophical beliefs, one may adopt mathematical realism and hold that sets, numbers and other entities are ontologically real.

Of course, one can also treat mathematics as a social construction created by humans, and those for whom Kant's beliefs resonate may find a compromise between the two, holding axioms as analytic *a priori* and theorems as synthetic *a priori* (see Chapter 3). The vigilant reader will have guessed that mathematical realism, too, comes in varieties, for we can be realists about some entities but not others (Nola & Sankey, 2007).

Our everyday world seems objective and predictable in the sense that we know that every effect has a cause. Newton's laws and the laws of relativity advocated by Einstein enable us to predict events accurately and reliably. Our reality is local and we can explain it. However, the quantum world is filled with uncertainty, probabilities, and nonlocal influences. Davies and Brown (1986: 25) put it nicely: '[Observer-dependent reality] seems, perhaps, alien to us because, in most cases, the world still behaves *as if* it had an independent existence. It is actually only when we witness quantum phenomena that this impression looks untenable'. The point of including quantum mechanics in our overview of metaphysical and epistemological problems in this book is not to argue that our everyday world is imaginary or that we have to accept Berkeley's idealism. It is rather that the notions of objectivism, absolutism, and universalism are undermined by quantum mechanics. Of course, it is possible that the search for a Theory of Everything will eventually end in success, but even the best contender (i.e., String Theory) could take decades, possibly centuries, before it is fully developed (Greene, 2003).

Quantum anti-realisms, including quantum idealism and subjectivism, invite important questions. For example, if at a quantum level things-in-themselves do not conform to the traditional realist outlook, what then are the implications for other kinds of realities, including the phenomenal and everyday realities? What guarantees do we have that at the macro and micro levels, the states of entities can be said to be objective beyond their appearances? How do we reconcile the notions of 'objective', 'absolute' and 'universal'? In the opinion of the 'father' of quantum mechanics, Niels Bohr, it was not up to physics to provide the answers to such questions. He held that physics 'tells us not about what *is* but what we can *say* to each other concerning the world' (Davies & Brown, 1986: 11).

--------------------------------- **Recommended reading** ---------------------------------

Davies, P.C.W. & Brown, J.R. (eds) (1986) *The Ghost in the Atom*. Cambridge: Cambridge University Press.

Greene, B.R. (2004) *The Fabric of the Cosmos: Space, Time and the Texture of Reality*. New York: Random House.

Herbert, N. (1985) *Quantum Reality: Beyond the New Physics*. New York: Anchor.

Notes

1. It would be incorrect to reduce atomists to only this view; however, any detailed discussions are beyond the scope of this book. Holden (2004) points out that we can observe a distinction between metaphysical and physical atomism. Historically, in some systems these are one and the same, but in others, they form quite distinct views. For Epicureans (the followers of the Greek philosopher Epicurus, ca. 341 BCE, who was an atomic materialist), for example, the physical atoms were constructed from metaphysical (here the term had spiritual connotations) atoms (Holden, 2004). Centuries later, Leibniz rejected the notion of physical atomism, instead maintaining *metaphysical atomism*, where the atom or *monad* is a creation by God: an indivisible 'metaphysical point, or center of an active force from which all phenomena begins, the "absolute first principle of the composition of things"' (Kavanaugh, 2007: 145). It is vital to appreciate that in this sense the word 'metaphysical' bears a spiritually infused meaning, which is not how we have employed it in this book. The term 'metaphysical', similarly to the word 'ontological', captures the philosophical inquiry into issues of existence and being, as outlined in Chapter 1.
2. Bohr has also been described as an anti-realist and instrumentalist for believing that there is a real atom but disputing the literal representation of the quantum world (see Faye, 2014).
3. In String Theory point-like particles (e.g., quarks and electrons) take the form of one-dimensional vibrating strings (see Greene, 2003).
4. The percentages do not add up to 100 per cent because the survey allowed multiple answers.

PART IV
Philosophy in Qualitative Research

Friendship is unnecessary, like philosophy, like art [...] It has no survival value; rather it is one of those things which give value to survival.

(C.S. Lewis, *The Four Loves*, 2010 [1960])

Eight

Conclusions: On Academic Creativity and Philosophical and Methodological Freedom

The preceding chapters examined the core epistemological concerns and outlined a range of conundrums which philosophers have encountered on their quest to obtain knowledge about the world. The aim before us in this concluding chapter is twofold: to accentuate the integral role philosophical concerns play in the research process, and to engage with some of the deeper problems facing qualitative inquiry. We will first cement in the view that qualitative research can stem from a vast array of epistemological stances. To help navigate this heterogeneous landscape, it is proposed that qualitative inquiry can be imagined on a continuum ranging from *means* to *orientation*, and that the way in which qualitative research manifests is determined by a combination of motivational factors and one's philosophical outlook. A set of probing questions is offered to assist novice researchers in deliberating their own position toward an assortment of philosophical and methodological problems. The second part of this chapter hopes to engage the reader with broader issues around academic creativity. Researchers are called to cultivate a vision of epistemological and methodological freedom, and build a less fractured, and perhaps even a post-paradigmatic, future.

Part one: Philosophy, truth and qualitative inquiry

All research commences with philosophical assumptions, although these may not be explicitly articulated by the researcher or brought to her reflexive fore. The lack of philosophical reflexivity is most notable in some domains of the natural sciences, but dismissive attitudes can also be found among social science scholars.[1]

In qualitative inquiry, philosophy forms the core around which all other decisions in the research process revolve. In this regard, there is a wide consensus (e.g., Denzin & Lincoln, 2011a; Flick, 2009; Guba & Lincoln, 2004; Hesse-Biber & Leavy, 2010; Leavy, 2014; Maxwell, 2013; Merriam, 2009; Patton, 2002; Silverman, 2013) on the necessity of engaging with ontological and epistemological views in the research design process. And so, as we approach the end of this book, it seems inevitable that we will return to a very basic and yet very important question: that of what philosophy is. This question may take years, perhaps even a lifetime, for a person to resolve. The answers, of course, are many and as varied as the intellectuals attracted to this mode of thinking. Here, we will consider the views of the French philosopher duo Deleuze and Guattari. They characterize philosophy as 'the art of forming, inventing, and fabricating concepts' (1991: 2). At the same time, however, they tell us that 'philosophy is not a simple art of forming, inventing, or fabricating concepts, because concepts are not necessarily forms, discoveries, or products. More rigorously, philosophy is the discipline that involves *creating* concepts' (1991: 5, emphasis in original). In other words, philosophy is a high-level endeavour in creative thinking. Philosophical concepts are 'not waiting for us ready-made, like heavenly bodies. There is no heaven for concepts. They must be invented, fabricated, or rather created and would be nothing without their creator's signature'

Table 8.1 Different approaches to 'truth'

Scientific Realism	There is only one true, correct interpretation; scientific theories describe the world as it truly is, objectively.
Structural Realism	Truth extends only to the mathematical and structural content of theories.
Logical Positivism	Propositions are verified in sense experience; the method of verification.
Constructive Empiricism	Theories are empirically adequate; there are no universal truths, only empirically adequate truths about observable events.
Postpositivism	Propositions are *provisionally* valid (true) until refuted; the method of falsification.
Pragmatism	It is needless to speak of absolute truth; it is more beneficial to talk of usefulness and utility – i.e., theories are useful if they solve problems.
Instrumentalism	Truth is replaced with *successful prediction* of what can be observed; a form of pragmatism.
Idea-ism	We can only know our ideas and sense data – i.e., no truth claims can be made in isolation of the ideas we have about the world.
Relativism	Truth is relative or contingent upon different frames of reference (e.g., a conceptual scheme, context, historical period, culture).
Pluralism	There may be several true interpretations – i.e., multiple and equal claims on truth.
Scepticism	We shall either suspend all judgement about knowledge and truth (Pyrrhronian scepticism) or abandon the quest for knowledge altogether, as there is no secure path to discerning truth from falsehood (Academic scepticism).
Solipsism	Only my mind exists; I have no reason to believe in anything else but my subjective thoughts, hence truth is egocentric.

(1991: 5). We are being reminded by Deleuze and Guattari of the creative ability of human beings to cast a web of complex thought to grapple with the possibilities and limits of knowledge – a notion to which we will return towards the closing of this chapter. In the noble pursuit of knowledge, there have been a number of philosophical responses to what true knowledge is. A selection of the most prevailing stances is summarized in Table 8.1.

In Table 8.1, we see that scientific realism is the strongest position, striving to give us literal truths about the world. It is a doctrine fuelled by the aim of science to produce *true* theories of both observable and unobservable entities. Structural realism is committed only to the mathematical or structural component of scientific theories; it doesn't seek to accurately describe the world, only the structure of its elements and the relations between them. Logical positivism or logical empiricism can be understood as the extension of the earlier empirical line of thought; however, as we saw in Chapter 2, it extends only to empirical truths about observable entities.

Constructive empiricism replaces truth with *empirical adequacy*, whereby theories are not true and accurate representations; rather, they are *successful* because they are empirically adequate. Postpositivism can be grasped as a form of rationalism advocated by Karl Popper, who argued that scientific theories or hypotheses ought to be possible to be proved false. The pragmatists replace the notion of *truth* with 'utility' and 'usefulness', and in so doing extend the discourse beyond a solely scientific realm (i.e., to social and moral concerns). In this regard, there are a variety of pragmatist approaches whose examination is beyond the scope of this book. Nevertheless, we can crudely state that the pragmatic theory of truth asks us to consider whether theories and beliefs acclaimed to be *true* allow us to function better, and whether this theory offers 'fruitful lines of inquiry to be pursued in the future' – i.e., to claim that something is *true* is to say that it is useful, beneficial, and promising (Solomon & Higgins, 2010: 173).

Instrumentalist approaches to knowledge can be classed as a variety of pragmatism because within them theories are judged on their success to predict. Moreover, instrumentalists are not interested in describing reality or giving us true accounts of how the world really is. Idea-ism tells us that we can only know our ideas, and that any truth claims to be had cannot be isolated from our sense data. Idea-ism, as we have seen, can accommodate a range of viewpoints. Constructionism, for example, is a form of idea-ism whereby we can only know socially constructed facts – the ideas we intend onto things and share with others. However, constructionism yields different varieties: from objective knowledge of social facts to relativist and pluralist readings. In this respect, the separation of each stance in Table 8.1 does not imply impermeable boundaries or mutual exclusivity; it is possible to arrive at different varieties within and across epistemologies. This way, *strong* constructionism starts in idea-ism and combines with relativism (i.e., what is true is relative to a reference frame). *Weak* constructionism, manifested in Searle's claims (covered in Chapter 6), starts in idea-ism and combines with epistemic realism. Therefore, it is possible to start with a core epistemology but end in different epistemic territories. Consider the following examples:

> **Idea-ism** → We can only know our ideas and sense data; no truth-claims can be made in isolation of the ideas we have about the world → Social constructionism (**weak**/realist) → Social facts are constructed but can be known objectively → We can know the ideas (social facts) people have constructed about things, places, people, and events objectively → Compatible with objective hermeneutics, hermeneutic realism, and epistemic objectivism.

> **Idea-ism** → We can only know our ideas and sense data; no truth-claims can be made in isolation of the ideas we have about the world → Social constructionism (**strong**) → Truth about social facts is socially agreed and always relative to the context according to which it is judged → Compatible with relativism (whether something is true or false is relative), and → also with pluralism (there may be multiple truths, all equally valid).

We must bear in mind that idea-ism is a vast doctrine. Aside from the main figures noted in this book, such as Locke, Berkeley, Hume, and Kant, idea-ism accommodates social constructionist approaches – i.e., social facts are the product of our minds – but can be also traced to the views of prominent scientists. The theoretical physicist David Bohm, for example, held that 'truth is a creative perception', and that scientific theories are a way of seeing rather than representing true knowledge (1994: 182). Hence, according to this conception, truth is fundamentally entwined with, and lies in, the act of perceiving – it is about the grasping of thoughts.

Moving on to the remaining philosophical outlooks in Table 8.1, the pluralists not only believe that truth is relative to contexts, they also purport that there may be multiple, equally valid true accounts. This is not to say that 'everything is true' or that 'anything goes', but rather that the distinct feature of pluralism is the demand for plurality encapsulated by the slogan 'many things go' (Chang, 2012: 261). Seen this way, pluralism is a thesis of diversity and cannot be reduced to mere relativism because it allows different viewpoints and theories to coexist: 'It allows for comparisons between different conceptual frameworks and perspectives' (Baghramian, 2004: 244). The sceptics are either 'mute' on the question of truth (Pyrrhonian scepticism) or reject the possibility of knowledge altogether (Academic scepticism). And finally, the proponents of solipsism (and also extreme forms of subjectivism) may be convinced that the objects of this world, including this book, are nothing more than the product of their own mind. For the solipsists, there is no reality and knowledge beyond one's individual consciousness, no objective knowing.

A key point to be made about the doctrines listed in Table 8.1 is that qualitative researchers can move from one philosophical outlook to another, depending on the problem they wish to address. For instance, one can be a realist through and through and across a range of domains (e.g., ontological, epistemological, semantic and moral realism). But one can also be a relativist about moral codes, a scientific realist about natural facts, an instrumentalist about quantum phenomena, and a *strong* social constructionist about social phenomena. In addition, we have seen that each doctrine encompasses a multiplicity of perspectives. And to complicate matters even further, it is possible to think about what is real in reference to different realms, as noted in Chapter 7. There is the realm of social realities and social facts, the realm of appearances and phenomena, the quantum realm of things in themselves, and the noumenal realm of universal laws and pure mathematics. In such a heterogeneous landscape, it is difficult to package philosophical assumptions in convenient 'lunch boxes'. And so, in responding to the kind of question that asks 'Are you a realist?', the careful reader may respond with a counter-question, 'A realist about what?'.

Qualitative research as a 'means' and 'orientation'

There is no single correct approach to qualitative research, rather numerous ways of engaging in it. Without wanting to expand the list of existing dichotomies (e.g., number vs narrative, objective vs subjective), it is possible to contemplate the decisions that shape one's research design and situate these on an attitudinal continuum. In Figure 8.1 it is shown that at one end of the continuum qualitative research can be conceived of as a *means* and on the other as *orientation*. When taken as a means, it is for the achievement of desired goals and we are generally speaking of a set of methods or 'tools'. Examples include methods for identifying and recruiting respondents, methods for collecting data, methods for making sense of the data (data analysis), and strategies for reporting the research findings.

Some writers on qualitative research, such as Silverman (2013), hold that the choice of qualitative methods must not be predetermined in advance but ought to be driven by the research question. He makes the following case: '[I]f you want to discover how people intend to vote, then a quantitative method, like a social survey, may seem the most appropriate choice. On the other hand, if you are concerned with exploring people's life-histories or everyday behaviour, then qualitative methods may be favoured' (Silverman, 2013: 11). This *practical* view is generally shared by mixed-methods researchers and pragmatist scholars for whom methods are more or less a 'matter of fit'. In this respect, the proponents of mixed methods have been described as the *connoisseurs of methods*, i.e., methodologically eclectic, knowledgeable, and well informed in their study design, aiming to best address the research problem at hand (Teddlie & Tashakkori, 2010). Within this perspective, qualitative research serves a functional purpose, a *means* to an end. We must remember, however, that there are no 'better' routes to qualitative research, and that a mixed-methods approach is one among many views about knowledge acquisition.

Moving along the line towards the other end of the attitudinal spectrum, qualitative research can also be conceived of as orientation. At this end of the spectrum, we are no longer speaking merely of 'means' and 'tools', but deeper concerns intertwined with the act of acquiring knowledge and the potential implications

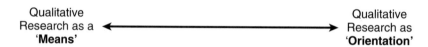

Figure 8.1 Attitudinal Continuum: qualitative research as a 'means' and 'orientation'

for various stakeholders. Qualitative research as *orientation* pays more attention to the ways in which knowledge is created – it is a more probing, critical, and discursive process. For instance, researchers can draw on various forms of reflexivity and reflectivity (for a comprehensive discussion of these issues, see Ashmore, 1989), pay specific attention to matters of politics and power, and also critically examine who is silenced, empowered, or disadvantaged.

In *The Qualitative Manifesto*, Denzin illustrates the extent to which qualitative research can be entangled with issues of social justice and thus become a moral and political activity; he declares that 'the qualitative researcher is not an objective, politically neutral observer who stands outside and above the study of the social world' (2010b: 23). In this text, Denzin's articulation of the *eighth* moment of qualitative research presents a strong view of qualitative inquiry as an activist and a political act, what he calls 'an invitation and a call to arms' (2010b: 10). Furthermore, when qualitative research is approached as *orientation*, researchers can be driven by deliberate strategies to positively impact the co-researchers' lives. In this respect, Denzin and Lincoln describe qualitative research as 'an inquiry project' that is 'also a moral, allegorical, and therapeutic project', motived by a 'humanistic and social justice commitment to study the social world' (2011b: xiii). For example, in the area of action and participatory research, the aim can be to positively alter social realities, and the research activity is seen as a collaboration between the knowing subject and the researcher (Bergold & Thomas, 2012). Last but not least, qualitative research as *orientation* may manifest as an emancipating, liberating, and creative endeavour, and it too can be a decolonizing venture (e.g., Denzin et al., 2008; Devy et al., 2014; Smith, 1999).

Of course, not every study is concerned with morality, politics, or empowering the co-researchers' community. Some investigators may simply wish to obtain richer data, triangulate methods, build new theories, or even generate and test hypotheses. For this reason, it is useful to think of qualitative inquiry in terms of the researcher's commitment to philosophical, moral, ethical, and political issues, which add to the fertile landscape of qualitative inquiry. On this note, it is necessary to emphasize that Figure 8.1 is not offered here as a prescriptive tool – it is a heuristic device whose purpose is to demonstrate the contrasting attitudes towards, and motivations behind, the engagement with qualitative research.

To put philosophy into practice, and to assist us with connecting philosophical problems with research design, consider the decision-making process in Figure 8.2 surrounding the use of interviews. Typically, participants are selected based on some shared characteristics, which are articulated within the overall premise of the research topic (e.g., cancer survivors, teachers, pilgrims, providers of luxury accommodation, artists).

In general, the recruitment strategies focus firstly on establishing commonalities, and then on selecting respondents who meet the criteria. Every interview, then, can be grasped as a unique account consisting of the participant's individual understanding, which may extend to a lived experience, beliefs, personal preferences, and so forth. This process is captured in Figure 8.2 by steps #1, #2 and #3.

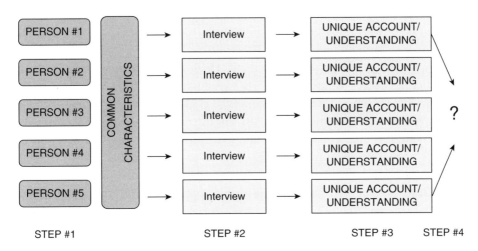

Figure 8.2 The philosophical and methodological considerations behind 'data'

One can go about this process mechanically and uncritically, and when reaching step #4, adopt a reductionist stance, i.e., pursue the reductionist instinct to identify common themes or keywords in order to provide a generic understanding of the phenomenon under scrutiny. However, it is also possible to critically and hermeneutically engage with each of these steps. Every time we specify a phenomenon we take a side – we make the choice to contribute to a particular understanding. Put another way, we express consensus on the ontological, semantic, and epistemic levels. For instance, the meaning of the word 'teacher' differs across cultures and contexts. In an indigenous community, what a teacher is and does doesn't have to conform to western ideals. Therefore, one can engage critically and ponder the construction, context, and magnitude of the ontological and semantic categories in step #1. Moreover, step #4 is an invitation to think about the underlying philosophical assumptions.

Some studies can draw on descriptive phenomenology – say, the phenomenology of teaching experience – in order to discover the *essence* of the phenomenon. In this instance, the researcher demonstrates an allegiance to the view that experiences have intrinsic features, or *essences*, which can be discovered by the method of phenomenological reduction (i.e., by following the philosophy of Edmund Husserl). Here the qualitative researcher would arrive at these essences by means of finding common themes and reducing these to generalized statements (see, for example, Van Manen, 1990). Contemplating and understanding the philosophical and methodological implications is vital, as it would be methodologically flawed if a descriptive phenomenological study were to proclaim that there are as many essences as there are respondents. Husserl held that the essences of phenomena are to be found in consciousness, but exist 'beyond' the individual, so to speak. Thus, his goal with this method was not to describe people's subjective accounts, rather he sought to describe *ideal forms* as they appeared in the subjects' consciousness. Husserl's view of phenomenology as the *science of consciousness* (Husserl, 1931), plus the role of *logic* (Husserl, 2001 [1900/1901]) in his work, mark a 'rationalist impulse in phenomenology' (Smith, 2013c: 367).

Of course, one can also draw on Gadamer, Heidegger, Habermas, or Ricoeur, and employ hermeneutics. This way, step #4 does not have to see the researcher committing to finding common themes or essences. It is indeed possible to treat each case as a unique account. In addition, scholars can use interviews to solely examine the processes of knowledge construction, i.e., scrutinize each of the steps in Figure 8.2 and make a theoretical contribution (as opposed to an empirical one). Fortunately, there are several insightful methodological texts that can assist researchers further in making sense of the complex philosophical and methodological decisions. Alvesson and Sköldberg (2000),[2] for example, note the differences between the line of philosophers who strove to objectively describe and understand the *true* meaning of texts, art, and experiences, and those who saw *truth* as something that emerges between subject and object. In summary, Figure 8.2, and the question mark in step #4 in particular, are an invitation to think about the research process and its alignment with the underlying philosophical assumptions. It should assist in achieving a level of philosophical and methodological rigour that can only be attained by confronting one's epistemological and ontological views.

Where to start?

To determine one's attitude towards qualitative inquiry requires ongoing reflexivity about a range of philosophical and methodological problems. The following probes bid us to contemplate an assortment of issues that we touched upon throughout this book. For each statement the aim is to work out where we sit on a spectrum, ranging from strong agreement to strong disagreement in terms of our research. It is proposed that a high score in 'strongly disagree' responses is likely to result in qualitative research approached as a *means*, whereas a high score in 'strongly agree' responses is indicative of qualitative research as *orientation*. The statements, as with Figure 8.1, are offered as a self-probing exercise. Students and instructors can create different and additional probes to explore their views.

The first statement in Probe #1 focuses on the conceptual framework by Lally (1981), introduced in Chapter 1, who distinguished between those scholars interested in the study of the structures (the *Object*) and those motivated to understand the individual (the *Self*). Strong agreement with this statement would suggest a tendency towards *orientation*; strong disagreement would situate the research close to a *means*. It is also possible to sit comfortably in the middle of the continuum on this issue, and take agency and structure to be mutually constitutive (see Giddens, 1984, for an exploration of this). The second statement centres on the issue of scientific knowledge and the applicability of the scientific method of the natural sciences to the social sciences. Proponents of the view that the methods of the social sciences (and, by extension, qualitative research) are *not* fundamentally different from the natural sciences are more likely to approach qualitative research as a *means*. Qualitative research then becomes the ground for rigorous, reliable, and objective study of human experience (through the use of surveys with open-ended questions, computer-aided qualitative analysis (see Kelle, 2007), and quanti-qualitative methodologies (Grim et al., 2006)).

───── **PROBE #1 Self vs. Structure; Subject vs. Object** ─────

1. I am most concerned about understanding the Subject/Self rather than the Object/Structure believed to influence the agency of individuals.
2. Social science and qualitative research are fundamentally different from the methods and approaches in the natural sciences.

Strongly disagree ◄───────► **Strongly agree**

The statements in Probe #2 tackle the problem of *truth*. As summarized in Table 8.1, researchers have an array of stances to choose from when confronted with epistemic objectivity. The point that deserves additional emphasis is that how one approaches truth determines not only how one deals with the question mark in Figure 8.2 (step #4), it also influences all methods-related choices. Investigators aiming at rich, multiple understandings which are not to be benchmarked or reduced to a common theme are closer to the *orientation* end on the attitudinal spectrum. Nonetheless, many qualitative researchers seek to identify commonalities in order to objectively describe a phenomenon, in which case they are adopting qualitative research as a *means*. Given that qualitative researchers study social phenomena, we can also consider questions about social facts. One may adopt the view that social realities are always changing, transforming and morphing into new realities, and therefore to speak of objectivity would be futile. Others might disagree, arguing that it *is* possible to study social facts objectively. For the latter, the task of qualitative methods is to assist in accomplishing this goal (i.e., objective hermeneutics, discussed in Chapter 5). Quantum mechanics can be included in the overall philosophical deliberations when considering the essence of things, objectivism, absolutism, and universalism.

PROBE #2: Truth
---

3. The function of qualitative research is to provide understanding/s, not to report objective truths.
4. There is no single true, absolute, or objective social fact; truth can only be judged within a given reference frame.
5. There may be more than one true account of social facts, and qualitative research can provide plural understandings.
6. What is claimed as true, moral, or just demands a close examination of the specific contexts, forces, and factors that constitute what is presented as true, moral, or just.
7. Quantum mechanics undermines the notion of the thing-in-itself and also the possibility of absolute and universal truths.

Strongly disagree ←————————→ Strongly agree

Statements 8 to 11 in Probe #3 reflect the role of the inquirer in the research process. The more engrossed a researcher is in the process, the more she moves towards qualitative research as *orientation*; conversely, the more distant one is from the process, the nearer one is to qualitative research as a *means*. Statement #10 attends to the problem of whether the choice of methods ought to be driven solely by the research question or determined by the inquirer. Consider, for example, the difference between studies underpinned by mixed methods and pragmatic approaches and inquiries that are highly reflexive, constructionist, and hermeneutic.

PROBE #3: The Researcher
---

8. I am a fundamental part of the research act, and therefore;
9. It is philosophically and methodologically naïve to bracket myself out of the process of creating knowledge.
10. Qualitative research is a creative scholarly activity capable of accommodating a wide range of methods, whose choice is determined by the researcher (rather than driven by the research problem).
11. My views, background, and existing knowledge influence the research design and hence the final outcome.

Strongly disagree ←————————→ Strongly agree

The statements in the final Probe #4 further ask us to consider the political and moral dimensions of our research. Scholars concerned with matters of social justice, human rights, and the empowerment of minority groups may be drawn to critical, hermeneutic, and constructionist philosophy. Consequently, they may scrutinize notions of objectivity, truth, and representation – i.e., whose views are represented, by whom, and for what purpose – and in so doing move from using qualitative research as a *means* of accurately representing how things are to qualitative research as *orientation*. Of course, what is termed here 'additional concerns' may indeed play a fundamental, if not decisive, role in one's research project. A qualitative study underpinned by indigenous epistemology is a case in point.

Probe #4: Additional Concerns

12. Qualitative research extends to the critical examination and promotion of issues of social justice and human rights; it seeks to give a voice to oppressed, disempowered, and marginalized minority groups.
13. The participants in my research should benefit from my research.
14. Indigenous epistemological and metaphysical views have an important place in qualitative research.

Strongly disagree ←————————→ **Strongly agree**

There are other areas one can reflect upon, including the motivation behind the use of qualitative research. While for some academics the reasons may be as simple as to wish to triangulate, others may be deeply invested in the narratives and viewpoints of the co-researchers on a case-by-case basis. Still, even with triangulation, we have to be vigilant. Triangulation, commonly understood as an approach that blends qualitative and quantitative data (Bryman, 2001), is underpinned by the need to increase confidence, credibility, validity, and robustness by employing more than one method. One can triangulate not only quantitative and qualitative data, but also research notes, documents, interviews, and participant observations (Patton, 2002), as well as theories, methodologies, and investigators (see Denzin, 1970, 1978). Where the motivation is to eliminate potential bias and increase the study's credibility and validity, the research moves to the *means* end of the attitudinal spectrum in Figure 8.1. However, some proponents of pluralist, relativist, constructionist, and hermeneutic approaches may oppose the notion of a privileged path to more objective or credible forms of knowledge. For instance, in collaborative inquiry the purpose of triangulating is not to 'verify or come up with the "truest" description, but rather to describe the multiple realities in a given situation' (Gehart et al., 2007: 384). Gomm further comments on constructionist attitudes toward triangulation, noting that:

> from a *social constructionist* point of view triangulation makes no sense, since each version will be regarded as the outcome of the way it was produced, and there is no particular expectation that any two versions will agree. And, from any

perspective, triangulation presumes some prior decision about what are the sorts of matters about which we can be right or wrong, and which matters will always be questions of interpretation or opinion. (2009: 367)

Thus, methodological or methods-related decisions, triangulation included, stem from the resarcher's philosophical stance. The rationale for the use of triangulation, as well as its role in the research process, can vary dramatically depending on the underlying epistemology. To avoid philosophical and methodological mishaps, a self-probing analysis – such as through the use of the examples shown here – may prove valuable for maintaining philosophical and methodological integrity across all aspects of the research process.

Part two: Post-paradigmatic qualitative research in a post-war future

We began this book by canvassing a selection of conceptual schemas to show that there are various strategies for making the decisions needed to produce knowledge in a scholarly fashion, and for integrating philosophy into research. Crotty (1998) devised a model that includes the four elements of epistemology, theoretical perspective, methodology, and methods; Lally's (1981) framework is centred on metatheoretical and epistemological assumptions; and Lincoln et al.'s (2011) matrix of 'alternative inquiry paradigms' (positivism, postpositivism, critical theory, constructivism, and participatory) is based on ontological, epistemological, and methodological decisions. It was suggested in Chapter 1 that the extent to which qualitative research has been conceptualized – and perhaps too easily accepted – in terms of paradigms, restricts the ways in which philosophical, theoretical, and methodological concerns structure qualitative inquiry. The argument put forth asserted that the use of paradigms represents a compartmentalized, inflexible approach to philosophy, and that as construed by Lincoln et al. (2011), paradigms are limited in their ability to thoroughly capture philosophical diversity.

The problem with laying down prescriptive rules about what qualitative research *is* and how it *ought* to proceed lies in the narrowing of the possibilities of an abundant and constantly evolving body of philosophical thought. When we accept paradigms uncritically as the 'givens', qualitative knowledge becomes habituated, and paradigms grow into hegemonic systems of organization. And when that moment of realization arrives, knowledge is already manufactured in set ways – reflecting the 'locally' cemented customs and practices. In this respect, paradigmatic thinking conditions the mind to 'see' through predetermined ontological, epistemological, and methodological lenses: it steers research into convenient matrices. And so paradigms are no less than the philosopher's carving tool.

Aware of the constructed nature of conceptual schemas, the probing, critical mind may choose to adopt a *post-paradigmatic* approach to qualitative research.

In its reach beyond paradigmatic thinking, such an approach recognizes that paradigms are the product of creative 'local' processes, i.e., the communities of qualitative practice in which they are founded, accepted, and maintained. Fuelled by the realization that there are continua, gradations, and subtle levels of complexity, a post-paradigmatic mind nurtures philosophical diversity. It resists the impulse to catalogue ideas into rigid compartments, instead seeking a critical, creative engagement with philosophy and methodology. It becomes a way of thinking not in terms of limitations but of possibilities.

The 'conceptual personae' in qualitative research

At the start of this chapter, it was suggested that philosophy is about the formation, invention, and fabrication of concepts. Yet there is more that goes into the making of philosophical concepts. Deleuze and Guattari further elaborate that philosophical concepts require 'conceptual personae', loosely translated as 'characters' (1991: 2). The Greeks, as they explain, used the conceptual persona of a *friend* who 'no longer stands for an extrinsic persona, an example or empirical circumstance, but rather for a presence that is intrinsic to thought, a condition of possibility of thought itself' (1991: 3). Qualitative research has, in a similar fashion, conceptually flourished with the assistance of conceptual personae. However, in the rhetoric of qualitative inquiry, these have been mainly 'enemies' and 'warriors'.

Much of the history of qualitative research has been written on the battlefield with the positivists, and even contemporary qualitative thinkers face a 'war' between 'evidence-based methodologists and the mixed methods, interpretive, and critical theory schools (2005 to present)' (Denzin, 2010a: 421). The ninth moment in qualitative research, we are told, has more conflict in store for us, a moment termed by Denzin and Lincoln (2005) as the 'fractured future'. But there is a price to be paid for the maintenance of such a mental imaginary, and the conceptual personae of enemies and warriors come at a great cost. The language of wars sustains a state of fear; it fuels separatism, nurtures isolation, and feeds into the processes of fragmentation:

> When the conceptual persona is a warrior, the thoughts are of a warrior;
>
> When the conceptual persona is a warrior, research becomes warfare;
>
> When the conceptual persona is a warrior, methodology becomes a defense mechanism;
>
> When the conceptual persona is a warrior, creativity gives way to reliable weaponry;
>
> When the conceptual persona is a warrior, there is no room for dialogue.

It is possible to foresee a different future. The imminent generations of qualitative researchers need not become warriors, nor do they have to be conditioned by prophecies of conflict and fragmentation. We can aspire to creating a future where the conceptual personae are 'friends', 'fellows' and 'respectful opponents'.

We can create an environment that nurtures academic freedom, creativity, and the expression of a range of philosophical orientations and methodological choices.

On the importance of philosophical and methodological freedom

Qualitative research comes in many shapes and forms. We must abandon the idea that there is a 'better', sturdier, or more important path to qualitative research. What there are, nevertheless, are different research aims, varying levels of usefulness, and a range of attitudinal factors that drive scholars to create knowledge that best conforms to their vision. Such visions are seldom subjective. Agreement as to what is acceptable on the level of method, epistemology, or paradigms occurs within communities of qualitative practice. By accepting without pause the ideals established as the 'norm', one risks producing research in a mechanical fashion. The cost is both epistemic and existential, for one compromises not only the possibility of original knowledge but also one's philosophical and methodological freedom.

Whilst we leave these thoughts to reverberate, it is fitting to conclude by noting a pair of methodological 'rebels': Paul Feyerabend (1924–1994) and Richard Cobb (1917–1996). Feyerabend, one of the most notorious figures of anti-realism, referred to his early philosophical aspirations as those of a 'raving positivist' (2010: 271). Preston (1997: S421) remarks that the young Feyerabend insisted that 'theories tell us about what things are, their very nature, in a world which exists independently of measurement and observation'. In philosophical terms, Feyerabend was a scientific realist. The later Feyerabend, however, advocated ontological pluralism, antireductionism, epistemic pluralism (the notion that science contains many epistemologies and not just one), and even social constructionism (as read by Preston). He saw the need for more discursive and dialogical approaches to science, and was opposed to any narrow, strict, or dogmatic approaches to truth-seeking. Hacking (2010: xiii) emphasizes that Feyerabend – who was condemned by many for his famous assertion that 'anything goes' – 'never meant for one minute that anything except the scientific method (whatever that is) "goes"'; he clarifies further that what Feyerabend did loathe was 'any kind of intellectual or ideological hegemony' (2010: xiii). The philosopher himself described his approach as a form of anarchism which campaigned against the 'enslaving' of everyone else with only a single set of ideas, and where nothing else was allowed to 'go'. His use of the motto 'anything goes' was to argue that openness to other ideas is important for (scientific) progress. He wrote the following on this matter:

> One of my motives for writing *Against Method* was to free people from the tyranny of philosophical obfuscators and abstract concepts such as "truth," "reality," or "objectivity," which narrow people's vision and ways of being in the world. (Feyerabend, 1996: 179)

The second anti-methodologist, Richard Cobb, was a well-respected British historian and a professor at the University of Oxford, whose research focused on French history and the French Revolution. He has been described by Cuttica as a thinker with a 'fierce aversion to methodological discussion as well as theoretical reflection in historical research' (2014: 96). Cobb was opposed to the application of sociological methods to historical research because these were 'too neat, too mechanical and too devoted to sterile laws far removed from the "sympathy" necessary to capture what was going on amongst idealist and unpredictable men and women at a given time in a given society' (2014: 95). In Cobb's opinion, the established methods and theoretical models led to inadequate generalizations, inert sociological categories, rigid classifications, and the portrayal of peoples in a homogeneous fashion. Cuttica brings to our attention that Cobb disregarded any forms of global history, rejected notions of professionalism, and saw theoretical discussions as being either 'pretentious, tail-chasing froth' or 'a restatement of the obvious' (2014: 94). In summary, Cobb was:

> a breaker of 'the signposts'; of 'the charts of collective identities'; of 'generalizations'; of 'easily assimilated general laws'. He rejected historical interpretations of the genesis of phenomena, especially revolutions, constructed on ideas of inevitable progress, fixed developments and pre-established courses of action dovetailed to fit implausible and irritatingly abstract theoretical 'models'. (2014: 95)

Despite Cobb's methodological approach being an 'anti-methodology', and although there is no easily identifiable theoretical framework to be distilled from his writing, his work made a major contribution to history – so much so that it led to new interpretations of the French revolutionary period (Cuttica, 2014). There is a similarity between these two intellectuals. The rebellious, anarchistic attitude that Feyerabend endorsed, Cobb, to an extent, executed with potent force throughout his academic career. Therefore, the take-home message here is that we must not be afraid of scholarly inventiveness and creativity. We ought to pursue inspired inclinations because there is every chance that some creations will turn out to be immensely valuable. This is not a claim that *all* qualitative inquiry must conform to defiant modes of thinking. The attitudinal continuum erected in this chapter accommodates all forms of qualitative knowledge. Qualitative research would be impoverished without the voices of the minority groups and the minds that wander off the well-travelled path. And so we ought to nurture a vision of epistemological and methodological freedom, and with this vista in mind, all that remains to be said is:

> *'Philosophers of the world, create!'*

Deleuze and Guattari[3] (1991: vii)

Notes

1. Sanderson (2007: 4095), for example, holds that natural scientists do not need philosophy of science 'because they have a keen sense of what they are doing, and they generally do it extremely well'. In his view, social scientists 'very badly need to study the history and philosophy of science because they need to gain a much better understanding of how real science actually works and try to emulate it' (2007: 4095).
2. They describe the first as the adherents of *objectivist hermeneutics* with figures such as Dilthey and Weber. The latter, Alvesson and Sköldberg (2000) note, are the proponents of *alethic hermeneutics* (i.e., alluding to something hidden) where the concern may be with the concealed aspects of interpretation – be they original structures (existential hermeneutics), patterns of metaphor or narrative (poetic hermeneutics), or hidden *other* interests (critical hermeneutics/ hermeneutics of suspicion).
3. This slogan is the interpretation offered by Tomlinson and Burchell as part of their effort to summarize the gist of the book (see Translators' Introduction in Deleuze & Guattari, 1991: vii).

Glossary

A *priori* justification Relies on rational intuitions or insights; based on reason alone and includes mostly abstract concepts and mathematical calculations (Russell, 2007).

A *priori* knowledge Relies on *a priori* justification; knowledge grounded in rational thought, as opposed to experience; associated with the doctrine of *rationalism*.

A *posteriori* knowledge Relies on empirical evidence or experience, such as perceptions from our senses (see also **empiricism** and **empirical research**).

Abduction A form of reasoning that moves from data to a hypothesis for explaining the data. The term was coined by C.S. Pierce and is also known as inference to the best explanation (of gathered evidence or facts): 'The governing idea is that explanatory considerations are a guide to inference, that the hypothesis that would, if correct, best explain the evidence is the hypothesis that is most likely to be correct' (Lipton, 2006: 2).

Absolutism An overarching philosophical view comprising objectivism, foundationalism, and universalism (Krausz, 2010a); it states that there is an independent, neutral, and final point of view (e.g., laws, moral principles).

Academic scepticism A philosophical view which states that no knowledge is possible.

Analytic philosophy A branch of philosophy that flourished in the twentieth century. Analytic philosophers apply logic to ensure the clarity of philosophical thought (e.g., the proponents of logical positivism).

Analytic statement A statement whose truth or falsity 'can be determined solely by the analysis of the meanings of the words in the sentence expressing it' (Hung, 2014: 135). For example, 'all bachelors are single' is an analytic statement.

Anti-realism An umbrella term that covers a variety of philosophical positions whose commonality is their objection to scientific realism.

Appearance That which appears to the human senses; sense data.

Atomism (in western philosophy) A view propagated in ancient Greece by the philosopher Democritus that asserts reality is composed of small entities called atoms, surrounded by void.

Axioms Statements of self-evident truth established by Euclid of Alexandria (e.g., if equals be added to equals, the wholes are equal).

Cartesian intuition/deduction 'Intuition is a faculty we have by virtue of which we are capable of grasping truths directly; deduction is a complementary faculty, by virtue of which we can intuit the connections between one proposition and another' (Garber, 2001: 117).

Cartesian scepticism A sceptical method of doubting all truth claims to eliminate all unreliable knowledge; not to be confused with **Academic** or **Pyrrhonian scepticism**.

Causality (philosophy) The idea that some events cause other events to occur. David Hume challenged the notion of causation and proposed that we only perceive one event followed by another, not the cause or 'necessary connection' itself (Jubien, 2004: 37).

Causality (physics) The relationship between cause and effect.

Causal realism Claims that 'there are external objects that exist independently of our minds and which cause our *indirect* perception of them via the senses' (Ladyman, 2002: 141); also known as **indirect** or representative **realism**.

Chaos and complexity theory Terms used in qualitative research, mostly as metaphors to study human complexities and the unpredictability in human behaviour (see Patton, 2002).

Chicago School A form of symbolic interactionism developed by Herbert Blumer; distinctive for use of the method of participant observation and a focus on the subject/Self. Within this school, the Self was understood to be the result of mutual interpretations (Herman, 1994); social structures were seen to be *emergent* phenomena, which come into being through the active agency of individuals.

Coherence theory of truth A view of truth as a matter of coherence with other propositions; a statement is true if it is consistent with other accepted propositions.

Consensus theory of truth A view of truth as a matter of agreement.

Constructionism A philosophical standpoint claiming that knowledge and/or social reality are socially constructed. See **social constructionism**.

Constructivism A philosophical outlook adopted by Immanuel Kant whereby a subject is actively involved in the construction of knowledge. Constructivism 'claims that a minimal condition of knowledge is that the subject must in some sense, which varies according to the thinker concerned, "construct" what it knows' (Rockmore, 2011: 11).

Constructive empiricism A form of empiricism introduced by Bas van Fraassen, who argued that observable evidence is not sufficient for determining the *truth* of theories about unobservable entities. Theories are not *true*, rather they are *empirically adequate* if they generate true predictions about observable entities (Bird, 2004).

Correspondence theory of truth A view that the truth of propositions depends on their relation to facts, i.e., how accurately statements correspond to reality.

Culture 'An integrated system of symbolic and material practices, that is ways of achieving goals and projects that are constrained by local norms, and which are historical in that they emerge from and continue traditions' (Harré & Krausz, 1996: 11).

Deduction A method of reasoning 'concerned with drawing logically valid conclusions that must follow from a set of premises' (Heit, 2007: 2).

Direct realism A view which states that the world is how we perceive it directly via our senses; also known as naïve realism.

Dogma A strong set of principles insisted upon by its adherents; for example, the outcome of **Academic scepticism** led to a dogmatic conclusion that nothing is knowable.

Dualism Two opposing parts or principles; for example, René Descartes maintained that the body is fundamentally different from the mind (mind–body dualism).

Ecological psychology The claim that perception and action are indissoluble, and that the distinction between an observer and the environment is blurred; based on the work of J.J. Gibson.

Empirical research Research based on empirical evidence, i.e., observation and experimentation.

Empiricism A philosophical doctrine whose central claim is that knowledge can only be derived from experience (see also *a posteriori* **knowledge**).

Entanglement A concept in *quantum mechanics* suggested by Erwin Schrödinger which states that subatomic particles (for example, two electrons) are instantaneously connected and have an immediate effect on one another, regardless of how physically far apart they are.

Epistemic Relating to 'some aspect of our actual knowing or believing'. Examples of epistemic questions are 'Should I believe this?' or 'Do I really know that?' (Crumley, 2009: 17).

Epistemological realism A philosophical stance which speaks of the ability to know the external world as it *truly* is; in its strongest form it manifests as **scientific realism**.

Epistemology The theory of knowledge, including issues such as the nature, scope, justification, and the limits of knowledge.

Ethnography The study of peoples and cultures. Ethnography has two meanings: it is a field of study and also a descriptive account of a culture prepared by an anthropologist. As a field, it originated in the disciplines of social anthropology (UK) and cultural anthropology (USA) with the aim of providing descriptive accounts of cultural groups. Contemporary ethnography is multi-disciplinary and draws on a wide range of methods.

Facts (epistemic) In epistemology, facts are statements believed to be true. Epistemic facts are also called natural facts, i.e., facts about the world that are confirmed by scientific methods.

Fact (social) In social ontology, a social fact is 'any fact involving collective intentionality of two or more animals' (Searle, 2014: 18). 'US dollar banknote', 'professor', 'student', 'president of the United States', 'homework', 'sustainability', 'blogger', and 'Afghan citizen' are all examples of social facts.

Falsification A methodological feature of Karl Popper's *postpositivist* approach to knowledge; specifically, Popper's claim that 'the criterion of the scientific status of a theory is its falsifiability, or refutability, or testability' (1999b: 69), i.e., that scientific theories or hypotheses ought to be possible to be proven false.

Foundationalism An epistemological position about the justification of knowledge: 'Foundationalists maintain that some beliefs are properly basic and that the rest of one's beliefs inherit their epistemic status (knowledge or justification) in virtue of receiving proper support from the basic beliefs' (see Poston, 2015).

Global scepticism See **Academic scepticism**.

Hermeneutic circle A conceptual/philosophical tool used in the processes of understanding which 'describes how, in the process of understanding and interpretation, part and whole are related in a circular way: in order to understand the whole, it is necessary to understand the parts, while to understand the parts it is necessary to have some comprehension of the whole' (Hoy, 1982: vii).

Hermeneutic idea-ism A philosophical stance which asserts that interpretation is not to be discovered in the text, object, or event, instead it is entangled with the interpreter. Applied to research, it views the researcher as playing an active role in the process of meaning-making.

Hermeneutic phenomenology A branch of philosophy that sees social, cultural, and historical situatedness as necessary for the development of understandings (see also **hermeneutic circle**).

Hermeneutic realism A philosophical stance resting on the notion of 'correct interpretation', which states that there can be only one *truthful* account of an event, text, or object, and that the role of the researcher, and indeed the purpose of an inquiry, are to make this truthful account known.

Hermeneutics A philosophical doctrine dating back to Ancient Greece, where it denoted the interpretation of messages between gods and humans. In the Middle Ages it became the science of interpretation. Wilhelm Dilthey was one of the most influential philosophers within the hermeneutic tradition. He emphasized the drive for objectivity and reliability in interpretation, a notion that was challenged by other hermeneutic thinkers and critical theorists such as Gadamer, Foucault, and Derrida.

Hypotheses Statements that are subject to testing, verification, and proof, which commonly take the form of prediction. They are relativized to people and scientific communities, and can be either true or false (Hung, 2014).

Hypothetico-deductive method A method of formulating theories or hypotheses so they can be tested and potentially falsified by experimentation and observation. The hypothetico-deductive method and **falsificationism** are methodological features ascribed to **postpositivism** (see also **deduction**).

Idea-ism An epistemological thesis which holds that what appears to us through our perception 'are not external objects but rather appearances or ideas or sense-data produced in our minds by external objects' (Musgrave, 1993: 89).

Idealism A metaphysical claim which asserts that objects in the external world exist independent of the mind.

Immaterialism (metaphysical) The view that 'everything is mental or an aspect of, or dependent on, the mental' (Alston, 2002: 97); also called **metaphysical idealism**.

Indirect realism The view that we can only have indirect knowledge of the external world as things may not always be how they appear to us.

Induction A logical process of arriving at knowledge about observed phenomena by moving from the particular to the general, i.e., from individual observations to general principles (see also **verificationism**).

Innate knowledge A concept used by some rationalist philosophers to argue that some forms of knowledge are *inborn* or innate, that we have a mental disposition which does not require experience (e.g., 2 + 2 = 4, the triangle, God).

Instrumentalism A claim that states that both observable and unobservable entities are *instruments* 'whose value consists in their ability successfully to predict what can be observed, that is, the outcomes of experiments rather than in their description of the fundamental structure of reality' (Ladyman, 2002: 266).

Iowa School A form of symbolic interactionism developed by Manford Kuhn. Its distinctive feature was the development and testing of hypotheses to make generalized statements about human behaviour. The programme was driven by 'quantifiable measurements within target samples' (Katovich et al., 2003: 119).

Logically necessary True by definition (see also **analytic statement**).

Logical positivism A form of empiricism in twentieth-century philosophy grounded in logical and empirical science. It is based on three core principles: the distinction between analytic and synthetic statements, the principle of verification, and a reductive thesis (Stroll, 2000).

Materialism (metaphysical) The view that material objects exist independent of human beings and their mental processes.

Matter A loose term used in physics to denote the substance of observable entities.

Metaphysical idealism See **immaterialism (metaphysical)**.

Metaphysical realism A claim about the mind-independent existence of objects; it 'affirms the existence (or reality) of a largely mind-, experience-, language-, concept-, theory-, and practice-independent world' (Pihlström, 2014: 252).

Metaphysics The 'part of philosophy that treats the concept of *existence* (or *being*) [emphasis in original]' (Jubien, 2004: 36); it includes both physical entities (e.g., table, people, stone) and abstract entities (e.g., quarks, number, mind, God), which form ontological hierarchies (see also **ontology**).

Necessary statement In philosophy, a 'statement is **necessary** if its truth or falsity cannot but be as it is, otherwise it is said to be **contingent**' [emphasis in original] (Hung, 2014: 136).

Nominalism A thesis which states that all things that exist are particulars: 'Nominalists deny that there is any genuine or objective identity in things which are not identical. Realists, on the other hand, hold that the apparent situation is the real situation. There genuinely is, or can be, something identical in things which are not identical. Besides particulars, there are universals' (Armstrong, 1978: 12).

Noumena A concept used by Kant (sing. noumenon) to explain an aspect of reality that exists mind-independent of the observer, i.e., 'thought entities' or 'objects of pure understanding' that are conceivable by the mind but beyond the reach of experience (see Dilworth, 2013).

Objectivism A thesis that states the way things are in the world is independent of the human mind and any reference frame: on the level of ontology, objectivism affirms that external objects exist irrespective of reference frames; on the level of epistemology, it asserts that a statement or a claim is epistemologically objective if it holds regardless of any reference frame (Krausz, 2010a).

Objectivity (in the research process) A notion of distance between the researcher and the researched, whereby 'scientists make observations in such a way that they do not distort or misread what they observe as a result of tradition, values, emotions, or other subjective influences' (Slife & Williams, 1995: 193).

Observable entity In the philosophy of science, the observable is 'that which can, under favourable conditions, be perceived using the unaided senses (for example, planets and platypuses)' (see Chakravartty, 2013: section 1.1, para. 1).

Ontological realism A philosophical stance that forms a broader realist doctrine; the claim that reality and objects exist independent of the human mind (see also **metaphysical realism**).

Ontology A field of metaphysics that is concerned with the study of being, or that which is; it includes a hierarchy of levels of reality to determine what exists, undeniably, in the external world (Solomon & Higgins, 2010).

Paradigm From the Greek *paradeigma* (exemplar), this term was popularized by Thomas Kuhn, who used it to denote 'accepted examples of actual scientific practice' (2012 [1962]: 11). In qualitative research, it is used to encapsulate a unique set of ontological, epistemological, and methodological assumptions (Denzin & Lincoln, 2011a).

Phenomena The cognitive grasping of appearances (in Kantian terms).

Phenomenalism The empirical thesis that states that unless statements are confirmed or verified by experience they are nonsensical.

Phenomenology The study of the structures of conscious *experience* as they manifest in people's mind; developed by Edmund Husserl.

Pluralism A philosophical stance whose adherents believe in 'multiple investigative approaches and representational systems' (Kellert et al., 2006: xi). Pluralism about truth, for example, states that there can be multiple truths that are equally valid.

Positivism 'A model of the research process which treats "social facts" as existing independently of the activities of both participants and researchers' (Silverman, 2013: 379).

Post-paradigmatic approach A philosophical and methodological approach to research stemming from the critical awareness that there are continua, gradations, and subtle levels of complexity which are not captured by paradigms.

Postpositivism A view of the scientific method as a hypothetico-deductive process underpinned by falsificationism; it arose from the critique of logical positivism by Karl Popper (see also **falsification**).

Postulates Basic suppositions of geometry.

Pragmatist theory of truth A view of truth as 'practice-oriented, situational, provisional, experimental and processual in the sense that it is constantly emerging anew in never-ending processes of adaptation to experience and readjustment to intersubjective encounters' (Fluck, 1999: ix).

Pyrrhonian scepticism A variety of scepticism that asks us to suspend judgement if there is conflicting evidence; it is based on the doctrines of Pyrrho of Elis.

Quantum mechanics The study of physical entities at very small atomic and subatomic levels.

Quon A generic term for a quantum object; 'any entity, no matter how immense, that exhibits both wave and particle aspects in the peculiar quantum manner' (Herbert, 1985: 64).

Rationalism A philosophical tradition characterized by the primacy of rational thought, reason, or intellect in receiving and holding knowledge (see Nelson, 2013a). In epistemology, rationalism states that knowledge is the product of reason alone (see also *a priori* **knowledge**).

Realism A family of philosophical views which includes metaphysics, ontology, epistemology, methodology, and semantics. Realism is an opposing stance not only to instrumentalism and relativism, but also to phenomenalism, pragmatism, verificationism, reductionism, internal realism, constructive empiricism, and many more (see Nola, 1988).

Reference frame A term used by the proponents of relativism to argue that truth, moral values, or beauty, for example, exist relative to something else, such as a historical period, culture, paradigms, or social norms.

Reflective research Research that comprises the dual characteristics of careful interpretation and reflection, whereby '[t]he first implies that all references – trivial and non-trivial – to empirical data are the *results of interpretation*' [emphasis in original], whilst the second 'turns attention "inwards" towards the person of the researcher, the relevant research community, society as a whole, intellectual and cultural traditions, and the central importance, as well as the problematic nature, of language and narrative (the form of representation) in the research context' (Alvesson & Sköldberg, 2000: 9).

Reflexivity An active process of examining one's assumptions and attitudes toward research. Reflexivity can be approached as self-reference, self-awareness, but also as 'the constitutive circularity of accounts' (for a comprehensive discussion of these issues, see Ashmore, 1989).

Relativism A family of philosophical views which includes ontology, epistemology, methodology, and semantics. The varieties of relativism depend on the relativizers (e.g., social class, historical epoch, culture) and what is being relativized (e.g., truth, perceptual experience, methods of investigation) (see Nola, 1988).

Rigour The degree to which research methods are scrupulously and meticulously carried out.

Scepticism An epistemological doctrine characterized by a sceptical or doubting attitude toward knowledge (see also **Academic scepticism** and **Pyrrhonian scepticism**).

Scientific method A collection of general principles whose application are believed to produce reliable knowledge (see also **scientific realism**).

Scientific realism A philosophical doctrine whose proponents claim that scientific knowledge about both observable and unobservable (or theoretical) entities ought to be treated as a true and accurate description of reality (Sankey, 2008), i.e., the aim of science is to produce *true* theories of both observable and unobservable entities.

Semantic realism A philosophical branch of a broader realist doctrine which speaks to the truth-value of sentences/scientific theories (see Nola, 1988).

Social constructionism A philosophical stance that, in its basic form, claims that knowledge, social facts, or both are socially constructed. Social construction-ism comes in varieties and its claims can also extend to the facts of the natural sciences (strong constructionism).

Social fact See **fact (social)**.

Social ontology A branch of philosophy that deals with social reality; a broader philosophical project that seeks to understand 'the mode of existence of social entities such as governments, families, cocktail parties, summer vacations, trade unions, baseball games, and passports', termed by Searle (2010: 5) 'The Philosophy of Society'.

Solipsism A philosophical doctrine that denies the existence of matter and other thinking subjects.

Structural realism A form of realism proposed by John Worrall that states truth is limited to the structural and mathematical content of a theory (Ladyman, 2014).

Subatomic particle A particle smaller than a hydrogen atom (e.g., electrons, protons, neutrons).

Subjectivism A philosophical doctrine that states 'the subject has an immediate knowledge only of its own ideas, so that it has no knowledge beyond its circle of consciousness' (Beiser, 2002: 1).

Symbolic interactionism A sociological perspective that rests on three core assumptions: social reality is socially constructed; individuals have agency; people interact with each other and give rise to/manipulate symbols, languages, identities and meanings (see Denzin, 1978).

Synthetic statement A proposition that entails empirical investigation in order to confirm its truth.

Theoretical entity A term used in the philosophy of science to designate entities that are not observable (e.g., subatomic particles), as opposed to those that are (e.g., rocks).

Transcendental Independent of, or going beyond, experience (see also **phenomenology** and *a priori* **knowledge**).

Transcendental phenomenology A phenomenological philosophy developed by Edmund Husserl to study how phenomena manifest in consciousness; it is 'concerned with articulating the "conditions of the possibility" of experience' (Cerbone, 2006: 5).

Universalism A philosophical claim that there are *universals*, or properties and relations, which exist independent of the classifying mind (Armstrong, 1978).

Unobservable entity See **theoretical entity**.

Verificationism A method of verifying or confirming theories popular among the adherents of *positivism*.

Verisimilitude A concept in the philosophy of science that concerns the truth and the falsity of statements; it can be described as 'a measure of the extent to which a theory approaches the truth but falls short of it' (Nola & Sankey, 2007: 36).

References

Al-Khalili, J. & McFadden, J. (2014) *Life on the Edge: The Coming of Age of Quantum Biology*. London: Bantam.

Alston, W.P. (2002) What metaphysical realism is not. In W.P. Alston (ed.), *Realism and Antirealism* (pp. 97–118). Ithaca, NY: Cornell University Press.

Alvesson, M. & Sköldberg, K. (2000) *Reflexive Methodology: New Vistas for Qualitative Research*. London: SAGE.

Amoroso, L. (2015) Spinoza and Vico: A new science of interpretation. In J. Malpas & H.-H. Gander (eds), *The Routledge Companion to Hermeneutics* (pp. 39–49). Abingdon: Routledge.

Anderson, D.L. (2002) Why God is not a semantic realist. In W.P. Alston (ed.), *Realism and Antirealism* (pp. 131–46). Ithaca, NY: Cornell University Press.

Ankersmit, F. (1983) *Narrative Logic: A Semantic Analysis of the Historian's Language*. The Hague, The Netherlands: Martinus Nijhoff.

Anglin, W.S. (1994) *Mathematics: A Concise History and Philosophy*. New York, NY: Springer-Verlag.

Applebaum, W. (ed.) (2000) *Encyclopedia of the Scientific Revolution: From Copernicus to Newton*. New York: Garland.

Archer, M.S., Bhaskar, R.A., Collier, A., Lawson, T. & Norrie, A. (eds) (1998) *Critical Realism: Essential Readings*. London: Routledge.

Ariew, R. (2013) Pierre Duhem. In E.N. Zalta (ed.), *The Stanford Encyclopedia of Philosophy* (Summer, 2013 edn). Retrieved from http://plato.stanford.edu/archives/sum2013/entries/duhem/

Armstrong, D.M. (1978) *Nominalism and Realism: Universals and Scientific Realism, Volume 1*. Cambridge: Cambridge University Press.

Ashmore, M. (1989) *The Reflexive Thesis: Wrighting Sociology of Scientific Knowledge*. Chicago, IL: University of Chicago Press.

Aspect, A., Grangier, P. & Roger, G. (1982) Experimental realization of Einstein-Podolsky-Rosen-Bohm *Gedankenexperiment*: A new violation of Bell's inequalities. *Physical Review Letters*, 49 (2): 91–4.

Atkinson, P., Coffey, A. & Delamont, S. (1999) Ethnography: Post, past, and present. *Journal of Contemporary Ethnography*, 28 (5): 460–71. doi:10.1177/0891241 99028005004.

Atkinson, P., Coffey, A. & Delamont, S. (2003) *Key Themes in Qualitative Research: Continuities and Changes*. Walnut Creek, CA: AltaMira.

Atkinson, P., Coffey, A., Delamont, S., Lofland, J. & Lofland, L. (eds) (2007) *Handbook of Ethnography*. New York: SAGE.

Atkinson, P., & Housley, P. (2003) *Interactionism: An Essay in Sociological Amnesia*. London: SAGE.

Baert, P., Weinberg, D. & Mottier, V. (2011) Social constructionism, postmodernism and deconstructionism. In I.C. Jarvie & J. Zamora-Bonilla (eds), *The SAGE Handbook of the Philosophy of Social Sciences* (pp. 475–86). London: SAGE.

Baghramian, M. (2004) *Relativism*. Abingdon: Taylor & Francis.

Baghramian, M. (2009) 'From realism back to realism': Putnam's long journey. *Philosophical Topics*, 36 (1): 17–36. doi:10.5840/philtopics20083612.

Baghramian, M. (ed.) (2013) *Reading Putnam*. Abingdon: Routledge.

Beiser, F.C. (2002) *German Idealism: The Struggle against Subjectivism, 1781–1801*. Cambridge, MA: Harvard University Press.

Bell, J.S. (1964) On the Einstein-Podolsky-Rosen paradox. *Physics*, 1: 195–200.

Bell, J.S. (2004) *Speakable and Unspeakable in Quantum Mechanics* (2nd edn). Cambridge: Cambridge University Press.

Berger, P. & Luckmann, T. (1966) *The Social Construction of Reality: A Treatise in the Sociology of Knowledge*. Garden City, NY: Anchor.

Bergold, J. & Thomas, S. (2012) Participatory research methods: A methodological approach in motion. *Forum: Qualitative Social Research Sozialforschung*, 13 (1).

Berkeley, G. (2008[1710]) *A Treatise Concerning the Principles of Human Knowledge*. Rockville, MD: Arc Manor.

Bermúdez, J.L. (2008) Cartesian skepticism: Arguments and antecedents. In J. Greco (ed.), *The Oxford Handbook of Skepticism* (pp. 53–79). New York: Oxford University Press.

Bernstein, R.J. (1983) *Beyond Objectivism and Relativism: Science, Hermeneutics, and Praxis*. Oxford: Basil Blackwell.

Berryman, S. (2011) Ancient Atomism. In E.N. Zalta (ed.), *The Stanford Encyclopedia of Philosophy* (Winter, 2011 edn). Retrieved from http://plato.stanford.edu/archives/win2011/entries/atomism-ancient

Bevir, M. (1994) Objectivity in history. *History and Theory*, 33 (3): 328–44. doi:10.2307/2505477.

Bhaskar, R.A. (1997) *A Realist Theory of Science*. London: Verso.

Bird, A. (2004) Philosophy of science. In J. Shand (ed.), *Fundamentals of Philosophy* (pp. 297–325). London: Taylor & Francis.

Bloor, D. (2011) Relativism and the sociology of scientific knowledge. In S.D. Hales (ed.), *A Companion to Relativism* (pp. 433–55). Oxford: Wiley-Blackwell.

Blumer, H. (1979) Comments on 'George Herbert Mead and the Chicago Tradition of Sociology'. *Symbolic Interaction*, 2 (2): 21–2. doi:10.1525/si.1979.2.2.21.

Blumer, H. (1986 [1969]) *Symbolic Interactionism: Perspective and Method*. Berkeley, CA: University of California Press.

Bogdan, R.C. & Biklen, S.K. (2007) *Qualitative Research for Education: An Introduction to Theories and Methods* (5th edn). Boston, MA: Pearson.

Boghossian, P. (2006) *Fear of Knowledge: Against Relativism and Constructivism*. Oxford: Oxford University Press.

Bohm, D. (1994) *Thought as a System*. New York: Routledge.

Bohm, D. (2002 [1980]) *Wholeness and the Implicate Order*. Abingdon: Routledge.

Bokulich, A. & Bokulich, P.J.M. (eds) (2011) *Scientific Structuralism*. New York: Springer.

Bolyard, C. (2013) Medieval Skepticism. In E.N. Zalta (ed.), *The Stanford Encyclopedia of Philosophy* (Spring, 2013 edn). Retrieved from http://plato.stanford.edu/archives/spr2013/entries/skepticism-medieval/

Born, M. (1951) *The Restless Universe*. Mineola, NY: Dover Publications.

Bourdeau, M. (2013) Auguste Comte. In E.N. Zalta (ed.), *The Stanford Encyclopedia of Philosophy* (Winter, 2013 edn). Retrieved from http://plato.stanford.edu/archives/win2013/entries/comte/

Braver, L. (2007) *A Thing of this World: A History of Continental Anti-realism*. Evanston, IL: Northwestern University Press.

Brinkmann, S., Jacobsen, M.H. & Kristiansen, S. (2014) Historical overview of qualitative research in the social sciences. In P. Leavy (ed.), *The Oxford Handbook of Qualitative Research* (pp. 17–42). New York: Oxford University Press.

Brown, C. (1988) Internal realism: Transcendental idealism? *Midwest Studies In Philosophy*, 12 (1): 145–55. doi:10.1111/j.1475–4975.1988.tb00163.x.

Brown, H.I. (1992) Direct realism, indirect realism, and epistemology. *Philosophy and Phenomenological Research*, 52 (2): 341–63.

Bryman, A. (2001) *Quantity and Quality in Social Research* (revised edition). London: Routledge.

Burnham, D. (2015) *Gottfried Leibniz: Metaphysics*. Retrieved 22 May 2015 from www.iep.utm.edu/leib-met/

Burr, V. (1998) Overview: Realism, relativism, social constructionism and discourse. In I. Parker (ed.), *Social Constructionism, Discourse and Realism* (pp. 13–26). London: SAGE.

Burr, V. (2003) *Social Constructionism* (2nd edn). New York: Routledge.

Carey, S.W. (1988) *Theories of the Earth and Universe: A History of Dogma in the Earth Sciences*. Stanford, CA: Stanford University Press.

Carlino, A. (1999) *Books of the Body: Anatomical Ritual and Renaissance Learning* (J. Tedeschi & A.C. Tedeschi, Trans.). Chicago, IL: University of Chicago Press.

Carnap, R. (1937) *The Logical Syntax of Language*. (A. Smeaton, Trans.). London: Kegan Paul, Trench, Trubner and Co.

Carter, R., Lubinsky, J. & Domholdt, E. (2013) *Rehabilitation Research: Principles and Applications*. St Louis, MO: Elsevier Health Sciences.

Cassam, Q. (2009) *The Possibility of Knowledge*. Oxford: Oxford University Press.

Caves, C.M., Fuchs, C.A. & Schack, R. (2007) Subjective probability and quantum certainty. *Studies in History and Philosophy of Science, Part B: Studies in History and Philosophy of Modern Physics*, 38 (2): 255–74. doi:10.1016/j.shpsb.2006.10.007.

Cerbone, D.R. (2006) *Understanding Phenomenology*. Stocksfield: Acumen.

Chakravartty, A. (2013) Scientific realism. In E.N. Zalta (ed.), *The Stanford Encyclopedia of Philosophy* (Summer, 2013 edn). Retrieved from http://plato.stanford.edu/archives/sum2013/entries/scientific-realism/

Chalmers, A. (2014) Atomism from the 17th to the 20th Century. In E.N. Zalta (ed.), *The Stanford Encyclopedia of Philosophy* (Winter, 2014 edn). Retrieved from http://plato.stanford.edu/archives/win2014/entries/atomism-modern

Chang, H. (2012) *Is Water H_2O? Evidence, Realism and Pluralism*. Dordrecht, The Netherlands: Springer.

Chappell, V. (1994) *The Cambridge Companion to Locke*. Cambridge: Cambridge University Press.

Clark, D.H. & Clark, M.D.H. (2004) *Measuring the Cosmos: How Scientists Discovered the Dimensions of the Universe*. Piscataway, NJ: Rutgers University Press.

Collins, R. (2005) The Durkheimian movement in France and in world sociology. In J.C. Alexander & P. Smith (eds), *The Cambridge Companion to Durkheim* (pp. 101–35). New York: Cambridge University Press.

Comte, A. (1858) *Positive Philosophy* (H. Martineau, Trans.). New York: Calvin Blanchard.

Comte, A. (1875) *System of Positive Polity*. London: Longmans, Green and Co.

Cook, H.J. (2010) Victories for empiricism, failures for theory: Medicine and science in the seventeenth century. In C.T. Wolfe & O. Gal (eds), *The Body as Object and Instrument of Knowledge: Embodied Empiricism in Early Modern Science* (pp. 9–32). London: Springer.

Copleston, F.C. (1958) *History of Philosophy: Descartes to Leibniz*. Mahwah, NJ: Paulist.

Creswell, J.W. (2010) Mapping the developing landscape of mixed methods research. In A. Tashakkori & C. Teddlie (eds), *SAGE Handbook of Mixed Methods in Social and Behavioral Research* (pp. 34–68). Thousand Oaks, CA: SAGE.

Creswell, J.W. (2013) *Qualitative Inquiry & Research Design: Choosing Among Five Approaches* (3rd edn). London: SAGE.

Crombie, I.M. (2013) *An Examination of Plato's Doctrines: Volume 1 Plato on Man and Society*. Abingdon: Routledge.

Crotty, M. (1998) *The Foundations of Social Research: Meaning and Perspective in the Research Process*. St Leonards, NSW: Allen & Unwin.

Crumley, J.S. (2009) *An Introduction to Epistemology* (2nd edn). Peterborough, Ontario: Broadview.

Cuttica, C. (2014) Anti-methodology par excellence: Richard Cobb (1917–96) and history-writing. *European Review of History: Revue européenne d'histoire*, 21 (1): 91–110. doi:10.1080/13507486.2013.857644.

Dahlstrom, D. (2014) Martin Heidegger. In S. Luft & S. Overgaard (eds), *The Routledge Companion to Phenomenology* (pp. 50–61). Abingdon: Routledge.

Dauenhauer, B. & Pellauer, D. (2014) Paul Ricoeur. In E.N. Zalta (ed.), *The Stanford Encyclopedia of Philosophy* (Summer, 2014 edn). Retrieved from http://plato.stanford.edu/archives/sum2014/entries/ricoeur/

Davies, P.C.W. & Brown, J.R. (1986) The strange world of the quantum. In P.C.W. Davies & J.R. Brown (eds), *The Ghost in the Atom* (pp. 1–39). Cambridge: Cambridge University Press.

Davisson, C.J. (1928) The diffraction of electrons by a crystal of nickel. *The Bell System Technical Journal*, 7 (1): 90–105. doi:10.1002/j.1538-7305.1928.tb00342.x.

Delamont, S., Coffey, A. & Atkinson, P. (2000) The twilight years? Educational ethnography and the five moments model. *International Journal of Qualitative Studies in Education*, 13 (3): 223–38. doi:10.1080/09518390050019640.

Deleuze, G. & Guattari, F. (1991) *What is Philosophy?* (H. Tomlinson & G. Burchell, Trans.). New York: Columbia University Press.

Deleuze, G. & Guattari, F. (2014) *A Thousand Plateaus: Capitalism and Schizophrenia*. (B. Massumi, Trans.). London: Bloomsbury Academic.

DeLong, H. (1998) *A Profile of Mathematical Logic*. Mineola, NY: Dover.

Denzin, N.K. (1970) *The Research Act: A Theoretical Introduction to Sociological Methods*. Rutgers, NJ: Transaction.

Denzin, N.K. (1978) *The Research Act: A Theoretical Introduction to Sociological Methods* (2nd edn). New York: McGraw-Hill.

Denzin, N.K. (1997) *Interpretive Ethnography: Ethnographic Practices for the 21st Century*. Thousand Oaks, CA: SAGE.

Denzin, N.K. (2001) *Interpretive Interactionism* (2nd edn). Thousand Oaks, CA: SAGE.

Denzin, N.K. (2010a) Moments, mixed methods, and paradigm dialogs. *Qualitative Inquiry*, 16 (6): 419–27. doi:10.1177/1077800410364608.

Denzin, N.K. (2010b) *The Qualitative Manifesto: A Call to Arms*. Walnut Creek, CA: Left Coast.

Denzin, N.K. & Lincoln, Y.S. (eds) (1994) *Handbook of Qualitative Research*. Thousand Oaks, CA: SAGE.

Denzin, N.K. & Lincoln, Y.S. (1998) *The Landscape of Qualitative Research: Theories and Issues*. Thousand Oaks, CA: SAGE.

Denzin, N.K. & Lincoln, Y.S. (eds) (2000) *Handbook of Qualitative Research* (2nd edn). Thousand Oaks, CA: SAGE.

Denzin, N.K. & Lincoln, Y.S. (2003) The discipline and practice of qualitative research. In N.K. Denzin & Y.S. Lincoln (eds), *Handbook of Qualitative Research* (2nd edn, pp. 1–46). Thousand Oaks, CA: SAGE.

Denzin, N.K. & Lincoln, Y.S. (eds) (2005) *The SAGE Handbook of Qualitative Research* (3rd edn). Thousand Oaks, CA: SAGE.

Denzin, N.K. & Lincoln, Y.S. (2011a) Introduction: The discipline and practice of qualitative research. In N.K. Denzin & Y.S. Lincoln (eds), *The SAGE Handbook of Qualitative Research* (4th edn, pp. 1–20). Thousand Oaks, CA: SAGE.

Denzin, N.K. & Lincoln, Y.S. (eds) (2011b) *The SAGE Handbook of Qualitative Research* (4th edn). Thousand Oaks, CA: SAGE.

Denzin, N.K. & Lincoln, Y.S. (2013) *The Landscape of Qualitative Research* (4th edn). Thousand Oaks, CA: SAGE.

Denzin, N.K., Lincoln, Y.S. & Smith, L.T. (eds) (2008) *Handbook of Critical and Indigenous Methodologies*. Thousand Oaks, CA: SAGE.

Descartes, R. (2008) *Meditations on First Philosophy with Selections from the Objections and Replies* (M. Moriarty, Trans.). New York: Oxford University Press.

Devitt, M. (1984) *Realism and Truth*. Oxford: Blackwell.

Devy, G.N., Davis, G.V. & Chakravarty, K.K. (eds) (2014) *Knowing Differently: The Cognitive Challenge of the Indigenous*. Abingdon: Routledge.

Dewey, J. (1938) *Logic: The Theory of Inquiry*. New York: Henry Hold and Company.

Dewey, J. (1979) *The Middle Works, 1899–1924, Volume 7:1912–1914* [Edited by Jo Ann Boydston. Introduction by Ralph Ross.]. Carbondale, IL: Southern Illinois University Press.

Dicker, G. (2004) *Kant's Theory of Knowledge: An Analytical Introduction*. New York: Oxford University Press.

Dilworth, C. (2013) *Simplicity: A Meta-metaphysics*. Lanham, MD: Lexington.

Douglas, H. (2011) Facts, values, and objectivity. In I.C. Jarvie & J. Zamora-Bonilla (eds), *The SAGE Handbook of the Philosophy of Social Sciences* (pp. 513–29). London: SAGE.

Dreyfus, H.L. (1991) Heidegger's hermeneutic realism. In D.R. Hiley, J.F. Bohman & R. Shusterman (eds), *The Interpretive Turn: Philosophy, Science, Culture* (pp. 25–41). Ithaca, NY: Cornell University Press.

Dreyfus, H.L. (1993) Heidegger's critique of the Husserl/Searle account of intentionality. *Social Research*, 60 (1): 17–38. doi:www.jstor.org/stable/40970727.

Duhem, P. (1969) *To Save the Phenomena: An Essay on the Idea of Physical Theory from Plato to Galileo* (E. Dolan & C. Maschler, Trans.). Chicago, IL: University of Chicago Press.

Durkheim, E. (1982) *The Rules of Sociological Method and Selected Texts on Sociology and Its Method* (W. D. Halls, Trans.). New York: Free Press.

Eldridge, M. (1998) *Transforming Experience: John Dewey's Cultural Instrumentalism*. Nashville, TN: Vanderbilt University Press.

Ellis, R.R. (1999) Solipsism. In H. Gordon (ed.), *Dictionary of Existentialism* (pp. 439–40). Westport, CT: Greenwood.

Embree, L. (ed.) (1997) *Encyclopedia of Phenomenology*. Dordrecht, The Netherlands: Springer.

Faye, J. (2014) Copenhagen interpretation of quantum mechanics. In E.N. Zalta (ed.), *The Stanford Encyclopedia of Philosophy* (Fall, 2014 edn). Retrieved from http://plato.stanford.edu/archives/fall2014/entries/qm-copenhagen/

Feagin, S.L. (2002) Tossed salad: Ontology and identity. In M. Krausz (ed.), *Is There a Single Right Interpretation?* (pp. 360–80). University Park, PA: Pennsylvania State University Press.

Ferguson, H. (2006) *Phenomenological Sociology: Experience & Insight in Modern Society*. London: SAGE.

Feyerabend, P. (1996) *Killing Time: The Autobiography of Paul Feyerabend*. Chicago: University of Chicago Press.

Feyerabend, P. (2010) *Against Method* (4th edn). London: Verso.

Fick, A. (1851) *Da errone quodam optic asymmetria bulbi effecto*. Marburg: Koch.

Field, R. (2015) *John Dewey (1859–1952)*. Retrieved from www.iep.utm.edu/dewey/ 1 May 2015.

Figal, G. (2010) *Objectivity: The Hermeneutical and Philosophy* (T.D. George, Trans.). Albany: State University of New York Press.

Figal, G. & Espinet, D. (2014) Hermeneutics. In S. Luft & S. Overgaard (eds), *The Routledge Companion to Phenomenology* (pp. 496–507). Abingdon: Routledge.

Fine, G. (2014) *The Possibility of Inquiry: Meno's Paradox from Socrates to Sextus*. New York: Oxford University Press.

Fisher, S. (2003) John Locke. In W. Applebaum (ed.), *Encyclopedia of the Scientific Revolution: From Copernicus to Newton* (pp. 578–81). New York: Taylor & Francis.

Fleck, L. (1979) *Genesis and Development of a Scientific Fact* [Entstehung und Entwicklung einer wissenschaftlichen Tatsache: Einführung in die Lehre vom Denkstil und Denkkollektiv, 1935] (F. Bradley & T. J. Trenn, Trans.). Chicago, IL: University of Chicago Press.

Flick, U. (2009) *An Introduction to Qualitative Research*. London: SAGE.

Fluck, W. (ed.) (1999) *Pragmatism and Literary Studies*. Tübingen, Germany: Gunter Narr Verlag.

Forrai, G. (2001) *Reference, Truth and Conceptual Schemes: A Defense of Internal Realism*. Dordrecht, The Netherlands: Kluwer Academic.

Foucault, M. (1977) *Discipline and Punish: The Birth of the Prison*. (A. Sheridan, Trans.). New York, NY: Random House.

Frede, M. (1990) An empiricist view of knowledge: Memorism. In S. Everson (ed.), *Epistemology* (pp. 225–50). Cambridge: Cambridge University Press.

Freedman, S.J. & Clauser, J.F. (1972) Experimental test of local hidden-variable theories. *Physical Review Letters*, 28 (14): 938–41. doi:10.1103/PhysRevLett.28.938.

French, S. & Ladyman, J. (2011) In defence of ontic structural realism. In A. Bokulich & P.J.M. Bokulich (eds), *Scientific Structuralism* (pp. 25–42). New York: Springer.

Fuchs, C.A., Mermin, N.D. & Schack, R. (2014) An introduction to QBism with an application to the locality of quantum mechanics. *American Journal of Physics*, 82 (8): 749–54. doi:10.1119/1.4874855.

Fuller, S. (1993) *Philosophy of Science and Its Discontents* (2nd edn). New York: Guilford.

Gadamer, H.-G. (1976) *Philosophical Hermeneutics* (D.E. Linge, Trans.). Berkeley, CA: University of California Press.

Gadamer, H.-G. (2004 [1960]) *Truth and Method* (J. Winsheimer & D. G. Marshall, Trans., 2nd edn). New York: Continuum.

Garber, D. (2001) *Descartes Embodied: Reading Cartesian Philosophy Through Cartesian Science*. Cambridge: Cambridge University Press.

Gehart, D., Tarragona, M. & Bava, S. (2007) A collaborative approach to research and inquiry. In H. Anderson & D. Gehart (eds), *Collaborative Therapy: Relationships and Conversations that Make a Difference* (pp. 367–87). Abingdon: Routledge.

George, J. (1999) Indigenous knowledge as a component of the school curriculum. In L. Semali & J. Kincheloe (eds), *What is Indigenous Knowledge? Voices from the Academy* (pp. 79–94). New York: Falmer.

Gergen, K.J. (1994) *Realities and Relationships: Soundings in Social Construction.* Cambridge, MA: Harvard University Press.

Gergen, K.J. (1998a) Constructionism and realism: How are we to go on? In I. Parker (ed.), *Social Constructionism, Discourse and Realism* (pp. 147–55). London: SAGE.

Gergen, K.J. (1998b) Constructionist dialogues and the vicissitudes of the political. In I. Velody & R. Williams (eds), *The Politics of Constructionism* (pp. 33–48). London: SAGE.

Gergen, K.J. (2001) *Social Construction in Context.* London: SAGE.

Gergen, K.J. (2009) *An Invitation to Social Construction* (2nd edn). London: SAGE.

Giddens, A. (1984) *The Constitution of Society.* Cambridge: Polity.

Giere, R.N. (2005) Scientific realism: Old and new problems. *Erkenntnis,* 63 (2): 149–65. doi:10.1007/s10670-005-3224-9.

Glaser, B.G. & Strauss, A.L. (1967) *The Discovery of Grounded Theory: Strategies for Qualitative Research.* New Brunswick, NJ: Aldine.

Godfrey-Smith, P. (2009) *Theory and Reality: An Introduction to the Philosophy of Science.* Chicago, IL: University of Chicago Press.

Golinski, J. (2005) *Making Natural Knowledge: Constructivism and the History of Science.* Cambridge: Cambridge University Press.

Gomm, R. (2009) *Key Concepts in Social Research Methods.* Basingstoke: Palgrave Macmillan.

Gonzalez, G. (2015) Hermeneutics in Greek philosophy. In J. Malpas & H.-H. Gander (eds), *The Routledge Companion to Hermeneutics* (pp. 13–22). Abingdon: Routledge.

Goodman, N. (1978) *Ways of Worldmaking.* Indianapolis, IN: Hacket.

Goodman, N. (1996) The way the world is. In P. J. McCormick (ed.), *Starmaking: Realism, Anti-Realism, and Irrealism* (pp. 3–10). Cambridge, MA: MIT Press.

Gorman, J. (1992) *Understanding History: An Introduction to Analytical Philosophy of History.* Ottawa, Canada: University of Ottawa Press.

Goswami, A. (1995) *The Self-Aware Universe: How Consciousness Creates the Material World.* New York: Penguin Putnam.

Gozza, P. (2000) Introduction. In P. Gozza (ed.), *Number to Sound: The Musical Way to the Scientific Revolution* (pp. 1–63). Dordrecht, The Netherlands: Kluwer Academic.

Graham, P.J. (2008) The relativist response to radical skepticism. In J. Greco (ed.), *The Oxford Handbook of Skepticism* (pp. 392–414). New York: Oxford University Press.

Greene, B.R. (2003) *The Elegant Universe: Superstrings, Hidden Dimensions, and the Quest for the Ultimate Theory.* New York: W.W. Norton & Company.

Greene, B.R. (2004) *The Fabric of the Cosmos: Space, Time and the Texture of Reality.* New York: Random House.

Greenstein, G. & Zajonc, A.G. (2006) *The Quantum Challenge: Modern Research on the Foundations of Quantum Mechanics* (2nd edn). Sadbury, MA: Jones and Bartlett.

Grim, B.J., Harmon, A.H. & Gromis, J.C. (2006) Focused group interviews as an innovative quanti- qualitative methodology (QQM): Integrating quantitative elements into a qualitative methodology. *The Qualitative Report*, 11 (3), 516–37. Retrieved from: http://nsuworks.nova.edu/tqr/vol11/iss3/5.

Grinnell, F. (1992) *The Scientific Attitude* (2nd edn). New York: Guilford.

Groarke, L. (2009) *An Aristotelian Account of Induction: Creating Something from Nothing*. Montreal, Canada: McGill-Queen's University Press.

Guba, E.G. (ed.) (1990) *The Paradigm Dialog*. London: SAGE.

Guba, E.G. & Lincoln, Y.S. (1989) *Fourth Generation Evaluation*. London: SAGE.

Guba, E.G. & Lincoln, Y.S. (1994) Competing paradigms in qualitative research. In N.K. Denzin & Y.S. Lincoln (eds), *Handbook of Qualitative Research* (pp. 105–17). Thousand Oaks, CA: SAGE.

Guba, E.G. & Lincoln, Y.S. (2004) Competing paradigms in qualitative research: Theories and issues. In S.N. Hesse-Biber & P. Leavy (eds), *Approaches to Qualitative Research: A Reader on Theory and Practice* (pp. 17–38). Oxford: Oxford University Press.

Gubrium, J.F. & Holstein, J.A. (2008) The constructionist mosaic. In J.A. Holstein & J.F. Gubrium (eds), *Handbook of Construcionist Research* (pp. 3–10). New York: Guilford.

Habermas, J. (1987 [1968]) *Knowledge and Human Interests* (J.J. Shapiro, Trans.). Cambridge: Polity.

Hacking, I. (1983) *Representing and Intervening: Introductory Topics in the Philosophy of Natural Science*. New York: Cambridge University Press.

Hacking, I. (2010) Introduction to the fourth edition. In P. Feyerabend (ed.), *Against Method* (4th edn, pp. vii–xvi). London: Verso.

Hacking, I. (2012) Introductory essay. In T. S. Kuhn (ed.), *The Structure of Scientific Revolutions: 50th Anniversary Edition; With an Introductory Essay by Ian Hacking* (4th edn, pp. vii–xxxvii). Chicago, IL: University of Chicago Press.

Harré, R. & Krausz, M. (1996) *Varieties of Relativism*. Cambridge, MA: Blackwell.

Hatch, J.A. (2002) *Doing Qualitative Research in Education Settings*. Albany: State University of New York Press.

Hausman, D.M. & McPherson, M.S. (2006) *Economic Analysis, Moral Philosophy, and Public Policy* (2nd edn). New York: Cambridge University Press.

Hayles, N.K. (2012) *How We Think: Digital Media and Contemporary Technogenesis*. Chicago, IL: University of Chicago Press.

Heidegger, M. (1962) *Being and Time* (J. Macquarie & E. Robinson, Trans.). Oxford: Basil Blackwell.

Heidegger, M. (1988) *The Basic Problems of Phenomenology* (A. Hofstadter, Trans., Revised edn). Bloomington: Indiana University Press.

Heit, E. (2007) What is induction and why study it? In A. Feeney & E. Heit (eds), *Inductive Reasoning: Experimental, Developmental, and Computational Approaches* (pp. 1–24). New York: Cambridge University Press.

Held, C. (1995) Bohr and Kantian idealism. In H. Robinson (ed.), *Proceedings of the Eighth International Kant Congress* (Vol. II, pp. 397–404). Milwaukee, WI: Marquette University Press.

Hellman, G. (1983) Realist principles. *Philosophy of Science,* 50 (2): 227–49. doi:10.1086/289107.

Herbert, N. (1985) *Quantum Reality: Beyond the New Physics.* New York: Anchor.

Herman, N.J. (1994) Interactionist research methods: An overview. In N.J. Herman & L.T. Reynolds (eds), *Symbolic Interaction: An Introduction to Social Psychology* (pp. 90–111). Dix Hills, NY: General Hall.

Herman, N.J. & Reynolds, L.T. (1994) *Symbolic Interaction: An Introduction to Social Psychology.* Dix Hills, NY: AltaMira.

Herman-Kinney, N.J. & Verschaeve, J.M. (2003) Methods of symbolic interactionism. In L.T. Reynolds & N.J. Herman-Kinney (eds), *Handbook of Symbolic Interactionism* (pp. 213–52). Lanham, MD: AltaMira Press.

Hersh, R. (1997) *What is Mathematics, Really?* Oxford: Oxford University Press.

Hesse-Biber, S.N. & Leavy, P. (2010) *The Practice of Qualitative Research* (2nd edn). Thousand Oaks, CA: SAGE.

Hildebrand, D.L. (2003) *Beyond Realism and Antirealism: John Dewey and the Neopragmatists.* Nashville, TN: Vanderbilt University Press.

Hirsch, E.D. (1967) *Validity in Interpretation.* New Haven, CT: Yale University Press.

Hoitenga, D.J. (1991) *Faith and Reason from Plato to Plantinga: An Introduction to Reformed Epistemology.* Albany: State University of New York Press.

Holden, T. (2004) *The Architecture of Matter: Galileo to Kant.* Oxford: Oxford University Press.

Holzhey, H. & Mudroch, V. (2005) *Historical Dictionary of Kant and Kantianism.* Oxford: Scarecrow.

Howson, C. (ed.) (2000) *Hume's Problem: Induction and the Justification of Belief.* New York: Oxford University Press.

Hoy, D.C. (1982) *The Critical Circle: Literature, History, and Philosophical Hermeneutics.* Berkeley, CA: University of California Press.

Huerta, R.D. (2005) *Vermeer and Plato: Painting the Ideal.* Cranbury, NJ: Associated University Press.

Hughes, J. (ed.) (2012) *SAGE Visual Methods.* London: SAGE.

Hung, E. (2014) *Philosophy of Science Complete: A Text on Traditional Problems and Schools of Thought* (2nd edn). Boston, MA: Wadsworth.

Husserl, E. (1931) *Ideas: General Introduction to Pure Phenomenology* (W.R.B. Gibson, Trans.). London: Allen & Unwin.

Husserl, E. (1965 [1910]) Philosophy as rigorous science (Q. Lauer, Trans.). In Q. Lauer (ed.), *Phenomenology and the Crisis of Philosophy* (pp. 71–147). New York: Harper.

Husserl, E. (1970) *The Idea of Phenomenology.* The Hague, Netherlands: Martinus Nijhoff.

Husserl, E. (2001 [1900/1901]) *Logical Investigations* (D. Moran, ed.). Abingdon: Routledge.

Jammer, M. (1979) A consideration of the philosophical implications of the new physics. In G. Radnitzky & G. Andersson (eds), *The Structure and Development of Science* (pp. 41–61). Dordrecht, The Netherlands: D. Reidel Publishing Company.

Jeans, J.H. (2012) *Physics and Philosophy* [Unabridged republication of the work co-published in 1943 by Cambridge University Press and the Macmillan Company]. Mineola, NY: Dover.

Jones, R.H. (2000) *Reductionism: Analysis and the Fullness of Reality*. Cranbury, NJ: Associated University Presses.

Jubien, M. (2004) Metaphysics. In J. Shand (ed.), *Fundamentals of Philosophy* (pp. 36–63). London: Taylor & Francis.

Kant, I. (2012 [1781]) *The Critique of Pure Reason*. New York: Start.

Katovich, M.A., Miller, D.E. & Stewart, R.L. (2003) The Iowa School. In L.T. Reynolds & N.J. Herman-Kinney (eds), *Handbook of Symbolic Interactionism* (pp. 119–40). Lanham, MD: AltaMira.

Kavanaugh, L.J. (2007) *The Architectonic of Philosophy: Plato, Aristotle, Leibniz*. Amsterdam, The Netherlands: Amsterdam University Press.

Kelle, U. (2007) Computer-assisted qualitative data analysis. In C. Seale, D. Silverman, J.F. Gubrium & G. Gobo (eds), *Qualitative Research Practice: Concise Paperback Edition* (pp. 443–60). London: SAGE.

Kellert, S.H., Longino, H.E. & Waters, C.K. (2006) *Scientific Pluralism*. Minneapolis: University of Minnesota Press.

Kincheloe, J.L. (2008) *Critical Pedagogy Primer* (2nd edn). New York: Peter Lang.

Kincheloe, J.L. & Steinberg, S.R. (2008) Indigenous knowledges in education. In N.K. Denzin, Y.S. Lincoln & L.T. Smith (eds), *Handbook of Critical and Indigenous Methodologies* (pp. 135–56). Thousand Oaks, CA: SAGE.

Kline, M. (1982) *Mathematics: The Loss of Certainty*. Oxford: Oxford University Press.

Kockelmans, J.J. (1985) *Heidegger on Art and Art Works*. Dordrecht, The Netherlands: Martinus Nijhoff.

Kockelmans, J.J. (1993) *Ideas for a Hermeneutic Phenomenology of the Natural Sciences*. Dordrecht, The Netherlands: Kluwer Academic.

Kolakowski, L. (1968) *The Alienation of Reason: A History of Positivist Thought* (N. Guterman, Trans.). Garden City, NY: Doubleday.

Krausz, M. (ed.) (2002) *Is There A Single Right Interpretation?* University Park: Pennsylvania State University Press.

Krausz, M. (2010a) Mapping relativisms. In M. Krausz (ed.), *Relativism: A Contemporary Anthology* (pp. 13–30). New York: Columbia University Press.

Krausz, M. (ed.) (2010b) *Relativism: A Contemporary Anthology*. New York: Columbia University Press.

Kuhn, T.S. (1962) *The Structure of Scientific Revolutions*. Chicago, IL: University of Chicago Press.

Kuhn, T.S. (2012 [1962]) *The Structure of Scientific Revolutions: 50th Anniversary Edition; with an Introductory Essay by Ian Hacking*. Chicago, IL: University of Chicago Press.

Kukla, A. (2000) *Social Constructivism and the Philosophy of Science*. London: Routledge.

Ladyman, J. (2002) *Understanding Philosophy of Science*. London: Taylor & Francis.

Ladyman, J. (2014) Structural realism. In A.N. Zalta (ed.), *The Stanford Encyclopedia of Philosophy* (Spring, 2014 edn). Retrieved from http://plato.stanford.edu/archives/spr2014/entries/structural-realism

Lakoff, G. & Núñez, R.E. (2000) *Where Mathematics Comes From: How the Embodied Mind Brings Mathematics Into Being.* New York: Basic.

Lally, J. (1981) Philosophical questions underpinning sociology: Some suggestions for presenting a course. *Teaching Sociology,* 9 (1): 3–14.

Lammenranta, M. (2008) The Pyrrhonian problematic. In J. Greco (ed.), *The Oxford Handbook of Skepticism* (pp. 9–33). New York: Oxford University Press.

Laudan, L. (1996) *Beyond Positivism and Relativism: Theory, Method, and Evidence.* Cumnor Hill: Westview.

Laudan, L. (1997) Explaining the success of science: Beyond epistemic realism and relativism. In A.I. Tauber (ed.), *Science and the Quest for Reality* (pp. 137–61). New York: New York University Press.

Lawson, T. (2015) A conception of social ontology. In S. Pratten (ed.), *Social Ontology and Modern Economics* (pp. 19–52). Abingdon: Routledge.

Leavy, P. (ed.) (2014) *The Oxford Handbook of Qualitative Research.* New York: Oxford University Press.

Leeming, D. (2005) *The Oxford Companion to World Mythology.* New York: Oxford University Press.

Lennon, T.M. & Hickson, M. (2014) Pierre Bayle. In E.N. Zalta (Ed.), *The Stanford Encyclopedia of Philosophy* (Fall, 2014 edn). Retrieved from http://plato.stanford.edu/archives/fall2014/entries/bayle/

Leplin, J. (ed.) (1984) *Scientific Realism.* Berkeley, CA: University of California Press.

Leplin, J. (1987) Surrealism. *Mind,* 96 (384): 519–24.

Leplin, J. (1997) *A Novel Defense of Scientific Realism.* New York: Oxford University Press.

Leplin, J. (2007) Enlisting Popper in the case for scientific realism. *Philosophia Scientiæ,* 11 (1): 71–97. Retrieved from: http://philosophiascientiae.revues.org/323 doi:10.4000/philosophiascientiae.323.

Levin, M. & Greenwood, D. (2011) Revitalizing universities by reinventing the social sciences: *Bildung* and action research. In N.K. Denzin & Y.S. Lincoln (eds), *The SAGE Handbook of Qualitative Research* (4th edn, pp. 27–42). Thousand Oaks, CA: SAGE.

Levine, N. (2006) *Divergent Paths: Hegel in Marxism and Engelsism. Vol 1: The Hegelian Foundations of Marx's Method.* Oxford: Lexington.

Lewis, C.S. (2010 [1960]) *The Four Loves.* London: HarperCollins.

Lightbody, B. (2013) *The Problem of Naturalism: Analytic Perspectives, Continental Virtues.* Plymouth: Lexington.

Lincoln, Y.S. & Guba, E.G. (1985) *Naturalistic Inquiry.* London: SAGE.

Lincoln, Y. S. & Guba, E.G. (1998) Competing paradigms in qualitative research. In N.K. Denzin & Y.S. Lincoln (eds), *The Landscape of Qualitative Research: Theories and Issues* (pp. 195–220). Thousand Oaks, CA: SAGE.

Lincoln, Y.S. & Guba, E.G. (2000) Paradigmatic controversies, contradictions, and emerging confluences. In N.K. Denzin & Y.S. Lincoln (eds), *Handbook of Qualitative Research* (pp. 163–188). Thousand Oaks, CA: SAGE.

Lincoln, Y.S., Lynham, S.A. & Guba, E.G. (2011) Paradigmatic controversies, contradictions, and emerging confluences, revisted. In N.K. Denzin & Y.S. Lincoln (eds), *The SAGE Handbook of Qualitative Research* (pp. 87–127). Thousand Oaks, CA: SAGE.

Lipton, P. (2006) Abduction. In S. Sarkar & J. Pfeifer (eds), *The Philosophy of Science: An Encyclopedia* (pp. 1–3). New York: Routledge.

Lock, A. & Strong, T. (2010) *Social Constructionism: Sources and Stirrings in Theory and Practice.* Cambridge: Cambridge University Press.

Locke, J. (1836) *An Essay Concerning Human Understanding* (27th edn). Glasgow: T. Tegg and Son.

Lodge, R.C. (2001) *The Philosophy of Plato.* Abingdon: Routledge.

Loeb, L.E. (1986) Is there radical dissimulation in Descartes' *Meditations*? In A. Rorty (ed.), *Essays on Descartes' Meditations* (pp. 243–70). Berkeley and Los Angeles, CA: University of California Press.

Long, A.A. (2006) *From Epicurus to Epictetus: Studies in Hellenistic and Roman Philosophy.* Oxford: Oxford University Press.

Lorenz, C. (1994) Historical knowledge and historical reality: A plea for 'internal realism'. *History and Theory,* 33 (3): 297–327. doi:10.2307/2505476

Losonsky, M. (2006) *Linguistic Turns in Modern Philosophy.* New York: Cambridge University Press.

Love, R.S. (2008) *The Enlightenment.* Westport: Greenwood.

Luft, S. & Overgaard, S. (eds) (2014) *The Routledge Companion to Phenomenology.* Abingdon: Routledge.

Lüth, H. (2012) *Quantum Physics in the Nanoworld: Schrödinger's Cat and the Dwarfs.* Heidelberg: Springer.

Lynch, M.P. (2002) Pluralism, metaphysical realism, and ultimate reality. In W.P. Alston (ed.), *Realism and Antirealism* (pp. 57–78). Ithaca, NY: Cornell University Press.

Lyons, T.D. & Clarke, S. (2002) Introduction: Scientific realism and commonsense. In S. Clarke & T.D. Lyons (eds), *Recent Themes in the Philosophy of Science: Scientific Realism and Commonsense* (Vol. 17, pp. ix–xxiii). Dordrecht, The Netherlands: Springer Netherlands.

Mach, E. (1919) *The Science of Mechanics: A Critical and Historical Account of Its Development* (T.J. McCormack, Trans., 4th edn). Chicago, IL: The Open Court Publishing Co.

Maffie, J. (2013) Ethno-epistemology. In B. Kaldis (ed.), *Encyclopedia of Philosophy and the Social Sciences* (pp. 277–79). Thousand Oaks, CA: SAGE.

Mailloux, S. (1989) *Rhetorical Power.* Ithaca, NY: Cornell University Press.

Manning, A.G., Khakimov, R.I., Dall, R.G. & Truscott, A.G. (2015) Wheeler's delayed-choice gedanken experiment with a single atom [Letter]. *Nat Phys,* 11 (7): 539–42. doi:10.1038/nphys3343.

Margolis, J. (2002) 'One and only one correct interpretation'. In M. Krausz (ed.), *Is There a Single Right Interpretation?* (pp. 26–44). University Park: Pennsylvania State University Press.

Markie, P. (2015) Rationalism vs. empiricism. In E.N. Zalta (ed.), *The Stanford Encyclopedia of Philosophy* (Spring, 2015 edn). Retrieved from http://plato.stanford.edu/archives/spr2015/entries/rationalism-empiricism/

Maxwell, G. (1962) The ontological status of theoretical entities. In H. Heigl & G. Maxwell (eds), *Minnesota Studies in the Philosophy of Science* (Vol. III, pp. 3–27). Minneapolis: University of Minnesota Press.

Maxwell, J.A. (2012) *A Realist Approach for Qualitative Research.* Thousand Oaks, CA: SAGE.

Maxwell, J.A. (2013) *Qualitative Research Design: An Interactive Approach* (3rd edn). Thousand Oaks, CA: SAGE.

Mayr, E. (1982) *The Growth of Biological Thought: Diversity, Evolution, and Inheritance.* Cambridge, MA: Harvard University Press.

McGrew, T., Alspector-Kelly, M. & Allhoff, F. (eds) (2009) *Philosophy of Science: An Historical Anthology.* Chichester: Wiley-Blackwell.

McNeill, W.H. (1986) *Mythistory and Other Essays.* Chicago, IL: University of Chicago Press.

Mead, G.H. (1913) The social self. *Journal of Philosophy, Psychology and Scientific Methods,* 10 (14): 374–80. doi:10.2307/2012910.

Mead, G.H. (1934) *Mind, Self, and Society.* Chicago, IL: University of Chicago Press.

Meltzer, B. & Petras, J. (1970) The Chicago and Iowa schools of symbolic interactionism. In T. Shibutani (ed.), *Human Nature and Collective Behavior* (pp. 3–17). Englewood Cliffs, NJ: Prentice-Hall.

Mermin, N.D. (2014) Physics: QBism puts the scientist back into science. *Nature,* 507 (7493): 421–23. doi:10.1038/507421a

Merriam, S.B. (2009) *Qualitative Research: A Guide to Design and Implementation* (2nd edn). San Francisco, CA: Jossey-Bass.

Meyer, M.A. (2003) *Ho'oulu: Our Time of Becoming: Hawaiian Epistemology and Early Writings.* Honolulu, HI: 'Ai Pohaku Press Native Books.

Mill, J.S. (1843) *A System of Logic, Ratiocinative and Inductive: Being a Connected View of the Principles of Evidence and the Methods of Scientific Investigation.* London: John W. Parker, West Strand.

Mill, J.S. (1858) *A System of Logic, Ratiocinative and Inductive: Being a Connected View of the Principles of Evidence and the Methods of Scientific Investigation.* New York: Harper & Brothers.

Mohanty, J. (2002) Intentionality, meaning, and open-endedness of interpretation. In M. Krausz (ed.), *Is There a Single Right Interpretation?* (pp. 63–75). University Park: Pennsylvania State University Press.

Monton, B. & Mohler, C. (2012) Constructive empiricism. In E.N. Zalta (ed.), *The Stanford Encyclopedia of Philosophy* (Winter, 2012 edn). Retrieved from http://plato.stanford.edu/archives/win2012/entries/constructive-empiricism/

Moody, E.A. (1975) *Studies in Medieval Philosophy, Science, and Logic: Collected Papers, 1933–1969.* London: University of California Press.

Moore, G.E. (1903) The refutation of idealism. *Mind,* XII (4): 433–53. doi:10.1093/mind/XII.4.433.

Moran, D. (2002) Editor's introduction. In D. Moran & T. Mooney (eds), *The Phenomenology Reader* (pp. 1–26). Abingdon: Routledge.

Moran, D. (2005) *Edmund Husserl: Founder of Phenomenology.* Cambridge: Wiley.

Moran, D. & Mooney, T. (eds) (2002) *The Phenomenology Reader.* Abingdon: Routledge.

Moroni, P. (2000) The history of Bologna University's Medical School over the centuries: A short review. *Acta Dermatovenerol APA,* 9 (2): 73–5.

Mouton, J. & Marais, H.C. (1988) *Basic Concepts in the Methodology of the Social Sciences.* Pretoria, South Africa: Human Sciences Research Council.

Müller-Lyer, F.C. (1889) Optische Urteilstäuschungen. *Archiv für Physiologie,* Supplement Volume, 263–70.

Musgrave, A. (1988) The ultimate argument for scientific realism. In R. Nola (ed.), *Relativism and Realism in Science* (pp. 229–52). Dordrecht, The Netherlands: Kluwer Academic.

Musgrave, A. (1993) *Common Sense, Science and Scepticism: A Historical Introduction to the Theory of Knowledge.* Cambridge: Cambridge University Press.

Nelson, A. (2013a) The rationalist impulse. In A. Nelson (ed.), *A Companion to Rationalism* (pp. 3–11). Chichester: Wiley-Blackwell.

Nelson, A. (ed.) (2013b) *A Companion to Rationalism.* Chichester: Wiley-Blackwell.

Neuman, W.L. (2011) *Social Research Methods: Qualitative and Quantitative Approaches* (7th edn). Boston, MA: Pearson.

Nola, R. (ed.) (1988) *Relativism and Realism in Science.* Dordrecht, The Netherlands: Kluwer Academic.

Nola, R. & Sankey, H. (2007) *Theories of Scientific Method.* Montreal, Canada: McGill-Queen's University Press.

Norton, J.D. (2013) *Euclidean Geometry: The First Great Science.* Retrieved 15 January 2014 from www.pitt.edu/~jdnorton/teaching/HPS_0410/chapters/non_Euclid_Euclid/index.html

O'Leary, M. (2010) *Revolutions of Geometry.* Hoboken, NJ: Wiley.

Oevermann, U., Allert, T., Kona, E. & Krambeck, J. (1979) Die Methodologie einer 'objektiven Hermeneutik' und ihre allgemeine forschungslogische Bedeutung in den Sozialwissenschaften. In H.G. Soeffner (ed.), *Interpretative Verfahren in den Sozial- Und Textwissenschaften* (pp. 352–434). Stuttgart: Metzler.

Ozouf, M. (1988) *Festivals and the French Revolution* (A. Sheridan, Trans.). Cambridge, MA: Harvard University Press.

Pascale, C.M. (2011) *Cartographies of Knowledge: Exploring Qualitative Epistemologies.* Thousand Oaks, CA: SAGE.

Patomäki, H. & Wright, C. (2000) After postpositivism? The promises of critical realism. *International Studies Quarterly,* 44 (2): 213–37. doi:10.1111/0020-8833.00162.

Patton, M.Q. (2002) *Qualitative Research and Evaluation Methods* (3rd edn). Thousand Oaks, CA: SAGE.

Pawson, R. & Tilley, N. (1997) *Realistic Evaluation*. London: SAGE.

Payne, G. & Payne, J. (2004) *Key Concepts in Social Research*. London: SAGE.

Pernecky, T. (2012) Constructionism: Critical pointers for tourism studies. *Annals of Tourism Research*, 39 (2): 1116–37. doi:10.1016/j.annals.2011.12.010.

Pernecky, T. (2014) Realist and constructionist shades of grey. *Annals of Tourism Research*, 48 (5): 295–8. doi:10.1016/j.annals.2014.06.011.

Phillips, D.C. (2000) *The Expanded Social Scientist's Bestiary: A Guide to Fabled Threats To, and Defenses Of, Naturalistic Social Science*. Cumnor Hill, Oxford: Rowman & Littlefield.

Phillips, D.C. & Burbules, N.C. (2000) *Postpositivism and Educational Research*. Cumnor Hill, Oxford: Rowman & Littlefield.

Phillips, S.H. (2012) *Epistemology in Classical India: The Knowledge Sources of the Nyāya School*. New York: Routledge.

Pihlström, S. (2014) Pragmatic realism. In K.R. Westphal (ed.), *Realism, Science, and Pragmatism* (pp. 251–82). New York: Taylor & Francis.

Polanyi, M. & Prosch, H. (1975) *Meaning*. Chicago, IL: University of Chicago Press.

Popkin, R. (2003) *The History of Scepticism: From Savonarola to Bayle* (revised and expanded edn). New York: Oxford University Press.

Popper, K. (1972) *Objective Knowledge: An Evolutionary Approach*. Oxford: Oxford University Press.

Popper, K. (1999a) *All Life is Problem Solving*. Abingdon: Routledge.

Popper, K. (1999b) Falsificationism. In R. Klee (ed.), *Scientific Inquiry: Readings in the Philosophy of Science* (pp. 65–71). New York: Oxford University Press.

Popper, K. (2005) *The Logic of Scientific Discovery*. London: Taylor & Francis.

Popper, K. (2013 [1945]) *The Open Society and Its Enemies*. Princeton, NJ: Princeton University Press.

Poston, T. (2015) *Foundationalism*. Retrieved 23 September 2015 from www.iep.utm.edu/found-ep/

Pratt, D. (2008) *Nobel Wisdom: The 1000 Wisest Things Ever Said*. London: JR Books.

Pratten, S. (ed.) (2015) *Social Ontology and Modern Economics*. Abingdon: Routledge.

Preston, J. (1997) Feyerabend's retreat from realism. *Philosophy of Science*, 64 (Dec): S421–31. doi:10.2307/188422.

Priest, G. (1995) *Beyond the Limits of Thought*. New York: Cambridge University Press.

Prinz, J. (2010) Empiricism. In A. Barber & R.J. Stainton (eds), *Concise Encyclopedia of Philosophy of Language and Linguistics* (pp. 183–5). Oxford: Elsevier Science.

Prus, R.C. (1996) *Symbolic Interaction and Ethnographic Research: Intersubjectivity and the Study of Human Lived Experience*. Albany, NY: State University of New York Press.

Psillos, S. (1999) *Scientific Realism: How Science Tracks Truth*. New York: Taylor & Francis.

Psillos, S. (2005) *Scientific Realism: How Science Tracks Truth*. London: Taylor & Francis.

Putnam, H. (1981) *Reason, Truth and History*. Cambridge: Cambridge University Press.

Putnam, H. (1996) Is there still anything to say about reality and truth? In P.J. McCormick (ed.), *Starmaking: Realism, Anti-Realism, and Irrealism* (pp. 11–27). Cambridge, MA: MIT Press.

Putnam, H. (1999) *The Threefold Cord: Mind, Body, and World*. New York: Columbia University Press.

Ramberg, B. & Gjesdal, K. (2014) Hermeneutics. In E.N. Zalta (ed.), *The Stanford Encyclopedia of Philosophy* (Winter, 2014 edn). Retrieved from http://plato.stanford.edu/archives/win2014/entries/hermeneutics/

Ree, J. (1974) *Descartes*. London: Allen Lane.

Reichertz, J. (2004) Objective hermeneutics and hermeneutic sociology of knowledge (B. Jenner, Trans.). In U. Flick, E. v. Kardorff & I. Steinke (eds), *A Companion to Qualitative Research* (pp. 290–5). London: SAGE.

Reynolds, L.T. (1993) *Interactionism: Exposition and Critique*. Lanham, MD: General Hall.

Rickless, S.C. (2013) *Berkeley's Argument for Idealism*. Oxford: Oxford University Press.

Ricoeur, P. (2008) *From Text to Action: Essays in Hermeneutics* (K. Blamey & J.B. Thompson, Trans., Vol. 2). London: Continuum.

Robinson, J.O. (1998) *The Psychology of Visual Illusion*. Mineola, NY: Dover Publications.

Rockmore, T. (2007) *Kant and Idealism*. New Haven, CT: Yale University Press.

Rockmore, T. (2011) *Kant and Phenomenology*. Chicago, IL: University of Chicago Press.

Rogers, K. (ed.) (2011) *Medicine and Healers Through History*. New York: Britannica Educational.

Rogers, R. (2013) *Digital Methods*. Cambridge, MA: MIT Press.

Rollinger, R.D. (1999) *Husserl's Position in the School of Brentano*. Dordrecht, The Netherlands: Kluwer Academic.

Rose, G. (2012) *Visual Methodologies: An Introduction to Researching with Visual Materials* (3rd edn). London: SAGE.

Rosenberg, A. (1999) The rise of logical positivism. In R. Klee (ed.), *Scientific Inquiry: Readings in the Philosophy of Science* (pp. 10–15). New York: Oxford University Press.

Rüegg, W. (ed.) (2004) *A History of the University in Europe*. Cambridge: Cambridge University Press.

Russell, B. (2007) A priori justification and knowledge. In E.N. Zalta (ed.), *The Stanford Encyclopedia of Philosophy* (Summer, 2014 edn). Retrieved from http://plato.stanford.edu/entries/apriori/

Ryan, P.J. (2009) *Euclidean and Non-Euclidean Geometry: An Analytic Approach*. Singapore: Cambridge University Press.

Sanderson, S.K. (2007) Science, proof, and law. In G. Ritzer (ed.), *Blackwell Encyclopedia of Sociology* (pp. 4091–6). Malden, MA: Blackwell.

Sandoval, C. (2000) *Methodology of the Oppressed: Theory out of Bounds*. Minneapolis, MN: University of Minnesota Press.

Sankey, H. (2008) *Scientific Realism and the Rationality of Science*. Aldershot: Ashgate.

Sarkar, S. (ed.) (1996) *Logical Empiricism at Its Peak: Schlick, Carnap, and Neurath*. New York: Garland.

Sasaki, C. (2003) *Descartes's Mathematical Thought*. Dordrecht, The Netherlands: Kluwer Academic.

Saunders, S. (2005) Complementarity and scientific rationality. *Foundations of Physics*, 35 (3): 417–47. doi:10.1007/s10701-004-1982-x.

Scheibe, E. & Falkenburg, B. (2001) *Between Rationalism and Empiricism: Selected Papers in the Philosophy of Physics*. New York: Springer-Verlag.

Scheibler, I. (2000) *Gadamer: Between Heidegger and Habermas*. Oxford: Rowman & Littlefield.

Schiller, F.C.S. (1896) Non-Euclidean geometry and the Kantian *a priori*. *The Philosophical Review*, 5 (2): 173–80. doi:10.2307/2175349.

Schlosshauer, M., Kofler, J. & Zeilinger, A. (2013) A snapshot of foundational attitudes toward quantum mechanics. *Studies in History and Philosophy of Science, Part B: Studies in History and Philosophy of Modern Physics*, 44 (3): 222–30. doi:10.1016/j.shpsb.2013.04.004.

Schneider, A. & Heise, D.R. (1995) Simulating symbolic interaction. *Journal of Mathematical Sociology*, 20 (2–3): 271–87. doi:10.1080/0022250X.1995.9990165.

Scholtz, G. (2015) Ast and Schleiermacher: Hermeneutics and critical philosophy. In J. Malpas & H.-H. Gander (eds), *The Routledge Companion to Hermeneutics* (pp. 62–73). Abingdon: Routledge.

Schouls, P.A. (1989) *Descartes and the Enlightenment*. Montreal, Canada: McGill-Queen's University Press.

Schrader, G. A. & Schrader, G. (1949) The thing in itself in Kantian philosophy. *Review of Metaphysics*, 2 (7): 30–44. doi:10.2307/20123133.

Schrödinger, E. (1926) An undulatory theory of the mechanics of atoms and molecules. *Physical Review*, 28 (6): 1049–70. doi:10.1103/PhysRev.28.1049.

Schütze, F. (1977) *Die Technik des narrativen interviews in Interaktionsfeldstudien – dargestellt an einem Projekt zur Erforschung von kommunalen Machtstrukturen*. Bielefeld, Germany: University of Bielefeld.

Schwandt, T.A. (2015) *The SAGE Dictionary of Qualitative Inquiry* (4th edn). Thousand Oaks, CA: SAGE.

Seale, C. (2002) Quality issues in qualitative inquiry. *Qualitative Social Work*, 1 (1): 97–110. doi:10.1177/147332500200100107.

Searle, J.R. (1969) *Speech Acts: An Essay in the Philosophy of Language*. Cambridge: Cambridge University Press.

Searle, J.R. (1996) *The Construction of Social Reality*. London: Penguin.

Searle, J.R. (2003) Social ontology and political power. In F.F. Schmitt (ed.), *Socializing Metaphysics: The Nature of Social Reality* (pp. 195–210). Lanham, MD: Rowman & Littlefield.

Searle, J.R. (2006a) Culture and fusion: Reply to D'Andrade. *Anthropological Theory*, 6 (1): 40–4. doi:10.1177/1463499606061733.

Searle, J.R. (2006b) Reality and social construction: Reply to Friedman. *Anthropological Theory*, 6 (1): 81–8. doi:10.1177/1463499606061738.

Searle, J.R. (2006c) Searle versus Durkheim and the waves of thought: Reply to Gross. *Anthropological Theory,* 6 (1): 57–69. doi:10.1177/1463499606061735.

Searle, J.R. (2006d) Social ontology: Some basic principles. *Anthropological Theory,* 6 (1): 12–29. doi:10.1177/1463499606061731.

Searle, J.R. (2010) *Making the Social World: The Structure of Human Civilization.* New York: Oxford University Press.

Searle, J.R. (2014) Are there social objects? In M. Gallotti & J. Michael (eds), *Perspectives on Social Ontology and Social Cognition* (pp. 17–26). Dordrecht, The Netherlands: Springer.

Searle, J.R. (2015) *Seeing Things As They Are: A Theory of Perception.* New York: Oxford University Press.

Semali, L. & Kincheloe, J. (eds) (1999) *What is Indigenous Knowledge? Voices from the Academy.* New York: Falmer.

Shapin, S. (1996) *The Scientific Revolution.* Chicago, IL: University of Chicago Press.

Shook, J. R. & Margolis, J. (eds) (2006) *A Companion to Pragmatism.* Oxford: Blackwell.

Siegel, H. (2004) Relativism. In I. Niiniluoto, M. Sintonen & J. Wolenski (eds), *Handbook of Epistemology* (pp. 747–80). Dordrecht, The Netherlands: Kluwer Academic.

Silverman, D. (1997) The logics of qualitative research. In G. Miller & R. Dingwall (eds), *Context & Method in Qualitative Research* (pp. 12–25). London: SAGE.

Silverman, D. (2013) *Doing Qualitative Research: A Practical Handbook* (4th edn). London: SAGE.

Silverman, D. (2015) *Interpreting Qualitative Data* (5th edn). London: SAGE.

Slife, B.D. & Williams, R.N. (1995) *What's Behind the Research? Discovering Hidden Assumptions in the Behavioral Sciences.* London: SAGE.

Smith, D.W. (2013a) *Husserl* (2nd edn). Abingdon: Routledge.

Smith, D.W. (2013b) Phenomenology. In E.N. Zalta (ed.), *Stanford Encyclopedia of Philosophy* (Winter, 2013 edn). Retrieved from http://plato.stanford.edu/entries/phenomenology

Smith, D.W. (2013c) Rationalism in the phenomenological tradition. In A. Nelson (ed.), *A Companion to Rationalism* (pp. 363–78). Chichester: Wiley-Blackwell.

Smith, J. (2015) Phenomenology. *Internet Encyclopedia of Philosophy.* Retrieved from www.iep.utm.edu/phenom/

Smith, L.T. (1999) *Decolonizing Methodologies: Research and Indigenous Peoples.* London: Zed.

Smith, M.J. (1998) *Social Science in Question: Towards A Postdisciplinary Framework.* London SAGE.

Sokal, A. & Bricmont, J. (2004) Defense of a modest scientific realism. In M. Carrier, J. Roggenhofer, G. Küppers & P. Blanchard (eds), *Knowledge and the World: Challenges Beyond the Science Wars* (pp. 17–45). Heidelberg: Springer.

Solomon, R. C. & Higgins, K.M. (2010) *The Big Questions: A Short Introduction to Philosophy* (8th edn). Belmont, CA: Wadsworth, Cengage Learning.

Sparrow, T. (2014) *The End of Phenomenology*. Edinburgh: Edinburgh University Press.

Spencer, R., Pryce, J. M. & Walsh, J. (2014) Philosophical approaches to qualitative research. In P. Leavy (ed.), *The Oxford Handbook of Qualitative Research* (pp. 81–98). New York: Oxford University Press.

Steel, D. (2001) *Eclipse: The Celestial Phenomenon That Changed the Course of History*. Washington, DC: National Academies.

Stoljar, D. (2009) Physicalism. In E.N. Zalta (ed.), *The Stanford Encyclopedia of Philosophy* (Fall, 2009 edn). Retrieved from http://plato.stanford.edu/archives/fall2009/entries/physicalism/

Stroll, A. (2000) *Twentieth-Century Analytic Philosophy*. New York: Columbia University Press.

Stroud, B. (1980) Berkeley v. Locke on primary qualities. *Philosophy*, 55 (212): 149–66. doi:10.1017/S003181910004897X.

Tappen, R. (2010) *Advanced Nursing Research: From Theory to Practice*. Sudbury, MA: Jones & Bartlett Learning.

Tashakkori, A. & Teddlie, C. (eds) (2010) *SAGE Handbook of Mixed Methods in Social and Behavioral Research* (2nd edn). Thousand Oaks, CA: SAGE.

Teddlie, C. & Tashakkori, A. (2010) Overview of contemporary issues in mixed methods research. In A. Tashakkori & C. Teddlie (eds), *SAGE Handbook of Mixed Methods in Social and Behavioral Research* (pp. 1–41). Thousand Oaks, CA: SAGE.

Titscher, S., Meyer, M., Wodak, R. & Vetter, E. (2000) *Methods of Text and Discourse Analysis* (B. Jenner, Trans.). London: SAGE.

Trudeau, R.J. (1987) *The Non-Euclidean Revolution*. Boston, MA: Birkhäuser.

Uebel, T. (2013) Logical empiricism. In M. Curd & S. Psillos (eds), *The Routledge Companion to Philosophy of Science* (2nd edn, pp. 90–102). Abingdon: Taylor & Francis.

Uebel, T. & Richardson, A.W. (2007) *The Cambridge Companion to Logical Empiricism*. New York: Cambridge University Press.

Uzgalis, W. (2014) John Locke. In E.N. Zalta (ed.), *The Stanford Encyclopedia of Philosophy* (Winter, 2014 edn). Retrieved from http://plato.stanford.edu/archives/win2014/entries/locke/

van Fraassen, B.C. (1980) *The Scientific Image*. Oxford: Clarendon.

van Fraassen, B.C. (1989) *Laws and Symmetry*. Oxford: Clarendon.

van Fraassen, B.C. (1999) Alternatives to realism. In R. Klee (ed.), *Scientific Inquiry: Readings in the Philosophy of Science* (pp. 322–9). New York: Oxford University Press.

van Inwagen, P. (2013) Metaphysics. In E.N. Zalta (ed.), *The Stanford Encyclopedia of Philosophy* (Winter, 2013 edn). Retrieved from http://plato.stanford.edu/archives/win2013/entries/metaphysics/

Van Manen, M. (1990) *Researching Lived Experience: Human Science for an Action Sensitive Pedagogy*. London, Ontario, Canada: Althouse.

Vasterling, V. (2014) Hannah Arendt. In S. Luft & S. Overgaard (eds), *The Routledge Companion to Phenomenology* (pp. 82–91). Abingdon: Routledge.

Vernes, J.-R. (2000) *The Existence of the External World: The Pascal-Hume Principle* (M. Baker, Trans.). Ottawa: University of Ottawa Press.

Vickers, J. (2013) The problem of induction. In E.N. Zalta (ed.), *The Stanford Encyclopedia of Philosophy* (Spring, 2013 edn). Retrieved from http://plato.stanford.edu/archives/spr2013/entries/induction-problem/

von Glasersfeld, E. (1984a) An introduction to radical constructivism. In P. Watzlawick (ed.), *The Invented Reality: How Do We Know What We Believe We Know? (Contributions to Constructivism)* (pp. 17–40). New York: Norton.

von Glasersfeld, E. (1984b) On constructing a reality. In P. Watzlawick (ed.), *The Invented Reality: How Do We Know What We Believe We Know? (Contributions to Constructivism)* (pp. 41–61). New York: Norton.

Wachterhauser, B.R. (1986) Introduction: History and language in understanding. In B.R. Wachterhauser (ed.), *Hermeneutics and Modern Philosophy* (pp. 5–62). Albany: State University of New York Press.

Watzlawik, P. (1984) *The Invented Reality: How Do We Know What We Believe We Know? (Contributions to Constructivism)*. New York: Norton.

Weckroth, K. (1989) Book review: *Studies in Symbolic Interactionism* by Carl J. Couch, Stanley L. Saxton, Michael A. Katovich. *Acta Sociologica*, 32 (2): 213–15. doi:10.2307/4200745.

Weinberg, D. (2008) The philosophical foundations of constructionist research. In J.A. Holstein & J.F. Gubrium (eds), *Handbook of Constructionist Research* (pp. 13–40). New York: Guilford.

White, H. (1987) *The Content of the Form: Narrative Discourse and Historical Representation*. Baltimore, MD: Johns Hopkins University Press.

Wilson, E.J. & Reill, P.H. (eds) (2004) *Encyclopedia of the Enlightenment*. New York: Facts On File.

Winch, P. (2008 [1958]) *The Idea of a Social Science and Its Relation to Philosophy*. New York: Routledge.

Woleński, J. (1997) Haller on Wiener Kreis. In K. Lehrer & J.C. Marek (eds), *Austrian Philosophy Past and Present: Essays in Honor of Rudolf Haller* (pp. 45–54). Dordrecht, The Netherlands: Kluwer Academic.

Wolfe, C.T. & Gal, O. (eds) (2010) *The Body as Object and Instrument of Knowledge: Embodied Empiricism in Early Modern Science*. London: Springer.

Worrall, J. (1989) Structural realism: The best of both worlds? *Dialectica*, 43 (1–2): 99–124. doi:10.1111/j.1746-8361.1989.tb00933.x.

Young, T. (1807) *A Course of Lectures on Natural Philosophy and the Mechanical Arts* (Vol. II). London: Printed for Joseph Johnson, St Paul's Church Yard, by William Savage, Bedford Bury. Retrieved from www.biodiversitylibrary.org/item/63006. doi:10.5962/bhl.title.22458.

Zahavi, D. (2003) *Husserl's Phenomenology*. Stanford, CA: Stanford University Press.

Index

Page references are annotated as follows: f=figure; g=glossary entry; n=note; t=table